JOHN LOCKE
AND THE WAY OF IDEAS

JOHN LOCKE
AND THE WAY OF IDEAS

BY

JOHN W. YOLTON

OXFORD
AT THE CLARENDON PRESS

Oxford University Press, Ely House, London W.1

GLASGOW NEW YORK TORONTO MELBOURNE WELLINGTON
CAPE TOWN SALISBURY IBADAN NAIROBI LUSAKA ADDIS ABABA
BOMBAY CALCUTTA MADRAS KARACHI LAHORE DACCA
KUALA LUMPUR HONG KONG TOKYO

FIRST PUBLISHED 1956 IN THE
Oxford Classical and Philosophical Monographs
REPRINTED LITHOGRAPHICALLY IN GREAT BRITAIN
AT THE UNIVERSITY PRESS, OXFORD
BY VIVIÁN RIDLER
PRINTER TO THE UNIVERSITY
1968

TO PROFESSOR
JULIUS R. WEINBERG

PREFACE

LOCKE is usually treated by intellectual historians as a member of the philosophical tradition stemming from Descartes and going on to Berkeley, Hume, and Kant. There can be very little doubt that his *Essay Concerning Human Understanding* defined the area of problems for his successors and specified the terminology in which those problems were to be discussed. From the time of Locke to the present day it is possible to trace a steady empirical descent which, though it would be extravagant to claim it as the sole direction of Locke's own thought, owes its impetus to the formulation Locke gave to many empirical doctrines. The roots of Locke's analyses in his predecessors cannot so readily be traced. The terminology of ideas which found its most forceful statement in the *Essay* finds many prior formulators both in England and in France. The Cartesian influence seems most evident here. There are many other doctrines invoked by Locke which also had had a long history before he began to reflect about problems of knowledge and reality, a history which in some cases goes back into the Middle Ages. Locke was widely read and his travels in France in 1675-9 brought him into contact with many ideas which found a sympathetic exposition in the *Essay*. It is correct, then, to treat the *Essay* as a major philosophical work related to the traditional problems of philosophy handled by his predecessors and successors.

But there is another side to Locke's philosophical analyses which is usually ignored or only insufficiently remarked. For all the cosmopolitanism of his analysis of knowledge, it had an immediate effect upon his own contemporaries in England, the nature of which strongly suggests that Locke himself was not unmindful of the relevance of his theory of knowledge to the problems and debates on morality and religion engaged in by his friends and associates. Locke in fact tells

us that the need for such an analysis as the *Essay* makes
was first brought home to him after a discussion with certain
friends on some problems in morality and religion. The
initial purpose of his thought was not to extend the traditional analyses of the Cartesians or the medievalists: it was
more simply to arrive at a way of dealing with important
difficulties in normative conduct and theological discussion.
During the course of composition Locke discovered that
his designs were to grow, that the simple difficulties which
first gave rise to his reflections were almost becoming lost
in the maze of theoretical problems in metaphysics and
epistemology. It was his careful extension of his first
analysis of knowledge which brought the *Essay* fully into
the philosophical tradition. But if one examines the moral
and religious context in which Locke was living at the time
of his initial reflections, it becomes quite clear that one of the
traits of the *Essay* which created such an active interest in
Locke's contemporaries was the way in which its philosophical
doctrines were almost always directly related to the moral and
religious disputes of the day. This relevance gave to Locke's
work an immediate importance for his readers. What came to
fan the flames of controversy and invective was the solutions
he proposed to the traditional disputes.

But the solutions which disturbed his readers concerned
only indirectly the problems in morals and religion. The
Essay was primarily an examination into what has come to be
called 'epistemology', the study of man's processes of gaining
knowledge, the kinds and limits of this knowledge, and the distinction between knowledge and belief. In such an examination
ontological questions inevitably arise, such as the nature of
the objects of knowledge, their relation to our knowledge, and
the different kinds of objects which man can be said to know.
Various subsidiary questions have also to be met, such as the
nature of cause, of substance, of power, of liberty and necessity. It was the solutions to these epistemological and metaphysical problems which Locke's contemporaries felt had a
crucial effect upon theological and ethical issues, reinforcing

many of the new trends in these areas. Not all of Locke's epistemological doctrines, however, received the same degree of attention: it was more the second book than the fourth which occupied the minds of most of his critics, although we shall see that almost all of the major epistemological views of the *Essay* figured in the debates. Knowledge by means of ideas which are causally connected with, but only representative of, objects distinct from the mind was the 'new' doctrine which aroused the attention of Locke's contemporaries. The subsidiary doctrines (with the exception of the doctrine of substance, which was more intimately related to his epistemology than the others) were for the most part left alone.

I have been concerned to present, in this study, the reception given to Locke's theory of knowledge in the seventeenth century, and its impact upon the religion and morality of that period, indicating wherever necessary the general lines this impact took in the early years of the eighteenth century. I have also argued that the full significance of Locke's epistemology can only be grasped once we have set the *Essay* within the context of its own century, studied the reactions of Locke's contemporaries, and thereby seen what meaning these doctrines held for the men of that century. The results of this analysis disclose that Locke's epistemological doctrines had a disturbing effect upon the traditional moral and religious beliefs of his day; that, being in the midst of many radical movements of the century (the new science, the growing naturalistic tendency in religion, the empirical foundation for all knowledge), Locke's doctrines were held suspect from the start; and that so forceful was his formulation of many of the principles presupposed by these movements that he was considered by his contemporaries one of the more dangerous and important writers of the day.

I wish to thank the Keeper of the Western Manuscripts of the Bodleian Library for permission to quote from material in the Lovelace Collection of Locke manuscripts, and the editor of the *Journal of the History of Ideas* for permission to reprint portions of an article of mine on Locke and

Sergeant. I am greatly indebted to Professor R. I. Aaron of University College, Aberystwyth, for reading the whole of an earlier version of this study and for making many invaluable suggestions for its improvement. I have also profited from many critical suggestions of Professor Gilbert Ryle, for whose guidance I am indebted. I wish to express my thanks to Professor H. H. Price for his encouragement of the publication of this study, and to Sir W. D. Ross for his careful reading of the proof-sheets. Professor E. A. Strong of the University of California was responsible for first directing my attention to the need and value of such an historical study of Locke as I have here made. My wife has helped throughout to make the prose more readable and is also responsible for the bibliography.

J. W. Y.

CONTENTS

THE NATURE AND SCOPE OF THE
REACTION TO THE *ESSAY*

A N examination of the contemporary scene surrounding
Locke's *Essay Concerning Human Understanding* reveals
that from the very first the responses to his doctrines
were highly critical. In his review in the May 1690 issue of his
Bibliothèque Universelle, Jean LeClerc says that the abridgement of the *Essay* which appeared in the January issue of 1688
of the same journal 'fut si bien reçu des Connoisseurs, que le
Livre même ne manquera pas de plaire, à ceux qui tâchent de
distinguer ce qui est connu de ce qui ne l'est pas, car c'est-là le
principal but de cet Oùvrage'.[1] However, the reactions to this
summary were not all favourable. Locke later wrote, 'I have
been told, that a short epitome of this treatise, which was
printed in 1688, was by some condemmed without reading,
because *innate ideas* were denied in it.'[2] The letters of Christian
Knorr von Rosenroth and Fredericus van Leenhof preserved in
the Lovelace Collection, both dated 1688 from Amsterdam, are
two of the earliest written reactions to this doctrine. Both men
favour innate ideas and principles. It may have been these men
to whom Locke referred in a letter to Lady E. Guise of Utrecht,
although the men of whom Lady Guise spoke were more
probably theologians of her own city. Locke's comments and
rejection of the criticism referred to in this letter, even before
he had seen or heard the discussion directly, are characteristic of
much of his reaction to his critics. It is significant to notice the
very early awareness of the disturbing effects of the *Essay* upon
religion.

I see by your Lady's letter there are men touchy enough to be put
into a heat by my little treatise which I think has none in it. If they are

---

[1] t. xvii, p. 400.
[2] 'Epistle to the Reader', in his *Essay*, in *Works* (1823), vol. i, p. li. All references to Locke's works are from the 1823 edition, unless otherwise noted.

soe concerned for truth & religion as becomes sober men, they will answer the end of its publication & show me the mistakes in it. But if they are of those religious men, who when they can shew noe faults in his book can look into the heart of the author & there see flaws in the religion of him that writ it, though there be noe thing concerning religion in it, only because it is not suited to the systems they were taught I leave them to bethink themselves whether they are his disciples whose command it was, Judg not. Such gossiping talkers who supply the want of knowledg with a shew of zeale, & who if censure & tatle were reason & argument would certainly be very infallible I leave to their own good humor & charity; It haveing seldom been observed that any are forward to suspect or question others religion but those who want such a masque to cover some defect in their own. I have soe sincerely proposed truth to myself in all I have writ & doe soe much prefer it to my owne opinion that I shall think myself obleiged to any one who will shew me where I have missed it.[1]

In her letter of 10 May 1688 to Locke, Lady Guise had remarked: 'I know not how fare Emulation or a mistaken Zeal may prevaile over the minds of some, to Cavill with your philosophy or question your relegion but I leave them to answare for their Ignorance.'[2] Locke had sent her a copy of the 1688 abridgement which she fully enjoyed and claimed to follow perfectly. She praised Locke for having

with such admirable fasility offer'd to our sences what has been but obscurely treated of by others, & tho I am perswaded your flight is not lesse Exalted than that of other Philosophers, yet does it not remain in the clouds; but desends with a quicke tho Easy touch upon the aprehention & if it leaves not an Impression, the fault must be wholly asigned to the reader, since I can't but believe you have Extreamly well perform'd your part. . . .[3]

Lady Guise's praise may have been elicited by the good opinion Locke expressed of her character,[4] but the 1688 abridgement of the *Essay* was much discussed by Locke's friends in Amsterdam. Limborch wrote that he and his associates had discussed its doctrines,[5] and Peter Guenellon indicated that

---

[1] Locke to Lady E. Guise, Rotterdam, 21 June 1688. MS. Locke, C. 24, ff. 51, 52. The references to Locke manuscript material thus indicated are to the Lovelace Collection in the Bodleian Library.

[2] Lady E. Guise to Locke, Utrecht, 10 May 1688. MS. Locke, C. 11, f. 130.

[3] Lady Guise to Locke, 17 April 1688. MS. Locke, C. 11, f. 129.

[4] Cf. Lady Guise's reference to Locke's praise in her letter of 17 April.

[5] Limborch to Locke, Amsterdam, 3 April 1688. MS. Locke, C. 14, f. 13.

Locke's discussions were followed with interest by members of his college.[1] Guenellon was the intermediary for Leenhof and transmitted the latter's criticisms to Locke. It was typical of the general reaction that, while his friends expressed unlimited praise for the *Essay* even in its abridged form, those readers who lay outside the orbit of Locke's direct and intimate friendship quite early found points of criticism. This situation was duplicated in Ireland, where Molyneux wrote nothing but commendation, while William King, a friend of Molyneux but no acquaintance of Locke, sent to Locke a series of critical comments indicating places in the *Essay* where he thought Locke had erred. It was in England, however, that this situation of praise from intimate friends and hostile criticism from those outside this circle proliferated into its widest and most extensive form. A friend of James Tyrrell wrote in 1690: 'Mr. Locks new Book admits of no indifferent censure, for tis either extreamly commended, or much deeny'd, but has ten Enemies for one friend; Metaphysics being too Serious a subject for this Age.'[2] But Tyrrell himself, the man who had been in Locke's confidence since the early days of the inception of the *Essay*, reported a different reception from Oxford. In December of 1689 he wrote Locke that many copies of his book were being sold '& I hear it is well approved of by those who have begun the reading of it'.[3] At that time, Tyrrell had read only the epistle and part of the preface of the published version. In February, after he had read and heard more, he told Locke that he had begun the serious reading of his book

and to refresh those Notions; which I had fro your Manuscript copy concerning that matter: and I must tell you that your booke is received here with much greater applause than I find it is at London; the persons here being most addicted to contemplation.[4]

[1] Guenellon to Locke, Amsterdam, 25 March 1687/8. MS. Locke, C. 11, f. 5.
[2] Enclosed in Tyrrell's letter to Locke, 27 January 1689/90. MS. Locke, C. 22, f. 80.
[3] Tyrrell to Locke, Oxford, 20 December 1689. MS. Locke, C. 22, f. 72. It is apparent from this letter of Tyrrell that the *Essay* was already appearing in its first edition form as early as the middle of December 1689.
[4] Tyrrell to Locke, 18 February 1689/90. MS. Locke, C. 22, f. 82. Cf. his letter of February 1683/4, MS. Locke, C. 22, f. 50, where he speaks of having seen an early draft of the *Essay*.

The reception from Oxford was not all praise, however, for Locke was even charged with plagiarism, a charge probably false, but one that shows the recognition by Locke's contemporaries of the continuity of his thought with that of his predecessors. Tyrrell wrote in March 1690 that

a friend told me the other day that he had it from one who pretends to be a great Judge of bookes: that you had taken all that was good in it; from ~~Descartes~~ [sic] divers moderne french Authours, not only as to the notions but the manner of connection of them.[1]

But as early as 1692 the *Essay* was being used by Dr. Ashe, friend of Molyneux, in the university of Dublin as required reading for all bachelors.[2] By 1697 it had made its appearance in the universities of Cambridge and Oxford and was exerting some influence deemed by not a few to be dangerous.[3] In 1699, Samuel Bold, one who was outside the orbit of intimate friends, wrote a defence of Locke in which he bestowed high praise upon the *Essay*, asserting that it 'is a Book the best Adapted of any I know, to serve the Interest of Truth, Natural, Moral, and Divine: And that it is the most Worthy, most Noble, and best Book I ever read, excepting those which were writ by Persons Divinely inspired'.[4] The *Essay* was cited by William Wotton in his *Reflections upon Ancient and Modern Learning* (1694), along with the works of Descartes and Malebranche, as representative of modern logic and metaphysics (pp. 156, 158). LeClerc dedicated his *Ontologia* (1692) to Locke, pointing out that he had borrowed many doctrines of the *Essay*, a borrowing which introduced the Lockean modifications of the Cartesian way of ideas into France.[5] Richard

[1] Tyrrell to Locke, 18 March 1689/90. MS. Locke, C. 22, ff. 86–87.

[2] Molyneux to Locke, 22 December 1692, in *Works*, vol. ix, p. 299. Thomas Hearne confirms this point. See *Hearne's Collections*, entry for 21 November 1734, vol. xi, p. 394.

[3] See John Sergeant, *Solid Philosophy Asserted* (1697), p. [xv]. Cf. *Hearne's Collections*, ibid., 'Mr. John Wynne . . . was a great Tutor in Jesus College when he abridged Locke's *Essay of Human Understanding*, and being a great Lockist, he read the same to his Pupils and got many other Tutors in the University to read it. . . .'.

[4] *Some Considerations On the Principal Objections* (1699), p. 1.

[5] An interesting absorption of the Lockean and Cartesian logics through the intermediary of LeClerc is to be found in J. P. de Crousaz's *La Logique* (1712).

Burthogge also dedicated his *Essay upon Reason* (1694) to Locke, not, as Leclerc had done, because he made use of many of Locke's principles, but rather because the way of ideas elaborated in the *Essay* of Locke reaffirmed many of Burthogge's own earlier ideas, as expressed in his *Organum Vetus & Novum*. William Molyneux's comment, made prior to his friendship with Locke, is by now well known. In the Dedication to his *Dioptrica Nova* (1692), Molyneux had given credit to Locke for making great strides forward in logic.

> But to none do we owe more for a greater Advancement in this Part of Philosophy, than to the incomparable Mr. *Locke*, Who, in his *Essay Concerning Humane Understanding*, has rectified more received Mistakes, and delivered more profound Truths, established on Experience and Observation, for the Direction of Man's mind in the Prosecution of Knowledge, (which I think may be properly term'd Logick) than are to be met with in all the Volumes of the Antients. He has clearly overthrown all those Metaphysical Whymsies, which infected mens Brains with a Spice of Madness, whereby they *feign'd a Knowledge where they had none, by making a noise with Sounds, without clear and distinct Significations*.[1]

After the correspondence had begun between Molyneux and Locke, he told Locke that 'Upon my reading your Essay, I was so taken with it, that when I was in London, in August, 1690, I made inquiry amongst some of my learned friends, for any other of your writings.'[2] We know from a letter which Locke wrote to Molyneux that the copies of the first edition were all sold out by September 1692.[3] In that same letter, he asked Molyneux for his suggestions of deletions, additions, or corrections for the second edition, which was then in preparation.

In his reply, Molyneux said he had not sufficient leisure to carry out Locke's request but that he had given the *Essay* to a learned friend who had kindly made some written comments which Molyneux enclosed with the letter. These remarks were made by William King, then Bishop of Derry

[1] p. [4] of the 'Dedication to the Royal Society'. Also quoted in Fraser's edition of the *Essay*, vol. i, pp. xl–xli, and in *Works*, vol. ix, p. 289.
[2] Letter of summer 1692. Reprinted in *Works*, vol. ix, pp. 291–2.
[3] Letter of 29 September 1692, in *Works*, vol. ix, pp. 292–3.

and later Archbishop of Dublin—brief remarks running from Book One of the *Essay* to the section on Freedom in Book Two.[1] King's remarks are highly critical of many of the epistemological doctrines, but Locke did not consider them valid. Replying to Molyneux, he wrote as follows about King's remarks:

> I return you my humble thanks for the papers you did me the favour to send me in your last: but am apt to think you agree with me that there is very little in those papers, wherein either my sense is not mistaken, or very little, wherein the argument is directly against me. I suppose that learned gentleman, if he had had the leisure to read my Essay quite through, would have found several of his objections might have been spared.[2]

King admitted that his remarks were written in a hurry and that he had not 'had the leisure to read them over or to make English of them where words were left out'.[3] But the criticisms he made, as we shall see in a later chapter, hardly merit the complete rejection which Locke gave them. Locke suggested to Molyneux that King was blinded by the fact that he was concerned to defend some theory of his own or that his expression was hampered by the use of words which 'signify nothing at all'. Locke insisted, as he had done earlier to Lady Guise, that he was not fond of his own principles because they were his but only because he believed they were true. He confessed that he did not understand why two thinking men should disagree or be unable to reach agreement if they were both devoted to the truth. It was Molyneux's devotion to truth which attracted him and led him to value his criticism. Collins and Tyrrell received similar praise from Locke: both men were fond of telling him about the criticisms levelled against his *Essay*, and, like Molyneux, they found them all fallacious, irrelevant, or nonsensical.[4] Molyneux finally wrote some comments of his own on the *Essay* in December 1692, but his remarks consisted of nothing more than praise for the *Essay* as

---

[1] These remarks are preserved in the Lovelace Collection, MS. Locke, C. 28, ff. 99 et seq.

[2] Letter of 26 December 1692, in *Works*, vol. ix, p. 300.

[3] King to Locke, 1692. MS. Locke, C. 13, f. 6.

[4] See MS. Locke, the Tyrrell–Locke and Collins–Locke correspondence.

it stood and the assurance that Locke was the person best fitted
to judge concerning alterations and additions. He made it plain
that he and his learned friends with whom he discussed the
Essay all thought well of Locke's book and could find nothing
to which to take exception. Molyneux did later take issue
with Locke's analysis of·personal identity; but in the end he
seems to have been convinced that Locke's arguments in this
connexion were, with one or two qualifications, sound. The
whole exchange of letters on the subject was friendly and co-
operative. Judging from Locke's letters to Molyneux, we can
say that Locke was always anxious to have Molyneux's reactions to his material before publication, ostensibly because he
felt him to be such a good critic. But Molyneux's 'criticisms'
were usually a restatement of Locke's doctrines and a condemnation of Locke's critics. Molyneux provided solace for
Locke in the face of·the many dissenting critics who questioned the teachings of the *Essay*. More than once, Locke
confided in him his disappointment over the kind of attacks
raised against him. It is significant that the critics whom
Locke acknowledged as valuable were those friends who very
seldom had anything more than praise for the *Essay*, and who
consistently made the assertion that the men who wrote against
Locke were incomprehensible.

The many criticisms which appeared after the publication
of the second edition were all considered by Locke to be
fallacious for one reason or another. They received much the
same treatment as the remarks of William King. In a letter to
Molyneux dated 28 June 1694, Locke said:

> There appears to me to be so little material in the objections that I
> have seen in print against me, that I have passed them all by but one
> gentleman's, whose book not coming to my hand till those parts of mine
> were printed that he questions, I was fain to put my answer in the latter
> end of the epistle.[1]

The critic in this case was James Lowde, author of *A Discourse
Concerning the Nature of Man* (1694), one of the many attacks
upon Locke's rejection of innate moral principles. The reply

---

[1] Reprinted in *Works*, vol. ix, p. 339.

to Lowde in 'Epistle to the Reader', in the second and subsequent editions of the *Essay*, is one of the few published reactions of Locke to his critics. By 1697 a storm of negative criticism had engulfed the *Essay*, but Locke failed to take up the challenge of the majority of these attacks. One explanation for this failure to respond to criticism was, of course, his long controversy with Stillingfleet, the Bishop of Worcester, who saw in the *Essay* doctrines of dangerous consequence to Christianity. Undoubtedly because of Stillingfleet's prominence as well as his own desire to protect religious doctrines and beliefs, Locke felt called upon to respond at length to the bishop's attacks, even though he considered the charges made by the Bishop of Worcester to be misdirected and even malicious. But the bishop's long attacks were by no means all misdirected nor were these the most important of the unfavourable reactions published by Locke's contemporaries. In a letter to Molyneux of 22 February 1696/7, Locke declared that a Dr. S., 'a man of no small name . . . has been pleased to declare against my doctrine of no innate ideas, from the pulpit in the Temple, and, as I have been told, charged it with little less than atheism'.[1] Moreover, Locke had by this time received Leibniz's comments, sent to him from the Continent through their mutual acquaintance, Thomas Burnet of Kemnay;[2] John Sergeant, a Catholic priest, had written his long and detailed criticism, *Solid Philosophy Asserted, Against the Fancies of the Ideists*

---

[1] *Works*, vol. ix, p. 396. Dr. S. is William Sherlock, later Bishop of London. He published his charge of atheism against Locke in 1704 in his 'Digression Concerning Connate Ideas, or Inbred Knowledge' (pp. 124–64 of his *Discourse Concerning the Happiness of Good Men*, part i).

[2] Leibniz wrote three short sets of remarks on the *Essay* which Gerhardt dates, with insufficient supporting evidence, 1696 and 1698. (Cf. *Die Philosophischen Schriften von Gottfried Wilhelm Leibniz*, ed. by C. J. Gerhardt, 1875–90, bd. v, p. 6 for his dating; and bd. v, pp. 14–25 for his reprinting of the remarks.) Locke was enabled to examine the first set of remarks on two different occasions. Leibniz sent them to Thomas Burnet in his letter of 7/17 March 1696, and Burnet sent them to Locke via Mr. Cunningham (letter of Burnet to Leibniz, 30 November 1696) and again in a letter to Locke directly (cf. Burnet to Leibniz, 3 May 1697). These letters are reprinted by Gerhardt in bd. iii, pp. 174–9, pp. 185–6, and pp. 197–9. Besides these and the 1698 remarks, Leibniz wrote long comments on the Locke–Stillingfleet controversy. (Cf. Leibniz to Burnet, 20/30 January 1699, Gerhardt, bd. iii, pp. 243–53, pp. 223–43, and pp. 256–61.)

(1697); John Norris, who had published the first criticism of the *Essay* in 1690,[1] was still reprinting the original edition of his objections. It is no wonder that Locke wrote to Molyneux in the following manner:

> My book crept into the world about six or seven years ago, without any opposition, and has since passed amongst some for useful, and, the least favourable, for innocent. But, as it seems to me, it is agreed by some men that it should no longer do so. Something, I know not what, is at last spied out in it, that is like to be troublesome, and therefore it must be an ill book, and be treated accordingly. It is not that I know anything in particular, but some things that have happened at the same time together, seem to me to suggest this: what it will produce, time will show.[2]

Locke was incorrect in claiming that his book crept into the world without any opposition, for even the short epitome in LeClerc's journal was subjected to criticism; but he was right in pointing out that criticisms had increased by 1697. Samuel Bold, whose defence I have already referred to, expressed the same surprise at the number of attacks which were being made on the *Essay* by the end of the century. Nor was he sure of the explanation for the great outcry against Locke's doctrines, but he suggests that the fact that so many 'hands should be employed, just at the same time, to Attack and Batter this *Essay*', is significant, implying, as Locke also had done, that some sort of malicious plot was under way to cry down the *Essay*.[3] Molyneux thought he could place his finger upon the disturbing features of the *Essay* which called forth these suspicions.

> I fancy I pretty well guess what it is that some men find mischievous in your *Essay*: it is opening the eyes of the ignorant, and rectifying the methods of reasoning, which perhaps may undermine some received errors, and so abridge the empire of darkness; wherein, though the subjects wander deplorably, yet the rulers have their profit and advantage.[4]

He considered it ridiculous that anyone could find the doctrines of the *Essay* dangerous to religion.

---

[1] 'Cursory Reflections', 44 pp. appended to his *Christian Blessedness* (1690).
[2] Letter of 22 February 1696/7, in *Works*, vol. ix, pp. 396–7.
[3] Op. cit., p. 2.
[4] Letter of 16 March 1696/7, in *Works*, vol. ix, pp. 401–2.

Locke had expressed the same fears in his short reply to the first of Thomas Burnet's attacks in 1697.[1]

> Before anything came out against my Essay concerning Human Understanding the last year, I was told, that I must prepare myself for a storm that was coming against it; it being resolved by some men, that it was necessary that book of mine should, as it is phrased, be run down.[2]

I have found no evidence to indicate that the doctrines of the *Essay* were plotted against in this manner by a group of men unconcerned with their truth or falsity. Many of the doctrines were felt to be dangerous to Christianity and to morality, being sympathetic to the Socinian interpretations of the Scriptures. This fact led some men to class Locke among the Socinian writers of the day and to view him with the same hatred as they held for all members of this class. But whereas many of the writers of this group were damned without much attention being paid to their principles, Locke (with the interesting exception of William Carroll, whom I shall discuss in a later chapter) had no undiscriminating critics. Specific charges were brought against his epistemological doctrines. Several writers tried to point out to Locke that he could easily throw off this charge of Socinianism by stating his views on the Holy Trinity and other Christian doctrines then being hotly debated. Locke candidly refrained from giving a clear answer to Stillingfleet's charge that he denied the Trinity, undoubtedly because he was very sympathetic to the naturalistic Socinian and deistical interpretations. His extended replies to Stillingfleet's charges are, on the whole, free from personal animosity: he tries to meet the challenges and to explain his position. But Locke's reaction to his critics was not always of this nature. Stillingfleet's position and the cogency and weight of his charges probably led Locke to consider him seriously. I have already referred to an early letter of Locke's to Lady

---

[1] There were two Thomas Burnets actively concerned with the *Essay*. The one of Kemnay already mentioned served as the intermediary between Locke and Leibniz; the other, who himself wrote against Locke, was of the Charterhouse, and author of *Telluris Theoria Sacra* (1681–9).

[2] 'An Answer to Remarks upon an Essay concerning Human Understanding', in *Works*, vol. iv, p. 186.

Guise showing his readiness to dismiss criticism from the men of religion. We have learned of his reactions to William King's brief remarks and have found that the number of criticisms made against him by 1697 led him to believe that the critics were out to undermine the *Essay* and to give it a bad name by foul means. If there was such a plot, it was at least partially successful at the turn of the century. The Grand Jury of Middlesex handed down a presentment on the last day of Easter term 1697 banning Locke's *Reasonableness of Christianity*, on the grounds that it denied the Trinity, appealed to reason as the sole criterion of religious truth, gave rise to Arianism, Socinianism, atheism, and Deism.[1] The *Essay* was the subject of a similar censure to the tutors of Oxford in 1703. About this matter Collins wrote in February 1704:

> I am promis'd by a Friend at Oxford a particular account of the Proceedings of the Heads of Colleges with relation to their forbidding any of your Booke to be read in the University. I should be very glad so considerable a recommendation might for the benefit of mankind be made publick to the World, for what they have done plainly shows that in the way of reason they are not to be dealt with which they very well approve of when it serves their purpose.[2]

Tyrrell referred to the incident in his letter of 28 February 1703/4 and in April 1704 he gave Locke the full account.

> That in the beginning of November last, there was a meeting of the Heads of Houses then in town; it was there propos'd by Dr. Mill, and seconded by Dr. Maunder, that there was a great decay of logical exercises in the university, which could not be attributed to any thing so much as the new Philosophy which was so much read, and in particular your Book and Le Clercs Philosophy: against which it was offred, that a Programma should publish, forbiding all tutors to read them to their Pupils.[3]

Tyrrell went on to point out that the order was not enforced. Although the proposal to ban the *Essay* at Oxford was

---

[1] J. Gailhard, *The Epistle and Preface To the Book against the . . . Socinian Heresie* (1698), reproduces the edict, pp. 82–83. It is also referred to in *A Free but Modest Censure On the late Controversial Writings and Debates* (1698) by one F.B., M.A., of Cambridge, p. 15.

[2] Collins to Locke, 18 February 1703/4, MS. Locke, C. 7, f. 18.

[3] Tyrrell to Locke, April 1704, MS. Locke, C. 22, f. 167. Reprinted in King's *Life of John Locke* (1830), vol. i, pp. 357–9.

not successful, those opposing the book were able to give it a bad reputation which did persuade some not to read it. Thomas Hearne recalled that when John Wynne had introduced the *Essay* for the first time, many students read it, but that he himself 'always declined it. For indeed I neither then nor ever since have had any good opinion of Locke, who though a man of parts, was, however, a man of very bad principles'.[1] The champions of Locke were described by Hearne as 'a set of men of republican Principles, but orthodox and truly honest men have detected his errors, and fallacies, and endeavoured . . . to obstruct his infection'. But, however much against Locke Hearne may have been, he did not fail to speak out against the attacks of William Lancaster (the Provost of Queen's College in 1706) against Locke. Hearne's opinion of Lancaster was not high.

This day at one of the Clock, that old, hypocritical, ambitious, drunken sot, Will. Lancaster Provost of Queen's College was admitted Vice-Chancellour, being the 4th Year of his entering upon that office. . . . It must be here observ'd that whereas he spoke now well of Dr. Wynne he spoke very scurvily of him sometime agoe, and was pleas'd to run down Mr. Lock in the Convocation-House.[2]

Wynne himself was criticized by Lancaster as being a Lockist.[3] Hearne reports on the Convocation House incident as follows: Lancaster assured the House that

he would take as much Care as possible, & endeavour all he could to manage the trust committed to him to the Honour & Credit of the university; & for that End he hop'd the Seniors of the university, especially those who had the more immediate Care of Youth, would join with him in stiffling the Mischiefs of ill & pernicious Books, written on purpose to ruin both the Church & university, & bring a Disgrace upon Learning & Religion, among which he nam'd Dr. *Tyndale's* Book of the Rights of the Church, in which are publish'd new Forms of Ecclesiastical & Civil Government & Mr. *Lock's* Humane Understanding, written to advance new Schemes of Philosophy & bring an *odium* upon Ancient Learning.[4]

---

[1] *Hearne's Collections*, vol. xi, p. 394. Entry for 21 November 1734.
[2] Ibid., vol. ii, pp. 281–2. Entry for 6 October 1709.
[3] Ibid., vol. ii, p. 283. Hearne to T. Smith, 6 October 1709.
[4] Ibid., vol. i, pp. 293–4. Entry for 9 October 1706.

William Carroll, who charged Locke with holding a Spino-zistic doctrine of one material substance, gives a slightly different version of this convocation address.

> And Since the Reverend Dr. *Lancaster*, Vice-Chancellor of *Oxford*, has been pleas'd to recommend the *Dissertation [upon the Tenth Chapter of the Fourth Book of Mr. Lock's Essay* (1706)] made upon that *Chap.* in his Speech to the University, as an *Antidote* against Mr. *L*'s Book, and a *Key* to understand it; I here publickly return him my Thanks.[1]

If Lancaster did in fact recommend Carroll's book in pre-ference to Locke's, Hearne's judgement of him was not as distorted as it might seem, for Carroll's dissertation on the *Essay* is one critical book of which Locke's friends could say with justice that it was incomprehensible or entirely irrelevant. But whatever be the full story about Lancaster's speech, it is clear that he was against Locke and his followers and that he had some sympathizers among his listeners. The *Essay* had acquired in the minds of many men the reputation of being a dangerous treatise.

The attacks of Lancaster and Carroll may have merited the charge suggested by Locke, that his critics were deter-mined to attack the *Essay* with any means at their disposal. John Edwards's attacks against Locke might also legitimately be included in this list.[2] But the truth of the matter is that Locke did not receive criticism well. When Tyrrell wrote to Locke about certain objections some friends of Tyrrell had made concerning the polemic against innate ideas, Locke apparently took Tyrrell for one of the objectors and criticized him for so being. Locke's tone was strong enough to cause Tyrrell to write back a letter in which he concludes: 'I have no more [to say] but if you do not like that I should tell you what objections the world make against what you write, I shall for the future be more reserved.'[3] Locke did, however, write a long reply to the arguments used by Tyrrell and his friends.[4]

---

[1] *A Letter to the Reverend Dr. Benjamin Prat* (1707), p. 24.
[2] Cf. his *Socinianism Unmask'd* (1696) and *Some Thoughts Concerning the Several Causes and Occasions of Atheism* (1695).
[3] Tyrrell to Locke, 27 July 1690. MS. Locke, C. 22, f. 93.
[4] Locke to Tyrrell, 4 August 1690, in King's *Life of Locke*, vol. i, pp. 366–7.

When Burnet wrote a mild, inquisitive letter to Locke (*Remarks upon an Essay concerning Humane Understanding*, 1697), raising quite legitimate questions about certain doctrines of the *Essay*, Locke appended a bitter, sarcastic note in reply, at the end of his *Letter to the Bishop of Worcester*. Burnet, like many other men of the century, found Locke's rejection of innate ideas, his treatment of conscience, and his dissociation of the law of nature from the inward principles commonly supposed to be inherent in man, dangerously challenging to the established morality and to revealed religion. He wrote seeking to obtain from Locke some indication as to how he felt his principles could protect these values. Instead of explanations, Burnet received from Locke the accusation of being malicious. It is not surprising to find Burnet astonished at Locke's attitude.

But I know no good Reason you can have for writing in such a snappish and peevish way. If you affect the Character of a Captious Disputant, I do not envy it you, I think you have taken the ready way to gain it, by your way of Writing, both here and elsewhere. If you have been so treated by other Pens, as to make you angry and out of humour, you ought not to take your Revenge or ease your Spleen upon an inoffensive Pen.[1]

Similarly, Leibniz's critical comments were completely rejected by Locke and their author condemned.

Mr. Burnet has had it this year or two, but never communicated it to me, till about a fortnight agone. Indeed Mr. Cunningham procured me a sight of it last summer, and he and I read it paragraph by paragraph over together and he confessed to me, that some parts of it, he did not understand; and I showed him in others, that Mr. L—'s opinion would not hold, who was perfectly of my mind. I mention Mr. Cunningham to you, in the case, because I think him an extraordinary man of parts and learning, and he is one that is known to Mr. L—. To answer your freedom with the like, I must confess to you, that Mr. L—'s great name had raised in me an expectation which the sight of his paper did not answer, nor that discourse of his in the Acta Eruditorum, which he quotes, and I have since read, and had just the same thoughts of it, when I read it, as I find you have. From whence I only draw this inference, that even great parts will not master any subject without great thinking, and even the largest minds have but narrow swallows.[2]

[1] *Second Remarks* (1697), p. 10.
[2] Locke to Molyneux, 10 April 1697. Reprinted in *Works*, ix, p. 407. The

Locke was careful, however, not to reveal his true opinion of these remarks to Leibniz. The joint efforts of Leibniz and Burnet to elicit Locke's judgement never succeeded in procuring any detailed comments from Locke. The most Locke ever said was that there were some things in the remarks which he did not understand, refusing to specify his judgement any further.[1] Molyneux had written to Locke in March that he would like to see Leibniz's paper, but he commented that he did not expect 'any great matters' from Leibniz, 'for methinks (with all deference to his great name) he has given the world no extraordinary samples of his thoughts this way, as appears by his two discourses he has printed, both in the Acta Erudit.'.[2] In a subsequent letter, Locke quoted LeClerc's comments upon Leibniz's observations on the *Essay*, substantiating his and Molyneux's opinion.

Mr. Leibnitz, Mathématicien de Hanover, aïant oüï dire, qu'on traduisoit vôtre ouvrage, et qu'on l'alloit imprimer, a envoié ici à un de mes amis ce jugement qu'il en fait, comme pour le mettre à la tête. Cependant il a été bien aise qu'on vous le communicât. Il m'a été remis entre les mains pour cela. On m'a dit mille biens de ce Mathématicien il y a longtemps que *magna & preclara minatur*, sans rien produire, que quelques demonstrations détachées. Je croi néanmoins qu'il ne vous entend pas, et ie doute qu'il s'entende bien lui-même.[3]

work referred to in the *Acta Eruditorum* (November 1684 issue) is the *Meditationes De Cognitione, Veritate, & Ideis*, which Leibniz had recommended to Locke in his first comments. Cf. Gerhardt, op. cit., bd. iv, pp. 422–6.

[1] Locke first declared that he was honoured that a man of Leibniz's stature had made remarks upon his work. Later he pleaded that he was too busy with other matters to find the time requisite for making proper and detailed comments. Cf. Burnet to Leibniz, 30 November 1696; Burnet to Leibniz, 3 May 1697; and Burnet to Leibniz, 23 October 1700 (Gerhardt, bd. iii, pp. 185–6; 197–9; and 273). Locke even solicited, indirectly, Leibniz's judgement on his controversy with Stillingfleet. Cf. Burnet to Leibniz, 26 July 1698, Gerhardt, bd. iii, p. 242. Locke continued to express to Leibniz his high esteem of his person and of his philosophy. Cf. Lady Masham to Leibniz, 3 June 1704, Gerhardt, bd. iii, pp. 348–52.

[2] Molyneux to Locke, 16 March 1696/7. Reprinted in *Works*, vol. ix, p. 404. The two discourses of Leibniz here referred to are the 'De primae philosophiae Emendatione, & de Notione Substantiae' (*Acta Eruditorum*, March 1694, pp. 110–12, reprinted in Gerhardt, bd. iii, pp. 468–70), and 'Specimen Dynamicum, pro admirandis Naturae legibus' (*Acta Eruditorum*, April 1695, pp. 145–57).

[3] LeClerc to Locke, 19 April 1697. MS. Locke, C. 13, f. 113. Locke's letter containing this quotation from LeClerc is reprinted in *Works*, vol. ix, p. 417.

Locke adds to what he has already said concerning Leibniz: 'I see you and I, and this gentleman, agree pretty well concerning the man; and this sort of fiddling makes me hardly avoid think-ing, that he is not that very great man as has been talked of him.'[1] One begins to wonder just what Locke would have con-sidered to be valid adverse criticism of his position. There is no indication in any of his published or unpublished remarks that he ever admitted the validity of his critics' observations.

Locke's own attitude towards the task of the critic is revealed in two passages, one from his brief reply to Burnet, the other from an early unpublished draft of his reply to John Norris. In the former he writes,

The world has now my book, such as it is: if any one finds, that there be many questions that my principles will not resolve, he will do the world more service to lay down such principles as will resolve them, than to quarrel with my ignorance (which I readily acknowledge) and possibly for that which cannot be done. I shall never think the worse of mine, because they will not resolve every one's doubts, till I see those prin-ciples, laid down by any one, that will; and then I will quit mine.[2]

Critics are not to raise questions, but to supply answers. Locke will not enter into discussion with anyone for the purpose of working out a better solution to his problems. He was faithful to this statement of his position, for in the few replies he did write, he always shows impatience at the critic's inability to understand his arguments or to see that they are true; he re-veals a slight bitterness at having to write replies. He wrote no reply with the idea in mind of benefiting from the pro and con of argumentation. But it must be admitted that such an attitude was in general vogue at the time. The thought of exchanging views for mutual benefit had not taken hold of the intellectual world. Moreover, in his unpublished early draft of his reply to Norris, he shows a more balanced attitude towards criticism.

I for my part have always thought if a writer were not guilty either of great disingenuity or great mistakes . . . his other marks of human frailty must be forgiven him & with me the obligation I had to him for what he taught or seemed sincerely to intend to teach me compensated for those

[1] Locke to Molyneux, 3 May 1697, in *Works*, vol. ix, p. 417.
[2] In *Works*, vol. iv, p. 188.

slips which perhaps I met with in him. Always I thinke this is due to
every one that his words should be understood in the most favourable &
most consistent meaning could be put upon them.[1]

Locke had been justly disturbed by Norris's failure to read to
the end of a sentence in the introduction to the *Essay*, taking
Locke to say that the mind never knows itself, when what
Locke said was that it takes great pains and hard work to know
one's own mind. There were undoubtedly people who condemned the *Essay* without reading it or without reading it
carefully. Mrs. Cockburn, in her *Defence* of the *Essay* (1702)
tells of having talked with several people who had read the
Remarks of Burnet and had from these 'concluded it [the *Essay*]
contain'd very dangerous Principles, and without farther Examination, condemn'd the *Essay*, having never read, or as
they own'd, very little consider'd it'. (Preface, p. [7].) But few
of the published or extant criticisms of Locke's book can be
written off as easily as Locke was wont to do, ascribing them to
blind desires to undermine the book, or to misguided understanding. Even within the seventeenth century, when polemics
were a popular form of writing and writers very seldom strove
to comprehend their objector's point of view, Locke's attitude
towards his critics seems unwarranted.

If any one find anything in my Essay to be corrected, he may, when he
pleases, write against it; and when I think fit I will answer him. For I do
not intend my time shall be wasted at the pleasure of every one, who may
have a mind to pick holes in my book, and shew his skill in the art of
confutation.[2]

In his opinion, almost all the criticisms brought against him
were examples of trifling and not worth his time. But many
sound criticisms of the doctrines, especially of the epistemological doctrines, were formulated by men like Norris, Henry

---

[1] MS. Locke, C. 28, f. 108.

[2] Locke's 'Answer' to Burnet's *Remarks*, in *Works*, vol. iv, p. 189. Locke was
of course justly disturbed by the rancour and ill will of the many religious controversies of his day. It was one of the aims of his *Letter on Toleration* to plead for
a wide, though clearly circumscribed, toleration in such matters. But appeal to
the *Letter* as a defence for Locke's disdain of his critics only provides a convenient though suspect excuse. Locke's attitude towards his critics was not just
that he did not wish to enter into polemics: he very clearly thought they were
wrong, biased, and unscrupulous.

Lee, Sergeant, Stillingfleet, Peter Browne, and lesser known or anonymous writers. Many of these, notably Norris, Lee, and Sergeant, exemplify the gradual growth of the recognition of the sceptical tendencies in the epistemology of the *Essay*, scepticism both as regards the abstract epistemological doctrines and as regards the effects of these doctrines upon morality and religion.

Stillingfleet charged the *Essay* with a propensity towards scepticism and the overthrow of important articles of the Christian faith; but Locke could not see that Stillingfleet had offered any arguments which proved this charge.

> I cannot see any argument your lordship has any where brought, to show its tendency to scepticism, beyond what your lordship has in these words in the same page, viz., that it is your lordship's great prejudice against it that it leads to scepticism; or, that your lordship can find no way to attain to certainty in it, upon my grounds.[1]

The pursuit of this type of scepticism in the *Essay* was carried forward by many writers into the eighteenth century. The seeds of the charge of scepticism against what we should call today Locke's epistemology, of epistemic scepticism as opposed to the religious and moral scepticism entailed in his epistemological doctrines, are to be found in Norris's first comments on the *Essay* when he criticized Locke's definition of truth as the 'joyning or separating of Signs, as the Things signified do Agree or Disagree with one another'. Such a definition, Norris pointed out, placed the emphasis on 'Truth of the *Mind* or of the *Subject*' instead of on 'Truth of the *Thing* or of the *Object*, which consists not in the minds joyning or separating either Signs or Ideas, but in the Essential Habitudes that are between the Ideas themselves.'[2] Norris went on to develop the sceptical direction of Locke's constant separation of things and ideas. The objections to this separation grew in the years between 1690 and 1700. By the turn of the century the charge of scepticism had become one of the most frequently repeated objections, a charge not always clearly divided into the two

---

[1] 'Mr. Locke's Reply to . . . the Bishop of Worcester's Answer to his Letter', in *Works*, vol. iv, p. 184.

[2] Norris, 'Cursory Reflections', in his *Christian Blessedness* (1690), pp. 37–38.

branches of scepticism which I have suggested. It had been the source of the original dispute between the Bishop of Worcester and Locke; William King made substantially the same accusation; Lee[1] wrote a careful commentary on each section of the *Essay* in an effort to combat its sceptical doctrines; and John Sergeant attacked the entire method of ideas, both in truth and in knowledge, as resulting in a vicious scepticism. Between 1696–7, the years of the publication of Sergeant's attack and of Toland's controversial book, *Christianity not Mysterious* (the latter of which borrowed the epistemological doctrines of Locke for an unorthodox form of religion), and 1704, the year of Locke's death, there are numerous tracts and pamphlets taking issue with one side or another of the epistemological doctrines of Locke; but Locke consistently failed to profit by a discussion or, in most cases, even a recognition of these criticisms. He penned many detailed replies to Sergeant's attack in the margins of his copy of *Solid Philosophy Asserted*;[2] the *Third Remarks* of Burnet also contain many marginalia in Locke's hand which were probably the preparation for an intended publication;[3] he wrote two drafts of a reply to Norris, the first still preserved in the Lovelace Collection, the second published after his death;[4] Stillingfleet drew considerable fire from Locke; and Bold, Mrs. Cockburn, and LeClerc sought to act as substitutes for Locke by replying to other critics.[5] Apart from

---

[1] *Anti-Scepticism* (1702).

[2] Locke's copy of this book is now in the St. John's College library at Cambridge. For a discussion of some of these marginal notes, see my article, 'Locke's Unpublished Marginal Replies to John Sergeant', *Journal of the History of Ideas* (October 1951), vol. xii, pp. 528–59.

[3] These have been published, not too satisfactorily, by Noah Porter, 'Marginalia Locke-a-na', in *New Englander and Yale Review*, July 1887, vol. xi, N.S. pp. 33–49.

[4] Locke also wrote a careful attack upon the philosophy of Malebranche, Norris's archetype. Neither this nor his reply to Norris was published during his lifetime. It is undoubtedly to one or the other of these papers that Robert South refers in his letter to Locke (6 December 1699, MS. Locke, C. 18, f. 173). Locke had apparently sent his remarks on Norris, or those on Malebranche, to South for his critical opinion. South recommended that Locke's opponent should not receive a reply, advice which Locke seems to have followed.

[5] The opponents of Locke to whom Bold replied in 1699 are not named. Mrs. Cockburn's defence was written against Burnet's *Remarks*, while LeClerc defended Locke, after his death, against Pierre Bayle. Tyrrell suggested that Mrs.

these replies, the frequent attacks relevant to his epistemological doctrines went unanswered.

The *Essay* had a wide circulation and received ample notices in the press. The popularity of the book was in some ways surprising. Other works in England dealing with the same problems, those of Glanvill, Norris, and Burthogge, for example, did not gain anything like the notoriety that the *Essay* of Locke did. Burthogge presents the most interesting case in this respect. His *Organum Vetus & Novum* (1678) was in many ways an anticipation of Locke's *Essay*, and a development of the way of ideas into a phenomenalism presaging Kant.[1] His later book, An *Essay upon Reason* (1694), carries forward the analysis of the 1678 work. But despite the fact that Burthogge's two works on the human understanding and the nature and role of ideas in knowledge cover much the same ground as did Locke, he failed to achieve that level of distinction which Locke acquired. His lack of fame was not due to inadequate announcements, for he received several notices in the English journals. His *Essay upon Reason* was advertised in the *Athenian Gazette* (vol. 13, no. 25, 1 May 1694) as being 'dedicated to Mr. Lock'. In the 5 May issue, it was again advertised with the comment: 'In this *Essay* the Author hath advanc'd many things *wholly new* . . . and concludes with Reflections on Dr. *Sherlock's* Notions about *Individuation*.' It was listed in the 12 May issue as being reviewed in the *Compleat Library* for May and June, another periodical of the time. A short notice of this book occurred in the 18 December 1694 issue of the *Athenian Gazette*, repeated in the 20 April 1695 issue and again in the 4 February 1695–6 issue. A long review appeared in the April 1694 issue of the *Compleat Library* (vol. iii, pp. 107–12), in which the reviewer called attention to Burthogge's debt to Locke, but no mention is made of the earlier work. In the

Cockburn's defence was ably done. Cf. his letter to Locke, 25 July 1703, MS. Locke, C. 22, f. 159.

[1] Burthogge's phenomenalism is developed in a summary fashion in several works. Cf. G. Lyon, *L'Idéalisme en Angleterre au XVIII* Siècle*, pp. 72–96; Cassirer's *Erkenntnisproblem*, bd. i, pp. 543–53; and M. W. Landes's reprinting of much of Burthogge's works, together with a long introduction, *The Philosophical Writings of Burthogge* (1921).

March 1694 issue of this same journal, the announcement of Burthogge's *Essay upon Reason* was made with the following praise:

There is in the Press an Essay upon Humane Reason. It is a very extraordinary Book, and as he treats all his things very learnedly and with great Conduct, so he hath handled abundance of things which have not yet fallen under the Consideration of any who have treated upon that Subject. It is a fine and Compleat System of thoughts, and the product of a long time and great experience in the World.[1]

It may have been that the failure to notice Burthogge's earlier work, combined with the attention Locke's *Essay* commanded, served to restrict him to an inferior status in terms of popularity.

Nicéron says that the followers of Malebranche claimed that Locke's book 'n'a eu de la réputation, que parce qu'il est fort bien écrit en Anglois'.[2] There can be no doubt that the style in which the *Essay* was written had much to do with its popularity. Burthogge probably suffered because his manner of writing was not so polished as that of Locke, but his obscurity was also very probably due to the way in which his epistemological discussions were obvious digressions from his main task, i.e. the presentation of a doctrine of a world soul or of the presence of spirits in the world.[3] His epistemology tended to become lost in these minor theological questions. Besides his style, another important factor accounting for Locke's popularity was the way in which he orientated his discussions around the religious and moral questions of great significance to the majority of people in the seventeenth century. Non-epistemological questions served as the stimulus for the discussion of problems of knowledge. It should have been no surprise to Locke to find his doctrines taken as applying to the context from which they originated. Those who had the

---

[1] This notice is found in the section 'News of Learning, from London'.

[2] *Memoires pour servir à l'Histoire des Hommes Illustres*, t. x, 1729 [part i], p. 7.

[3] It is curious that Locke, who had apparently read the *Essay upon Reason*, noted a quotation from p. 196 of that work dealing with witchcraft, a doctrine which concerned Burthogge considerably. See MS. Locke, C. 28, f. 114.

keenest interest in his book were theologians and moralists concerned with seeing what good or harm its principles would involve for their values. The seventeenth century was marked by a strong interest in science, but the interests of religion and morality were still paramount in most men's minds. Thus Locke's concern to solve problems of knowledge for the sake of these values went along with his literary style and fluency to give his book a wide popularity. Another important factor was the reception and publicity the *Essay* received in the journals of the day, a reception far outreaching that of Burthogge or any other similar writer on a kindred subject. The abridgement which Locke made for the *Bibliothèque Universelle* aided in the early dissemination of his doctrines outside England and stimulated many people to look with anticipation for the publication of the entire work. LeClerc was undoubtedly correct in remarking: 'Cet abregé plut à une infinité de gens et leur fit souhaiter de voir l'Ouvrage entier.'[1] This abridgement appeared in an English translation in 1692 in *The Young-Students-Library*, a publication of the Athenian Society (pp. 162–79). LeClerc's review of Norris's attack in 'Cursory Reflections' was also reprinted in English in another publication of this same society, *The Athenian Gazette*.[2] Thus within two years of its first appearance, the *Essay* and the first published attack on it had received close attention in a popular journal in England.

The widespread foreign reception of the *Essay* is traceable quite definitely to the publication of reviews of it in the French journals of Holland. It was the abridgement in the *Bibliothèque Universelle* that had first called Leibniz's attention to Locke.[3] Basnage de Beauval mentioned the *Essay* in a notice of the Coste French translation of Locke's *Some Thoughts Concerning Education*.[4] The publication and French translation of Locke's

[1] 'Eloge de feu M. Locke', *Bibliothèque Choisie*, t. vi, 1705, p. 377.
[2] 'Supplement to the Third Volume of the Athenian Gazette', 1691, pp. 2–3. Apparently Norris did not realize that this was a translation of the French review, for in the third edition of his *Practical Discourses* (1694) his 'Cursory Reflections' are reprinted with a reply to the Athenian Society against their unjust attack upon him.   [3] Cf. Gerhardt, op. cit., bd. v, p. 6.
[4] *Histoire des Ouvrages des Savans*, June 1695, p. 441.

other works and of the various attacks upon him were also
recorded by Basnage.[1] In the October 1697 issue of *Nouvelles
de la Republique des Lettres*, Jacques Bernard summarized the
Locke–Stillingfleet controversy at length, giving Locke more
credit than the bishop. This summary was continued in the
November issue. In June 1700, Bernard noticed the appearance
of the fourth edition of the *Essay* and called attention to the
Latin translation soon to appear, adding: 'Je crois qu'on ne
l'estimera pas moins au delà de la Mer, quand on aura lû la
Traduction Françoise, qu'en a faite Mr. *Coste*, à laquelle je sai
qu'il a travaillé avec la derniere exactitude' (p. 682). The Coste
translation was reviewed by Bernard in August 1700, with the
following words of praise for Locke:

> Un des plus pénétrans & des plus judicieux Ecrivains [i.e. Pierre
> Bayle, in his *Dictionnaire*, t. ii, p. 540] de ce siècle a remarqué; que *la
> plûpart des Savans ne sont propres qu'à cultiver les terres qui ont été déja
> défrichées. Il peuvent*, dit-il, *aplanir ou élargir un chemin que d'autres ont
> déja fait. Mais quelques-uns en très-petit nombre*, quibus arte benignâ &
> meliore luto finxit praecordia Titan, *peuvent défricher les terres les plus
> incultes, & faire une route dans des forêts où personne n'avoit passé*. Mr.
> *Locke* est sans doute de ce petit nombre.[2]

Basnage had been the first of the journalists to review Coste's
translation, opening his July 1700 review with the remark: 'Il
y a lon tems que cet Ouvrage fait du bruit & par le nom de
l'Auteur, & par la matiere.' He remarked upon the difficulty
that Coste had in translating the ideas and expressions of
Locke but felt that Coste had on the whole performed his task
well.[3] In September 1700 the Coste translation was carefully
and favourably reviewed by Leibniz in the German journal,
the *Monatlicher Auszug*.[4] In January of the following year, the
Mémoires pour l'Histoire des Sciences & des Beaux Arts (à
Trevoux) also gave it a brief review. The reviewer in the latter

[1] Cf. June 1695, pp. 435 ff.; November 1695, p. 135; May 1696, p. 419;
June 1700, p. 280; and July 1700, pp. 291 ff.

[2] *Nouvelles de la Republique des Lettres*, August 1700, pp. 123–4.

[3] Coste did have great difficulty in translating certain sections of the *Essay*,
difficulties which he and Pierre Bayle discussed together. See Bayle's *Œuvres
Diverses*, t. iv, letter to Coste, 30 August 1701, pp. 800–1.

[4] pp. 611–36. Reprinted in Gerhardt, op. cit., bd. v, pp. 24–37.

journal ends by excusing the brevity of his review and reminds the reader that this is only a summary and does not contain his, the reviewer's, own opinions: 'On prie le Lecteur de se souvenir qu'en faisant les extraits des ouvrages, on n'adopte pas les sentimens des Auteurs' (p. 131). The continental dissemination of Locke's doctrines was further aided by his friendship with Nicolas Thoynard and the Abbé Du Bos, both of whom saw the Coste translation as soon as the printer finished each section.[1] Du Bos was responsible for its introduction into the Royal Court of France.

Avant de partir de Paris javois promis mon exemplaire de Mr Locke pour lire a Mr. le duc de Chartres. Je vous seré bien obligé de scavoir de mr. l'abbé du Bois qui loge rue des bons enfans a lhotel de Malusine si son altesse Royalle en a encore a faire et de lui expliquer pourquoy je lai recu si tard.[2]

Pierre Bayle mentioned Locke several times in the 1702 edition of his *Dictionnaire* and discussed some of his doctrines, such as the ability of matter to think and his doctrine of substance. Locke is referred to as 'l'un des plus profonds Metaphysiciens du monde'.[3] Without a doubt Coste did Locke a great service by translating the *Essay* into French. The Latin edition further extended the range of Locke's doctrines and heightened interest in them.[4] By 1704, the year of Locke's death, his epistemological, moral, and religious doctrines were thoroughly disseminated both in England and abroad. These doctrines had been so much discussed, criticized, and praised by then, that

[1] Du Bos to N. Thoynard, 15 July 1699. 'M. Lock auoit toujours souhaité que l'on vous envoia les feuilles de la traduction de son traité de l'entendement humain a mesure quelles l'imprimoient, mais le libraire ne l'auroit point voulu faire crainte que son livre ne fut contrefait sur ces feuilles la.' (Bib. Nat., n.a. 560, f. 301. Reprinted by Paul Denis, *Lettres Autographes*, 1912, p. 97.)

[2] Du Bos to Thoynard, March 1701. Bib. Nat., ibid, f. 357. Reprinted in Denis, p. 115.

[3] Article on Dicaearchus, note M. Cf. also the article on N. Perrot d'Ablancourt, note L. There are other references which discuss Locke and refer to the Locke–Stillingfleet controversy.

[4] One of Locke's correspondents, Robert South, expressed what must have been a common belief among many of Locke's readers, i.e. that a Latin translation should be made in order to give the universally valid and appealing doctrines of the *Essay* their expression in a universal tongue. Cf. South to Locke, 22 September 1697, and 18 June 1699, MS. Locke, C. 18, ff. 169, 171.

no responsible thinker in the eighteenth century could afford to omit reference to Locke.

Many of the controversies in which the epistemological doctrines of the *Essay* became embroiled during Locke's lifetime continued over into the following century. Anthony Collins, Samuel Clarke, Isaac Watts, and others in and outside the clergy carried forward the discussion of mind and matter, the nature of substance, of liberty and free will. The epistemological and moral scepticism to which the doctrines of the *Essay* were believed by many to lead, especially within the context of deism, was further discussed by men like Peter Browne, John Witty, and Bishop Berkeley, the first of whom had written in 1697 one of the most penetrating of all the replies to Toland's use of Locke's principles in *Christianity not Mysterious*. The polemic against innate ideas had won general acceptance by the first years of the eighteenth century, although there were some outstanding exceptions who still defended innateness. Interest in Locke, however, began to wane towards the middle of that century. Philosophical discussion came to be centred in the new systems of Berkeley, Hume, and other Scottish thinkers. In religion, Deism, the movement to which Locke's doctrines, both religious and epistemological, gave such a strong impetus, had gained its ascendancy. Many of Locke's doctrines had been absorbed into the thought of his own century, even by those who most vehemently objected to his system. By the middle years of the following century, the fierceness of the debate over Locke's philosophy had abated. Isaac Watts's comment sums up the opinion of Locke held by many men around 1730.

His *Essay on the human Understanding* has diffused fairer Light through the World in numerous Affairs of Science and of human Life. There are many admirable Chapters in that Book, and many Truths in them, which are worthy Letters of Gold. But there are some Opinions in his Philosophy, especially relating to *intellectual Beings*, their Powers and Operations, which have not gain'd my Assent. (*Philosophical Essays*, 1733, p. viii.)

II

THE DOCTRINE OF INNATE
KNOWLEDGE

LOCKE was opposed to innate ideas as well as to innate principles. Both types of innateness were considered superfluous in accounting for human knowledge. The scholastic method of basing all knowledge upon maxims which were supposed to be intuitively known as certain was dangerous because it led us to be uncritical of the basic axioms of knowledge. Locke was seeking to introduce a new critical attitude towards all knowledge, its conclusions as well as its base. He thought he had been able to construct a system of knowledge in which appeals to maxims, to innate principles, or to innate ideas were no longer needed. He recognized that this jettisoning of the traditional grounds of knowledge leads to a restriction of knowledge, but he did not believe it opened the way for a defeating scepticism. Ethics, he thought, could still be placed on a deductive basis; and the three primary objects of knowledge—God, the self, and the external world—were all retained, the first two as certain, the third with a status stronger than ordinary probability. Innateness on the speculative and practical levels was not only false, it served to obscure the proper foundation of human knowledge, i.e. experience, taken in its broadest sense. Thus, the doctrine of innate knowledge had to be disposed of before Locke could develop his theory concerning the experiential basis of knowledge. But critics of Locke, even in his own day, were puzzled by the historical referents of Book One of the *Essay*; for, so they argued, no one ever held the naïve form of the doctrine of innateness as it was formulated by Locke. Modern critics have varied in their interpretations, from assigning Descartes as the opponent who is attacked in the *Essay*, to modifying this interpretation to include more directly the Cambridge Platonists and their

many followers in the pulpits of England, and the older scholastic philosophers who based all knowledge upon maxims.
Fraser is too anxious to defend the need for some sort of
rational principles presupposed in knowledge to think Locke
could have meant that anyone had ever held the naïve form
of the doctrine of innateness. He thinks Descartes was probably
in the forefront of Locke's mind while he was writing Book
One, but he points out that Descartes's theory of innateness is
much more subtle than that discussed by Locke. Fraser suggests that Locke could, upon a superficial reading of certain
passages in More, Hale, or Cudworth, 'have found expressions
of theirs which . . . appear to countenance the *sort* of innateness
which he attributes to the "established opinion"'.[1] He criticizes Locke for attacking the theory in its 'crudest form' and
for failing to recognize the need for a doctrine of innateness
in order to account for man's relations with the divine or the
infinite.[2] Gibson emphasizes the prevalence of the doctrine of
innateness in the seventeenth century, and its relations with the
doctrine of laws of nature. He cites Descartes and the Cambridge Platonists, and he also wisely calls attention to the fact
that the same kind of language, that of the stamp and its
impression upon the mind, was commonly employed in talking
about this doctrine.[3] Windelband names only Descartes and
the Cambridge Platonists,[4] Höffding rules out Descartes and
substitutes the scholastic philosophers with their dependence
on maxims,[5] while Rivaud has recently assumed that Locke
was opposing the Scholastics, Descartes, and Herbert of Cherbury.[6] Seth Pringle-Pattison agrees with Höffding and Gibson.[7]
Like Gibson, Lamprecht has argued that Locke was directing
his attack against the Cambridge Platonists 'and enthusias-
tic sectarians in religion and politics who abused the idea

[1] Fraser's edition of the *Essay*, vol. i, p. 37, note 1. Cf. his Prolegomena, vol. i,
pp. lxxi–lxxiii.
[2] Id., *Essay*, vol. i, p. 37, note 2.
[3] *Locke's Theory of Knowledge*, pp. 30–33.
[4] *Lehrbuch der Geschichte der Philosophie* (1950), p. 386.
[5] *Geschichte der neueren Philosophie*, bd. i, p. 429.
[6] *Histoire de la Philosophie*, t. iii, p. 389.
[7] Introduction to his edition of the *Essay*, pp. xxxi–xxxii.

badly',[1] showing Fraser's reluctance to believe the doctrine was ever held in its naïve form. Cassirer has advanced the novel suggestion that Locke really had no one in mind in Book One. 'Das System der "angeborenen Ideen" das Locke vor Augen hat, ist indessen in seinen Einzelheiten keine geschichtliche Realität, sondern eine polemische Konstruktion, die er als Erläuterung und als Gegenbild der eigenen Anschauung braucht.'[2] Aaron has returned to the traditional answer and names Descartes along with the 'various English thinkers and teachers, who, whilst not direct followers of Descartes, agreed with him in holding a theory of innate ideas'.[3] He cites Leibniz's and Voltaire's interpretation of Descartes's doctrine of innateness to show that Descartes was interpreted in the naïve way by prominent men of his country in touch with the various debates within the ranks of the Cartesians.

None of these identifications of 'these men of innate principles' of Book One of the *Essay* can be said to be wrong. Locke was writing to reveal certain implications of the belief in innate knowledge no matter how it was formulated, implications which were either entirely unwarranted and hence must be rejected, or which were important but not as radical as it might seem at first sight. He was not writing primarily as an historian, concerned to explain and refute the views of his predecessors. There is a certain amount of the 'constructivist' tendency in his thinking, as Cassirer suggests. But it is very doubtful whether any of the crucial problems discussed in the *Essay* would have occurred to his mind had they not been the subjects of debate in his own day. He looked to his society and to his predecessors in order to determine what the problems were and what solutions had been offered. When he scanned the literature of moralists and theologians of his century, he found that frequent appeals were made to a doctrine of innateness. Lamprecht, Aaron, and Gibson have been correct in suggesting that the doctrine had a wide circulation among the

[1] 'The Rôle of Descartes in Seventeenth-Century England', in *Studies in the History of Ideas*, vol. iii, p. 232.
[2] *Das Erkenntnisproblem*, bd. ii, pp. 230–1.
[3] *John Locke* (1937), pp. 77–80.

men of the period, but none of the critics of Locke has indicated just how prevalent its acceptance was. When we cease to search far and wide for opponents of Locke's polemic and concentrate our attention upon his own contemporaries and immediate predecessors in England, we find that the doctrine of innate knowledge was held, in one form or another, to be necessary for religion and especially for morality from the early years of the century right through to the end and into the beginning of the following century.[1] The doctrine underwent, in general, a transformation from its naïve form to a modified version. The naïve form claimed that God wrote into or impressed upon the soul or mind at birth certain ideas and precepts (or a developed conscience capable of deciding what is right and wrong, independent of custom or learning) for the guidance of life and the foundation of morality, even though we do not become aware of these innate principles (or of the conscience) until maturity. For those who questioned at all how we recognize these principles as innate, the reply was usually 'the ready and prompt assent we give to them upon first having them presented to us'. This form of the doctrine was modified, both before and after 1688, so that the claim for these principles being imprinted at birth was no longer included, and later, so that the name 'innate' was meant to apply only to those principles which we easily assent to. But the naïve form of the theory reappears even as late as the early years of the eighteenth century. In every case, it is invoked as a means of stabilizing morality and religion, of providing men with certain and sure foundations for the virtuous life. The principles which are listed as innate are always formulations of the existing values of the society. The listing of what Locke calls 'speculative' principles as innate is much less prevalent because they had less significance for his contemporaries.

[1] G. R. Cragg, in his *From Puritanism to the Age of Reason*, indicates an awareness of the pervasiveness of the doctrine, though he is not concerned with presenting a detailed account. 'Throughout the seventeenth century, many of the foremost religious writers had clung to the conviction that God had imprinted on the mind of man certain indelible truths, and that of these ideas the assurance of His own existence was at once the clearest and the most important' (pp. 115–16).

It is very difficult to doubt that it was against this firm
tradition in English moral and religious thought that Locke
was writing. He was probably not unmindful that Descartes
'and some of the Cartesians held a doctrine of the same genre
as many of his English contemporaries on this issue; but Locke
was primarily concerned to offer solutions to problems which
arose out of his own society. He was not concerned to go
abroad in his criticism, even though he looked to the Continent
in the development of his own epistemological principles.
Moreover, even his criticisms of the theory of innate knowledge
were not original. George Hickes claimed that 'there is scarce
one argument in it [the *Essay*] against *Innate Ideas*, which he
[Locke] had not heard, or read in the *University*, upon the
trite Question, commonly disputed on in the schools, *An dantur
innatae ideae?*'[1] Whether Hickes's charge is correct or not, it is
quite true that the issue of innate knowledge had been debated
extensively by Locke's contemporaries and many of his own
criticisms anticipated. No clearer evidence for the existence of
the naïve form of innateness could be found, save its formulation in the writings of many men, than the repeated denials of
its validity. The fact that we do find the theory formulated in
this form, that the language of these formulations and the
language of the criticisms against the naïve form made prior to
1688 are incorporated into the *Essay*, would seem to establish
the identity of the referents of Book One of that work. An
awareness of the role of the theory of innateness in the moralists and theologians of the early half of the century is essential
for a full appreciation of the intimate connexion between
Locke's epistemology and the contemporary debates of which
he was aware, and for understanding many of the criticisms
made against Locke's polemic by his contemporaries.

§ 1—*The Doctrine of Innate Knowledge Prior to 1688*

The doctrine of innate knowledge took several different
forms in England prior to 1688. Many writers who appealed to

[1] p. [34] of his 'Preliminary Discourse' in William Carroll's *Spinoza Reviv'd*
(1709).

the doctrine explicitly said that they did not mean that children are born with completed ideas ready for use. But even these writers employ a vocabulary for expressing the doctrine which must have been rigid and universally accepted. Some variant of the theory can be found in almost any pamphlet of the early part of the century dealing with morality, conscience, the existence of God, or natural law. For many men of the period, natural law required a natural conscience to enable men to recognize the laws laid down by God. Without a natural conscience supplied by God with the ability of leading men towards good and away from evil, there would be no sure foundation for morality. Richard Carpenter expressed this point of view in his *The Conscionable Christian* (1623), where, in the preface 'To the Reader', he says:

> Now the whole and intire work of conscience . . . consists, as I conceiue it, in a practicall syllogisme: the maior proposition whereof ariseth from the *Synteresis* or treasury of morall principles, and of sacred rules wherewith the practicall understanding is furnished, for the saving direction of us in all actions (p. [2]).

John Bullokar, in *An English Expositor* (1616), defined 'synteresie' as 'the inward conscience: or a naturall qualitie ingrafted in the soule, which inwardly informeth a man, whether he do well or ill'. Carpenter preserved the terminology of this definition in his description of conscience as

> a nobel and diuine power and faculty, planted of God in the substance of mans soule, working vpon itself by reflection, and taking exact notice, as a Scribe or Register, and determining as Gods Viceroy and deputy, Judge of all that is in the mind, will, affections, actions, and whole life of man (p. 41).

The conscience is 'borne with us', as a book 'euen in thine owne bosome, written by the finger of God, in such plaine Characters, and so legible, that though thou knowest not a letter in any other booke, yet thou maist reade this'. (pp. 43–44) The entire naïve form of the theory is to be found in Carpenter's book. Besides asserting conscience to be written by God into the heart of man in such plain language that even the ignorant could read its dictates, he specified the contents of this book of conscience as being 'sorted with singular precepts and principles concerning the knowledge and practice of good and euill' (p. 44). The term 'innate' carried the meaning of 'natural' in Bullokar's dictionary, and the conscience was the most natural of faculties. In Carpenter's opinion, the conscience was an indispensable factor for morality.

Even where not fully developed to the lengths of Carpenter's analysis, the theory of natural conscience and synteresis appears in places where it is clear that an elaborate theory is presupposed. For example, Burton, in his *The Anatomy of Melancholy* (1621), invoked the same principle of conscience and placed synteresis, which is for him the pure part of the conscience, in the understanding. Synteresis is asserted to be innate, along with the *dictamen rationis* and the conscience proper. 'Synteresie, or the purer part of the *Conscience*, is an innate habit, and doth signifie, *a conservation of the knowledge of the Law of God and Nature, to know good or evill.*'[1] Burton appeals to Plato for support of this view, revealing a common interpretation of Plato in Renaissance thought. The same point of view is presupposed by and given dramatic exposition in Thomas Nabbes's *Microcosmus, A Morall Maske* (1637), a play which seeks to depict the elements of the world and the moral development of man from his first state. In the last scene of the play, Conscience makes the following speech:

> Conscience the judge of actions
> Is neither power, nor habit, but an act;
> To wit an application of that knowledge
> That shewes the difference. Its Synteresis,
> Or purer part, is th' instigation
> Of will to good and honest things, and seates
> The mind in a rich throne of endlesse quiet. (Leaf G–2.)

It would be difficult to reconstruct the doctrine of synteresis from this oblique reference in Nabbes's play, but once we know the theory which this reference presupposes, its incorporation into a dramatic presentation reveals something of the extensive and pervasive acceptance of this point of view. Criticisms were

---

[1] p. 42, part i, member 2, subsection 10.

raised against this doctrine even in the early part of the century, but the essentials were retained. In his *A Key to the Key of Scripture* (1611), William Sclater couples conscience with the law of nature and asserts that 'The law of nature, is that rule of pietie, and honestie, that the Lord hath written in the hearts of all men: whereby they know confusedly, and in generall, what is good; what is euill; what to be done; what to be forborn.' (p. 170) But Sclater was reluctant to espouse the bold form of the theory, even though his use of the vivid language seemed to involve no other interpretation. The knowledge of the law of nature is, he said, 'vouchsafed vnto all by a generall influence of Gods grace, which is indeed as common as nature; and therefore called the law of nature'. (Ibid.) Just what form this influence takes was left obscure by Sclater, probably because he could think of no alternative save that of its being inborn in man. But conscience meant for him the same function as for Carpenter, informing man of good and evil. He never relinquishes the literal language, repeating many times that the principles of conscience are 'imprinted in the vnderstanding'.

The theory prevailed and grew as the century moved on. The language of conscience and synteresis was not always invoked; but the foundation of morality in the internal nature of man, the inscription of specific injunctions, was constantly championed. Writing in 1677, Sir Matthew Hale (*The Primitive Origination of Mankind*) distinguished between sensation, ratiocination, and intuition as sources of knowledge. Of intuition he said:

> There are some truths so plain and evident, and open, that need not any process of ratiocination to evidence or evince them; they seem to be objected to the Intellective Nature when it is grown perfect and fit for intellectual operation, as the Objects of Light or Colour are objected to the Eye when it is open (p. 2).

The movement from premise to conclusion is so swift, short, and clear in these cases that it seems to be instantaneous and without reasoning. Moral and intellectual truths are said to belong to this class. In virtue of the swiftness of assent to these truths, they 'seem upon this accompt to be congenite with us, connatural to us, and engraven in the very frame and compages

of the Soul'. (Ibid.) He compares these rational intuitions to
the involuntary instincts of man, those that are 'settled, con-
trived, implanted and directed there by a higher Wisdom'
(p. 30). Even though the principles said to be innate can be
deduced by rational arguments, Hale insisted that this fact
did not nullify their innateness.

> I come now to consider of those rational Instincts as I call them, the
> connate Principles engraven in the humane Soul; which though they are
> Truths acquirable and deducible by rational consequences and Argu-
> mentation, yet they seem to be inscribed in the very *crasis* and texture
> of the Soul antecedent to any acquisition by industry or the exercise of
> the discursive Faculty in Man, and therefore they may be well called
> anticipations, prenotions, or sentiments characterized and engraven
> in the Soul, born with it, and growing up with it till they receive a check
> by ill customs or educations, or an improvement and advancement by
> the due exercise of the Faculties (p. 60).

Examples of such congenite truths are, 'There is a God', 'God
is all powerful', 'Promises are to be kept', 'the obscene parts
and actions are not to be exposed to publick view'. These are all
rational instincts or congenite notions whereby the soul is 'pre-
disposed, inclined, and byassed to the good and convenience
proportionable to a rational and intellectual life', truths which
incline man 'to such a trade and way as is suitable to the good
of his Nature; so that he is not left barely to the undetermina-
tion, incertainty, and unsteadiness of the operation of his
Faculties' (p. 61). Moral principles for Hale have two sources
of origin: divine revelation and the internal constitution of
man's soul. To learn the principles by the first means man has
only to read the Bible; to learn them by the second he has only
to transcribe the original which is written in the heart (p. 63).
These engraven principles have three main functions: synteresis, syneidesis, and epicrisis; which shows the conscious
relation of his doctrine with the earlier versions of conscience
and synteresis.[1] The theory had undergone many more specific

---

[1] The body of doctrine of which these terms were an integral part is scholastic,
although uses of synteresis and prolepsis (another term in the doctrine) can be
traced to the Stoics. Liddell and Scott cite Periander and Bias as having used
syneidesis in the sense of conscience. Synteresis or synderesis is used by St.
Thomas as a habit of mind concerned with the precepts of the natural law

developments in Hale's hands than in those of any of its advocates earlier in the century, but he was not alone in this development. The author of 'Remarks upon the Nature and Office of Conscience' in *The Mischief of Persecution Exemplified* (1688) invoked the same sort of principles as did Hale, grouping them all under the 'universal and immutable Law engraven on the Mind of Man', principles which are said to have been 'known to the generality of Mankind' by their effect, 'and by natural anticipations and common notions of Good and Evil imprinted in Humane Nature'. Even though the innate moral rules become confused by environment and bad precepts, they are a 'fixt and permanent Faculty in the rational Soul, a connate Habit in the Practical Understanding' (p. 2). The author speaks frequently of the law of conscience being 'written in the Heart'. All men partake of 'the universal law of Nature, engraven on the Heart, which no positive or revealed Institution discharges any Man from' (p. 5). The law of conscience is caused by 'little sparks of that greater light, wherewith the mind of man was invested before his fall' (p. 6).

Many writers were concerned to defend the doctrine of innate knowledge as a means of proving the existence of God. John Bachiler, in his edition of Philippe de Mornay's *The Soule's Own Evidence, for its Own Immortality* (1646)[1], prefaces the work with the observation:

the iniquity of the times, having so far corrupted the minds of some, that the very *innate and inbred principles of Nature* (especially about a

(*Summa Theologica*, PP, Q. 79, art. 12; PS, Q. 94, art. 1–2). *The Oxford English Dictionary* gives the meaning of syneidesis as 'that function or department of conscience which is concerned with passing judgement on acts already performed', in contrast with synteresis which passes judgements on the acts to be performed. The term epicrisis was obviously part of the same technical vocabulary but is not listed in the *OED*, and I have not been able to discover its use in any other contemporary tract. Liddell and Scott define it as determination or judgement. The doctrine of these terms was known and associated with that of innate knowledge as late as 1735, when Wollaston (*The Religion of Nature Delineated*, 6th edition) described synteresis as 'the set of those practical principles (or a habit flowing from them)' used in moral judgements (p. 23, note F).

[1] This work by Bachiler is a new edition of Sir Philip Sidney's translation of the *Traité de la vérité de la religion chrétienne* by Philippe de Mornay, published in 1581.

Deity, the *sovereign welfare*, and the *Immortality of the Soule*) seeme in a manner to be quite *obliterated and extinct* in them.

Edward Fowler, *The Principles and Practices Of certain Moderate Divines* (1670), voices the same resentment at the denial of the idea of God being innate.

> That doctrine [i.e. that we must be sceptics unless we can answer all questions concerning existence, e.g. why bodies cohere] doth as evidently contradict the natural notions God hath imprinted in the original constitution of humane souls, as can be . . . and I must adde, that I cannot question but it would to *all*, that will be but perswaded freely to consult those innate notions (pp. 212–13).

Similarly, arguing that the idea of God can be derived from the common consent of nations, William Bates, *Considerations of the Existence of God* (1676), defines universal consent as including all men 'in whom the sense of Nature is not perverted' (p. 85). True to the tradition of innate knowledge, Bates says that the idea of God is 'indelibly stamp'd on the minds of men', and argues that 'the author of the *Humane Soul* has so fram'd it, that by the free use of its faculties it necessarily comes to the knowledge of its original' (pp. 82–83). But the most forceful statement of the naïve form of the theory is that given by Stillingfleet, Locke's great antagonist. In his *Origines Sacrae* (1662) he uses the familiar language of the idea of God being stamped on the soul.

> I begin with the *first* of them, which concerns the *existence* of *God* and *immortality* of the *soul*; both which seem to be supposed as general *Prolepses* in the *writings* of *Moses*, and as *things*, so consonant to *humane nature*, that none to whom his *writings* should come could be *supposed* to *question* them (bk. iii, ch. i, no. 2, p. 363).

The doctrine of 'prolepsis' was current in the seventeenth century as 'a preassumed notion, a presupposition'.[1] Leibniz says that innate ideas were called 'prolepses' by the Stoics, 'c'est à dire des assumtions fondamentales, ou ce qu'on prend pour accordé par avance'.[2] But Rivaud has pointed out that the

---

[1] See *The Oxford English Dictionary*, article on 'prolepsis'. Cf. Thomas Jackson, *Works*, vol. vi, 1844, p. 279, containing a sermon originally preached in 1637, and John Ray, *Miscellaneous Discourses* (1692), p. 109.

[2] *Nouveaux Essais*, p. 42, in Gerhardt's edition, bd. v.

Stoic doctrine of 'prolepses' was not a genuine doctrine of innateness in its naïve form.

> Selon Zénon, l'homme possède, en raison de sa parenté divine, le pouvoir inné de comprendre certains principes métaphysiques et moraux, ou le bon sens. . . . Mais ce pouvoir ne s'exerce qu'à l'occasion des impressions sensibles. Chrysippe aurait substitué les 'prolepses' au bon sens. Mais la 'prolepse' ou 'anticipation' n'a rien d'une idée innée. Elle n'existe pas en nous au moment de la naissance, même à l'état virtuel, car il ne peut exister aucune réalité potentielle.[1]

It was to Cicero's formulation of the doctrine that Stillingfleet referred.

> And yet after all the labours of *Epicurus*, he knew it was to no purpose to *endeavour* to *root* out wholly the *belief* of a *Deity* out of the world, because of the unanimous *consent* of the *world* in it; and therefore he admits of it as a necessary *Prolepsis* or *Anticipation* of *humane nature*, *quod in omnium animis deorum notionem impressit ipsa natura*, that *nature* it self had *stamped* an *Idea* of *God* upon the minds of men (p. 365).

At one point Stillingfleet seems aware of the criticism this position invites, and so denies that the idea of God is connate to the soul in the usual sense, affirming only that 'there is a *faculty* in the *soul*, whereby upon the free use of *reason*, it can form within itself a settled *notion* of such a *Being*, which is as *perfect* as it is *possible* for us to conceive a *Being* to be' (p. 369). But only three pages later he affirms unconditionally that the idea is imprinted upon the soul, seeking to demonstrate the truth of this claim by appeal to the common agreement concerning it and to the clarity of this idea. He speaks frequently of the idea of God as a prolepsis, indicating in his usage that he has gone beyond the guarded Stoic application of that concept and has equated it with the ideas which are imprinted at birth. To the argument that not all peoples have an idea of God, he replies

> that the *dissent of these persons is not sufficient to manifest the consent not to be universal.* . . . For I demand of the greatest *Atheist*, Whether it be sufficient to say, that it is not *natural* for men to have *two legs*, because some have been *born* with *one* (p. 392).

[1] *Histoire*, t. i, p. 377. Cf. Cicero's *De Natura Deorum*, bk. 1, xvi, xvii.

This particular argument frequently appears in defence of universality of assent. In his *The Immortality of the Human Soul* (1657), Walter Charleton argues for the universality of the belief in immortality along the same lines. Even though there have been and are people and nations who lack this belief, it does not follow

that the perswasion of its Immortality ought not to be reputed General; and that the dissent of a few persons doth not make a General Consent not to be Natural. For, as, though some men are born only with one foot, and some lay violent hands upon themselves; it is not lawful for us thence to argue, that it is not natural to men to have two feet, or that the desire of life is not natural to all men (pp. 127–8).

The same defence of universal consent is found in John Wilkins's *Of the Principles and Duties of Natural Religion* (1675) (pp. 58 ff.). The reference to universal consent was a generalization about a class, but as with all generalizations exceptions were recognized within the class. The exceptions aside, Stillingfleet and a host of other theologians were convinced that the idea of God is an 'indelible character' upon the mind.

In the same year as Stillingfleet's *Origines Sacrae* was first published, Robert South preached a sermon at St. Paul's Cathedral on 9 November in which he advocated the naïve form of the theory of innateness almost as strongly as did Stillingfleet.[1] South claimed that the speculative branch of the understanding has several general maxims and notions 'which are the rules of Discourse, and the basis of all Philosophy'.[2] Examples of such speculative innate truths are 'the same thing cannot at the same time be, and not be', 'the whole is bigger than a part', 'two proportions severally equal to a third, must also be equal to one another'. He was concerned to argue for the innateness of such speculative truths in order to show the possibility of moral maxims being innate. He recognized that Aristotle affirmed 'the Mind to be at first a meer *Rasa tabula*; and that these Notions are not ingenite, and imprinted by the finger of Nature but by the latter and more languid impressions

[1] Sermon on Genesis i. 27. Reprinted in his *Twelve Sermons* (1692), pp. 53–91.
[2] Ibid., p. 62.

of sense; . . .'[1] But South argues (1) that since these notions are universal, they must proceed from some universal constant principle which can be nothing else but human nature; (2) that 'These cannot be infused by observation, because they are the rules by which men take their first apprehension and observations of things, and therefore in order of Nature must needs precede them', and (3) that therefore 'it follows that these were Notions not descending from us, but born with us; not our Offspring, but our brethren; and (as I may so say) such as we were taught without the help of a Teacher'.[2] He then goes on to make the same claims for practical principles which 'are treasured up' in the practical understanding and constitute the 'seeds of Morality'.[3] Many men who deny innate speculative principles admit, South says, innate practical principles. He offers as examples of the latter, 'God is to be worshipped', 'parents are to be honoured', 'a man's word is to be kept'. All of these are 'of universal influence, as to the regulation of the behaviour, and converse of mankind', and are 'the ground of all vertue, and civility, and the foundation of Religion'.[4]

Thus, in Carpenter, Stillingfleet, and South, the naïve form of the doctrine of innate knowledge found its strongest advocates. The various other men who espoused one form or another of the doctrine testify to its pervasiveness in the period before 1688. In every case, appeal to it was made to protect the existing values of the society, whether these were the very belief in the existence of a God or the various moral rules embedded in the religion of their faith. Not even Stillingfleet was ignorant of the objections which could be raised against the naïve form of the theory, but so necessary was the doctrine felt to be for morality and religion that objections were swept aside or incompletely met. But the tendency to modify the naïve form into a dispositional doctrine of innate knowledge was implicit as early as 1611 in William Sclater. Under this tendency the theory claimed not that men are born with completed ideas and principles of morality, but only that such

<hr>

[1] Ibid., pp. 62–63.
[3] Ibid., p. 67.
[2] Ibid., pp. 63–64.
[4] Ibid.

knowledge was implicit in the soul and merely required experience to elicit awareness of it. The Cambridge Platonists developed this particular twist to the theory with great care, showing at the same time an almost emotional attachment to the literal language of the naïve version. In *An Antidote against Atheisme* (1653), Henry More argued that the fact that the idea of God arises upon the occasion of external stimuli does not detract from its connaturality and essentiality to the soul. He compared this idea with the various ideas of geometry which are readily consented to. He argues for actual knowledge implicit in the soul but defines his position as follows:

> And when I say *actuall Knowledge*, I doe not mean that there is a certaine number of *Ideas* flaring and shining to the *Animadversive faculty* like so many *Torches* or *Starres* in the *Firmament* to our outward sight, or that there are any *figures* that take their distinct places & are legibly writ there like the *Red Letters* or *Astronomicall Characters* in an *Almanack*; but I understand thereby an active sagacity in the Soul, or quick recollection as it were, whereby some small businesse being hinted unto her, she runs out presently into a more clear & larger conception (bk. i, ch. v, p. 13).

He compares the mind to a musician who can sing a song upon being awakened and given a few notes of the tune. 'So the *Mind* of man being jogg'd and awakened by the impulses of outward objects, is stirred up into a more full and cleare conception of what was but imperfectly hinted to her from externall occasions' (p. 14). Two lines of proof are suggested by More: the first, that ideas of cause and effect, of whole, part, like and unlike, &c., cannot be derived from the senses and hence must find their origin within the soul itself; the second, that principles such as 'the whole is bigger than the part', 'if you take equals from equals, the remainders are equal', 'every number is either even or odd', are 'true to the soul at the very first proposal' (bk. i, ch. vi, p. 17). His main objective throughout is to show that the idea of God is '*Natural, necessary* and *essential* to the soul of man'. The light of nature in all men is the foundation of his doctrine. We even find him still speaking of the innate truths of the soul dictating laws to us. Like Stillingfleet, More recognized the objection against universal

consent; but unlike Stillingfleet, who gave an unsatisfactory
answer to this objection, More rejects universal consent as a
sign of innateness. The mark of innateness for him was immediate assent upon examining the reasons and nature of the
given concept or principle.

> And it is sufficient to make a thing true according to the *light of*
> *Nature*, that no man upon a perception of what is propounded & the
> Reasons of it (if it be not clear at first sight, and need reasons to back it)
> will ever stick to acknowledge for a Truth (bk. i, ch. x, p. 32).

More, in other words, was careful to formulate the doctrine in
as unobjectionable a manner as possible, but he was not willing
to relinquish the doctrine entirely. The terminology of 'red
letters' and 'torches', which More was careful to avoid, was less
clearly denied by Culverwel, who, in *An Elegant And Learned*
Discourse of the Light of Nature (1654), openly claimed that
'There are stamp't and printed upon the being of man, some
clear, and undelible principles, some first and Alphabetical
Notions; by putting together of which it can spell out the Law
of Nature' (p. 47). This vigorous and literal-sounding language
is carried on throughout Culverwel's book.

> There's scatter'd in the Soul of Man some seeds of light, which fill it
> with a vigorous pregnancy, with a multiplying fruitfulnesse, so that it
> brings forth a numerous and sparkling posterity of secondary notions,
> which make for the crowning and encompassing of the soul with happi-
> ness (p. 47).

But the language is deceptive, for, like More, Culverwel only
wished to stress the activity and spontaneity of the soul in
the generation of its ideas and in its ready and immediate
assent to certain moral and speculative principles. The discovery of these principles is made by 'an *Intellectual Lamp*'
which is set up in the soul (p. 53). He speaks, in this connexion,
of the

> heavenly beam which God has darted into the soul of man; from *the*
> *Candle of the Lord*, which God has lighted up for the discovery of his
> own Lawes; from that intellectual eye which God has fram'd and made
> exactly proportionable to this Light (p. 59).

But in chapter eleven he makes it quite plain that he did not accept the doctrine of connate species as it was generally formulated by his contemporaries. The soul does not bring any notions along with it from another world, as Plato was commonly interpreted as holding. Like More, Culverwel found it necessary to attack the naïve form of the theory:

do but analise your own thoughts, do but consult with your own breasts, tell us whence it was that the light first sprang in upon you. Had you such notions as these when you first peep't into being? at the first opening of the souls eye? in the first *exordium* of Infancy? had you these connate *species* in the Cradle? and were they rock't asleep with you? or did you then meditate upon these principles, *Totum est majus parte, & Nihil potest esse & non esse simul?* (p. 78.)

He asserts with the Aristotelians that all knowledge first enters by the senses, and, like Locke later in the century, asks for 'a catalogue of all these truths you brought with you into the world'. He denies that the idea of God is innate, asserting it to be only a power. In *The Darkness of Atheism Dispelled* (1652) Walter Charleton advanced a similar argument, insisting that the idea of God is not a signature impressed upon the minds of all men; and that, if it were, the impression 'would be one and the same in all men; that all men would then conceive God under the same *Form* and Idea' (p. 35). Even if the belief were universal, he argues, after the fashion of More, this would not be evidence that it is one of those '*Implantate Notions*, which the same hand, that made our nature, hath engraven on the table of our minds, and left it not in the power of our depraved Wills totally to obliterate' (p. 105). In a later work, *The Immortality of the Human Soul* (1657), he uses 'innate' in the sense of 'potential' only. This work is written in dialogue form, with Lucretius, Athanasius, and Isodicastes as participants. Athanasius seems to represent the views of Charleton. In opposition to Lucretius' assertion of the Aristotelian principle of 'nothing in the intellect but what is first in the senses', Athanasius cites as exceptions 'the Common Notions, that are as it were engraven on our Minds' (p. 92), but he hastens to explain that by 'innate' he means only that which is 'potential'. Later, arguing for the immateriality of the soul, Athanasius insists that it will not be accounted paradoxical in me to affirm, that Immaterial Objects are most genuine and natural to the Understanding; especially since *Des Cartes* hath irrefutably demonstrated, that the Knowledge we have of the existence of the Supreme Being, and of our own Souls, is not only Proleptical and Innate in the Mind of man, but also more certain, clear, and distinct, than the Knowledge of any Corporeal Nature whatever (p. 119).

The qualification of 'innate' as 'potential' is not repeated, but we may assume that Charleton meant it to be operative.[1]

The terminology of the doctrine which More, Culverwel, and Charleton all combatted was the same: it was the terminology of the naïve form of the theory of innateness. All three were concerned, however, to retain a modified version of the theory. Their example was followed by other writers of the period before 1688. In *The Interest of Reason in Religion* (1675) Robert Ferguson argues that one meaning of the term 'reason' is those truths which are 'so connate to Sense and Reason; that upon their bare Representation they are universally assented to'. Like More and Culverwel, he denies that we are born with these truths.

I do not say that we are brought forth with a List and Scroll of *Axioms* formally Imprinted upon our Faculties; but I say that we are furnished with such Powers, upon the first Exercise of which about such things without any Harangues of Discourse, or previous Ratiocinations, we cannot without doing Violence to our Rational Nature, but pay them an Assent (pp. 22–23).

He calls these truths 'natural' and makes them the foundation of all science, knowledge, and discourse. He cites the law of contradiction and the law of causality as examples, and concludes the argument with the observation:

I know no *Idea's* formally *Innate*; what we commonly call so, are the Results of the Exercise of our Reason. The Notion of God is not

[1] Charleton may have changed his views, for in a still later work, *Natural History of the Passions* (1674), in large part a translation of Jean François Senault's *De L'Usage des Passions* (1641), the early portions contain positive assertions of the naïve form of innateness which are not to be found in Senault's work. Equating innate knowledge with the natural instinct of animals, he speaks of such knowledge as 'being by the omnipotent Creator, in the very act of their Formation, infused, and as an indelible Character impress'd upon their very principles or natures' (p. 39). Later he writes of 'a law engraven upon their hearts' (p. 41).

otherwise inbred, then that the Soul is furnished with such a Natural Sagacity, that upon the Exercise of her rational Powers, she is Infallibly led to the Acknowledgement of a Deity (p. 41).

The same rejection of the idea of God as innate is present in John Pearson's *An Exposition of the Creed* (1659).

For although some have imagined that the knowledge of a Deity is connaturall to the soul of man, so that every man hath a connate inbred notion of a God; yet I rather conceive the soul of man to have no connaturall knowledge at all, no particular notion of any thing in it from the beginning, but to receive the first apprehensions of things by sense, and by them to make all rationall collections. If then the soul of man be at first like a fair smooth table without any actuall characters of knowledge imprinted in it; if all knowledge which we have comes successively by sensation, instruction, and rationall collection, then we must not referre the apprehension of a Deity to any connate notion or inbred opinion (p. 32).

Samuel Parker not only denied the doctrine of innateness in whatever form it was couched, but went on to develop the alternative in some detail and sought for an explanation of why men have held to the naïve form of the theory. It is significant that the argument Parker opposes is not the modified version but the naïve form. Ascribing to Plato the doctrine that all knowledge is obtained by comparing objects perceived with their 'Ideal Pictures or Images engraven on our understanding', he argues that all knowledge, even that supposedly drawn from maxims, is had from experience and observation.[1]

Now to what purpose should Providence imprint such obvious and apparent Notices as this [that the whole is greater than its parts] upon the minds of Men, when as but to open our eyes, is enough to discover their undoubted Truth and Evidence? . . . But suppose that we were born with these congenite Anticipations, and that they take Root in our very Faculties, yet how can I be certain of their Truth and Veracity? For 'tis not impossible but the seeds of Error might have been the natural Results of my Faculties, as Weeds are the first and natural Issues of the best Soyles, how then shall we be sure that these spontaneous Notions are not false and spurious?[2]

The only means of gaining such certainty is to test these truths by experience. Even if there are connate principles, they are of

[1] *A Free and Impartial Censure Of The Platonick Philosophie* (1666), p. 55.
[2] Ibid., p. 56.

no use since 'before I have made Tryal, I cannot use them'. No good purpose is served by invoking innate notions.

But when we begin our knowledge from Notions within our selves, besides that 'tis a difficult and nice dispute to prove that the mind of man is furnished with any such innate *Prolepses*, and that we are destitute of any sure κριτήριον to discern Natural Anticipations from Preconceptions of Custome and Education (unlesse we bring them to the Touchstone of Experience) 'tis doubtless that Generalities are not capable of so palpable and convictive an Evidence, as Single and particular Observations.[1]

He sought, in *A Demonstration of the Divine Authority of the Law of Nature* (1681), to account for the growth of the naïve form of the doctrine on the basis of the misuse of language.

As to the Sufficiency of the Publication of the Law of Nature, the plain Account of it has been obscured by nothing more, then that it has alwaies been described and discoursed of in metaphorical and allusive Expressions, such as *Engravings*, and *Inscriptions*, and the *Tables of the Heart*, &c. As if the Law of Nature consisted of a certain number of Propositions that were imprinted upon the Minds of Men, and concreated with their Understandings, by attending to and reflecting upon which they were instructed or bound to govern their moral Actions (p. 5).

No better statement of the naïve form of the argument and the reasons for its appeal can be found in the literature of the seventeenth century. Parker suggests here, as he had done earlier, that even though the law of nature is imprinted upon our minds, we can never know it to be so. For man, the law of nature has an empirical origin, is derived by man's own reasonings from his observations of nature.

Parker was, of course, strongly influenced by the new science and was himself a member of the Royal Society. The appeal to innate, pre-experiential principles was opposed to the empiricism of this new movement. When religion ceased to be an affair of the heart, a private, personal relation between a man and his God, men began to find God in nature. Religion became less complex, more open, and more rational. If God is Himself in nature, what need is there for His laws and commands to be

[1] Ibid., p. 57.

written in the heart? The function of these laws was usurped by reason and observation. In his own early *Essays on the Law of Nature*, Locke exemplified this externalizing tendency by argu-ing that from the reports of our senses we infer a God as maker of the world: 'as soon as this is laid down, the notion of a uni-versal law of nature binding on all men necessarily emerges....'[1] The law of nature accordingly lost its innate basis; but in the minds of those who defended this concept of a law of nature, the force and certainty of the law were not rendered any the less powerful. When Locke came to reflect upon the problems of knowledge and religion, he found appealing this new attitude towards a simple naturalistic religion and an empirical basis for values. The old naïve form of the doctrine of an innate basis for values had been thoroughly exploded by 1688. Locke merely gave to these arguments their classic and most thorough state-ment. He had been preceded in this statement of the arguments against the naïve form of the theory by More, Culverwel, and Parker, and a number of lesser-known men. Burthogge, too, had gone far towards summarizing the older point of view on this issue. In *Causa Dei* (1675), Burthogge had insisted that the general articles of religion

wherein all men the World over commonly agree, and which are there-fore called *common sentiments though* they be *not* (what by some they be imagined) *Innate Idea's* or Notions ingrafted and imprinted on the Minds of Men by Nature, but ... *main and substantial Points of the first Tradition* (pp. 340–1).

Like Locke, he put his finger upon the customary basis of the religious values of his age. In *Organum Vetus & Novum* (1678), Burthogge referred to both sides of the doctrine, to the prac-tical and speculative maxims claimed to be innate. He remarks that some men have been convinced that the understanding has been furnished with

Anticipations, that is, with Connatural and Ingrafted Notions; Principles designedly implanted in the Minde, to be a rule to it to direct it. Thus in the *speculative* Understanding they have set up a habit, which

---

[1] *Essays on the Law of Nature*, ed. by W. von Leyden, Oxford, 1954, p. 133; cf. p. 151.

they call *Intelligence*; in the *Practical* another which is called *Synteresis*; in both a Constellation of *Principles*, shining with their own Light, and imparting it to others that want it (p. 55).

The doctrine which we have found invoked by various writers in the century is well summarized by Burthogge. He rejects the theory entirely.

But were there really such a System of Notions and first Principles ingrafted in the Minde by Nature, in whose Light all others were to shine and to be seen, it would follow that Contemplation of our own mindes, acquainting us with the Chain, Concatenation, and Sorites of the Principles therein, and Propositions deducible therefrom, would more impart to the rendring us Philosophers (not to say Divines also) than observation of the World and Experience; and so the greatest School-men (those Metaphysical Alchymists) that insisted much on this Method, and spun out all their notions of their own Bowels, should have been the wisest and most fruitful of men (pp. 55–56).

Burthogge was not impressed with the systems of the schoolmen. Like Parker, he sought to relate all knowledge to experience.

Again, the Soul in its state of Union and Conjunction with the Body, is so dependent on it in all its Operations, that it exercises none without the Aids of it. Ratiocination it self it is an Animal act; not an abstract Action of the Soul, but a (Concrete) act of the Animal; it is the Man reasons. And in the ordinary method of Nature, we receive into our Mindes no Impressions, no Images, but what are handed to them by our Senses. I am apt to think that a person who should never have seen, nor heard, nor tasted, nor smelt, nor felt any thing, would have his minde as little furnish'd with Idea's or Notions, as his Memory with Images, and would understand as little as he had sensed (pp. 56–57).

He goes on to affirm that the propositions commonly assented to do not involve a natural or automatic assent but a judicial assent, based on the evidence which the propositions bring. 'For instance, that the whole is greater than the part, we assented not unto it on the first hearing, but first considering what was meant by Whole, what by Part, what by Greater, what by Lesser' (pp. 57–58). Such propositions are so easily assented to that some doubt arises as to just when we did first assent to them. But, he concludes, 'Beings are not to be multiplied without *Necessity*.' Hence, innate notions are to be dispensed with as unnecessary.

§ 2—*The Critics of Locke's Polemic*

An examination of the literature in England prior to 1688 reveals, then, a firm and pervasive acceptance of the doctrine of innate knowledge, a doctrine held by many in its naïve form, modified into a dispositional doctrine by others, and criticized thoroughly by still other men sympathetic to the new movements within science and religion. All mystery as to the referents of Book One of Locke's *Essay* would seem to be dispelled. To ask whom Locke was attacking in that book is like asking whom Parker, Burthogge, More, or Culverwel were attacking. These men were not writing about a mythical doctrine never held by anyone. They were all attacking a firmly established doctrine which they considered to be no longer useful, and even injurious to religion and to the values they held. But should any doubts still linger in our minds concerning the adherents to the naïve form of the doctrine, a close look at the reception accorded to Locke's polemic confirms the impression we acquire while examining the literature prior to 1688. Some of Locke's critics deny that anyone ever held the naïve form of the doctrine, referring only to the modified dispositional version which they still feel to be necessary for morality and religion. Others admit the cogency of Locke's criticisms but only grudgingly. A few others, even into the eighteenth century, still advance the naïve form in opposition to Locke's denial. None of the critics recognizes the validity of grounding values or the law of nature in experience.

The doctrine of innate knowledge is found in some men after 1688 who make no reference to Locke. Of these, John Hartcliffe, *A Treatise of Moral and Intellectual Virtues* (1691), sought to defend the naïve form of the theory.

First there is a secret impression upon the Minds of Men, whereby they are naturally directed to approve some things as *good*, and avoid other things as *evil*. . . . Now these inclinations do not proceed from Reason, but from Nature, and are antecedent to all Discourse, as it is

manifest from hence, that they are as strong, and do put forth themselves
as vigorously in young persons, as in those that are older; they do shew
themselves as much in the rude and ignorant sort of People, as in those
who are more refined, and better instructed (pp. 352–3).

To the suggestion that this doctrine is contradicted by the fact
that some men have ideas of good and evil different from those
of others, he replies that there is a paucity of such men and that
they are no less than monsters, 'and no more to be drawn into
an argument against the truth of this assertion, than a Man
being born with three legs can be an argument, that Men
naturally have not two' (p. 358). There is a natural instinct in
man in terms of which 'we know what we ought to do, antecedent to all Reason & Discourse' (p. 359). Richard Bentley, in
the first of his Boyle lectures, *The Folly of Atheism* (1692),
speaks favourably of the 'commonly received notion of an
Innate Idea of God, imprinted upon every Soul of Man at their
Creation, in Characters that can never be defaced' (p. 4).
William Nicholls, *A Conference with a Theist*, Part iii (1697),
remarks that the alternative to innateness 'may be subject to as
many difficulties' as inhere in the doctrine of innateness (p. 33).
William King, *De Origine Mali* (1702), was concerned to defend
the modified version of the doctrine (pp. 7–9). In the remarks
which he sent to Locke via Molyneux in 1692, he charged
Locke with confusing the observation or recognition of a
principle as innate with the use of such a principle. He there
defined 'innate' as 'a thought that the natural frame of the mind
& circumstances in which God and nature has placed us, will
bring into our minds, if we do not do violence to our minds to
keep it out'.[1] Locke, King objected, 'will allow no idea innate
but such as a man brings coined in his mind like a shilling. So
that an innate idea is an actuall thought with him, which no
body, that I know of, ever said.'[2] He cites the example of a
child drawing back from fire the very first time it experiences
heat, thus showing that the child has an idea of heat framed in
his mind.

[1] MS. Locke, C. 28, f. 100.
[2] Ibid., ff. 99–100.

It is no argument that there are no notions graven in the mind by nature antecedent to all sense because men do not immediately think of them any more than it is an argument that a philosopher never knows any thing in his life because he is hard to be awakened out of sleep.[1]

Further, King does not believe Locke has explained sufficiently the origin of ideas or shown that, for example, the application of heat gives rise to the idea of heat.

Some will think all ideas preexisting in the soul, & that the application of outward objects only oblige the soul to attend to them; as letters written with the fluid of lemon are in the paper but not visible till fire make them so.[2]

Finally, the making of all ideas adventitious provides us with no certainty or assurance that men can have the same idea of heat, &c. This assurance is secured by the doctrine of innate ideas. In short, the doctrine of innate ideas, taken in its dispositional form, is both plausible and useful.

King borrowed other epistemological doctrines from the *Essay* and incorporated them in his *De Origine Mali*; but in the English translation of that work made after his death,[3] the notes on innate ideas have been removed and copious references to Locke's polemic inserted and quoted as authority to show that the doctrine of innate knowledge had been thoroughly exploded. His translators were working from manuscript material left by King, so it looks as if he altered his opinion on this doctrine after the first edition of his book. If so, we have an interesting example of Locke's persuasive powers. Locke was not so fortunate with his other critics. At the end of his abridgement of his *Essay* in the 1688 issue of LeClerc's *Bibliothèque Universelle*, he had asked for reactions and comments upon this outline to be sent to him in Amsterdam. At least two sets of comments were received by him in response to this suggestion. Both authors defend the doctrine of innate knowledge against Locke, the one with great detail, the other only in passing. Christian Knorr von Rosenroth begins his remarks, ' Observationes: In Tractatûm On. J. Locke de Intellectù:

[1] MS. Locke, C. 28, f. 99.   [2] Ibid., f. 100.
[3] *An Essay on the Origin of Evil* (1731), tr. by Edmund Law.

secûndûm doctrinam Hebraeorûm & Philosophorûm antiquorûm',[1] by pointing out that the *tabula rasa* doctrine does not find support in the old Hebrew texts or in Plato. He admits, however, two qualified senses in which one could speak of the mind as being a *tabula rasa*: one at the time of creation, where the mind 'nihil in se continebat, quàm quod à Luminibus divinis ipsi imprimeretur', the other at the time of the final reunion with God, 'ubi abrasis omnibus ideis prioribus, Intellectus iterum erit tabula rasa, nihilque contemplabitúr quam summùm illud Visionis suae beatificae Objectûm'. The nearer the mind ascends to the beatific vision, the more it merits to be called a *tabula rasa*. But minds of this calibre are rare. The ordinary man's mind is never a blank tablet, but always contains divine impressions.

The other reply to the abstract in LeClerc's journal was written by Fredericus van Leenhof at the instigation of a friend in Holland who knew Locke.[2] He was much impressed by the *Essay* and had many words of praise for Locke, but he admitted that he lacked the time required for making himself familiar enough with the terminology and the required distinctions to warrant his making extended and detailed criticisms. He does, however, indicate that he finds the rejection of innate ideas in the *Essay* difficult to accept, since for him the very concept of a soul entails the concept of ideas within the soul. To speak of the soul as a *tabula rasa* 'without previously created ideas' distorts the very meaning of the term. Leenhof belonged to a tradition in which the doctrine of innate knowledge was so firmly rooted that it was taken for granted. Although he does not indicate the specific details of the doctrine which he accepted, it is probable that it was similar to that formulated by Knorr von Rosenroth.

[1] MS. Locke, C. 13, ff. 14–15. Knorr von Rosenroth was a well-known Judaic scholar, author of *Kabbala Denudata* (1677–84).

[2] MS. Locke, C. 13, f. 152. These comments are in the form of a letter, the recipient of the letter being undoubtedly Peter Guenellon, friend of Locke and Leenhof. Guenellon also refers to them in one of his letters to Locke. (Cf. MS. Locke, C. 11, f. 5.) Leenhof was a prominent minister and mathematician of Holland (1647–1712), interested in Descartes and Spinoza, who got into trouble with his book, *Den Hemel op Aaide* (1703). For further information concerning him, cf. *Biographisch Woodenboek der Nederlanden.*

But the interesting aspect of these two comments from Holland
is that they show again the peculiar character of the appeal to
innate knowledge in England in the seventeenth century.
Among the Cartesians on the Continent, innateness was invoked
as part of the theoretical structure laid down by Descartes. The
two examples of advocates of the doctrine which we have from
Holland indicate that the doctrine there took the Cartesian form
as well as, in the case of Knorr von Rosenroth, being rooted in
the Judaic tradition. In England, the doctrine was always intimately bound up with the defence of the law of nature, with
the foundations of morality and religion. But in Holland as
well as in England it was the divines who reacted most strongly
against Locke's polemic. Tyrrell wrote in 1690 that the theologians were 'much scandalized that so sweet & easy a part of
their sermons: as that of the Laws written in the heart, is
rendered false & uselesse'.[1] One of the first attacks upon Book
One to which Locke replied was written by James Lowde
(*A Discourse Concerning the Nature of Man*, 1694), who was in
the heart of this English tradition. For Lowde, there were just
two basic sources of knowledge: the natural inscriptions on the
minds of men, and revelation (p. 51). Lowde denied that anyone ever held to the naïve form of the doctrine, indicating that
in accepting a doctrine of innate knowledge he did not mean
that the soul has an existence prior to this life or that all
knowledge is, as the Platonists say, a recollection.

> These natural Notions are not so imprinted upon the Soul, as that
> they naturally and necessarily exert themselves (even in Children and
> Ideots) without any assistance from the outward Senses, or without the
> help of some previous Cultivation (pp. 52–53).

He was an adherent of the dispositional modification. When
working properly, the understanding has

> a native power of finding or framing such Principles or Propositions, the
> Truth or Knowledge whereof no ways depends upon the evidence of
> sense or observation: thus knowing what is meant by a whole, and what
> by a part, hence naturally results the truth of this Proposition, *totum est
> majus suâ parte*, without any ways oblig'd to sense for it (p. 53).

[1] Tyrrell to Locke, 18 February 1689/90. MS. Locke C. 22, f. 82.

Lowde attacked Parker along with Locke, insisting that 'it must be granted, that it is at least possible for God to imprint truths upon the minds of Men: and if so then it cannot be done any other way, than by making 'em thus plain and self evident' (p. 56). It was Lowde's conviction that God 'hath communicated something of a Divine Ray, relating both to Intellectual and Moral Notices, into the very constitution of our humane Nature, something that is both a light and a law unto us' (pp. 63–64). Innate ideas are not 'super-induc'd or imprinted upon the Soul, *In esse completo*' but are 'native Properties and Qualifications of the Soul' (p. 82).

Lowde went on to charge Locke with reducing the foundation of morality to custom, a charge which Locke stoutly denied. Moral goodness and evil for Locke were grounded in the law of nature; but his denial of the naïve form of innateness led many of his readers to interpret him as uprooting the traditional and, in their eyes, the only legitimate basis for morality. Locke insisted that he was not opposed to the dispositional version of the theory of innateness. He only wished to point out that in this form the theory claimed so little that it no longer merited the name 'innate'. Lowde's doctrine asserted, he pointed out in his reply, that 'there are certain propositions which, though the soul from the beginning, or when a man is born, does not know, yet "by assistance from the outward senses, and the help of some previous cultivation", it may *afterwards* come certainly to know the truth of; which is no more than what I have affirmed in my First Book'. But Lowde did not wish to assert only this minimal claim. Locke was pointing out in effect that the test for dispositional innateness can only come after experience and that then, as Parker had observed, the claim for innateness becomes pointless. But with this interpretation Lowde did not agree. Like many other men in the period he believed that it was necessary and meaningful to adhere to the dispositional form of the theory. The revisions of Parker and Locke were too radical for most men of the century to follow. Once innate knowledge had been denied, in both its naïve and its dispositional forms, the readers of the

Essay looked about for Locke's substitute. The best they could find there as a basis for morality was custom or praise and blame. Tyrrell's friends, and even Tyrrell himself, found it difficult to construct any other interpretation of Book One.

> Since I came into the country I have begun again to read over your excellent Essay with great satisfaction; and discourseing with some thinking men at Oxford, no long since I found them dissatisfyed with what you have sayed concerneing the Law of nature (or reason) whereby wee distinguish moral good from evil & vertue from vice. For tho I confesse in your third chap p. 21 you thinke they equally forsake the truth, who running into the contrary extremes, either affirme an innate Law; or deny that there is a Law knowable by the light of nature; i.e. without the help of positive revelation. Yet they thinke you have in your second chap: p. 158, 159, 160 destroyed this reasonable concession, & resolved all vertue & vice & the law by which it is establisht out of a commonwealth, & abstracted from divine revelation; into the praise or dispraise that men give to certain actions in general.[1]

Thomas Becconsall in *The Grounds and Foundation of Natural Religion* (1698) saw the same dangers in the first book of the *Essay*. He was firmly convinced of the existence of a law of nature prior to revelation, a natural instinct for self-preservation being given to man which shows him upon reflection that he owes his present existence to God. From this fact alone, man is able to deduce what duties he owes to God, and from these to set up laws referring to God and man. Becconsall recognized that Locke did not deny the law of nature; but in undermining universal consent as its foundation, he believed Locke had in effect weakened the law and left the way open for the Latitudinarians and for those other men who wished to deny all such laws and base religion upon reason. Where is that universal consent which 'assures us there are Laws of Nature, or indispensable established Rules of Morality' (p. 46)? Like Parker, Becconsall tried to suggest reasons why laws of nature had been considered by so many as being innate, but in his suggestions he reveals a language which itself suggests reluctance to relinquish the doctrine.

[1] Tyrrell to Locke, 30 June 1690, MS. Locke, C. 22, ff. 90–91.

But further, that which in reality gives them the appearance of Innate Principles and the denomination of Laws of Nature, is the evidence and perspicuity of 'em. For since it is concluded, that Laws of Nature result from the very Frame and Order of Nature, from that state and condition of Things wherein we were born, and whereby we subsist; they must undoubtedly discover 'emselves to the Minds of Men, even tho' they were lodged in the *most simple and unimproved State of Nature.* . . . In a word, they are Laws of Nature, because they are *Impressions that are stamped on the Mind* from the most importunate cravings and exigencies of Nature; and they carry the appearance of Innate Principles, because they are certainly some of the first Suggestions that accompany a Mind after its arrived to a State of Thinking. (Pp. 67–68. My italics.)

Moreover, to Locke's dictum that there can be no ideas which are not actual and conscious perceptions of the mind, Becconsall replies that he can see no reason

why native Inscriptions may not remain without being actually attended to, as well as written Laws, or acquir'd Ideas. It's well known, those that contend for Innate Ideas, or Principles, do not think they discover 'emselves without the Exercise of our natural Powers and Faculties; and some of those external Means and Instruments that are necessary to acquired Knowledge (p. 73).

Becconsall makes a show of dispensing with the doctrine of innate knowledge, claiming that a fully rational religion can serve all the ends of the appeal to innateness; but the doctrine is not dead for him. Not only does it reappear in the terminology he employs, in his partiality for the criterion of universal consent for the laws of nature, but he defends a doctrine of natural conscience as well.

The dispositional version of the theory and the doctrine of natural conscience had been strongly defended the year before Becconsall's book by Thomas Burnet in a series of three *Remarks* on the *Essay*. Conscience for Burnet was 'a Natural Sagacity to distinguish Moral Good and Evil, or a different perception and sense of them, with a different affection of the Mind arising from it; and this so immediate as to prevent and anticipate all External Laws, and all Ratiocination'.[1] In the marginal replies in his copy of Burnet's third series of comments, Locke points out that 'It is not conscience that

[1] *Third Remark* (1699), pp. 7–8.

makes the distinction of good & evil, conscience only judging
of any action by that which it takes to be the rule of good &
evil' (note iii, p. 5).[1] Burnet confused the precepts by means of
which conscience works with the conscience itself. Like many
of his predecessors, he criticized Locke's formulation of the
doctrine of innate practical principles on the ground that
the adherents of this doctrine do not insist upon complete ideas
before the use of reason, but only on tendencies or instinct.
Burnet's own sympathies were clearly on the side of the dispositional analysis. He speaks of a natural sense of beauty and
order in all men and thence seeks to argue for a natural moral
sense. A list of innate rules, as Locke required, is not necessary,
since the natural moral conscience dictates anew each time it is
consulted. But such a position, such a modification of the naïve
form of the theory, cuts the ground from under the theory
itself; for, as Locke pointed out,

> Of those who say there are a set of fundamental propositions neces-
> sary to be believed by every one for salvation, it is reasonable to ask a
> list of them. And of those who say there are innate laws or rules of right
> or wrong, 'tis reasonable to demand a list of them, & he that cannot pro-
> duce what he soe tells of 'tis plain folly (note xxxv, p. 15).

For Locke there were just two alternatives. Either ideas and
principles are innate in the sense of full-blown and perfect
ideas, or they can be only tendencies which arise with experience. The former is absurd and false, the latter trivial and
of no consequence.

> If moral Ideas or moral rules (which are the moral principles I deny
> to be innate) are innate, I say children must know them as well as
> men. If by moral principles you mean a faculty to finde out in time the
> moral difference of actions. Besides that this is an improper way of
> speaking to cal a power principles; I never deny'd such a power to be
> innate, but that which I deny'd was that any Ideas or connection of
> Ideas was innate (note ix, p. 8).

[1] Locke's copy of Burnet's third set of *Remarks*, with Locke's marginal notes,
is in the Yale University Library. The manuscript notes have been published
by Noah Porter. The numbering of the notes is mine and refers to their order of
appearance in Locke's copy. The pagination refers to their location in Burnet's
text.

Moral good and evil must be learned before they can be achieved or avoided. Locke will allow a disposition towards good and evil if we mean by this only that men will be able in time to make the distinction between good and evil. He firmly denied that the soul has a natural disposition towards good and away from evil prior to experience.

Men have a natural tendency to what delights and from what pains them. This universal observation has established past doubt. That the soul has such a tendency to what is morally good & from what is morally evil has not fallen under my observation, & therefor I cannot grant it for as being (note xi, p. 9).

Writing in 1704, Anthony Collins observed that

1 there can be nothing advanced contradictory to the design of the *Essay of Human Und.* but on the Principle of Innate Ideas, in that sense they are refuted by the Author in the 1st book. 2 That Mr. Lee, Mr. Lowde, &c., who pretend to maintain Innate Ideas & by using the terms improperly, may seem to those, that will not examine, to be of a different opinion from him, do, notwithstanding their inclination to contradict him, state the Question so as to leave nothing contrary to what the Author has said.[1]

But Collins failed to see the very real antithesis which existed between Locke and his critics on this issue. The conviction held by Lowde, Burnet, and others was that there exists in the mind a disposition which, independent of experience, leads man towards good and away from evil. Locke was no more willing to subscribe to this dictum than he was to the naïve form of the theory of innate knowledge. John Milner (*An Account of Mr. Lock's Religion*, 1700) seems to have understood this fundamental difference which existed between Locke and those who held even to the dispositional form of the theory. Milner was concerned to defend Lord Herbert of Cherbury against Locke's analysis as well as to defend the modified version of the theory. But Milner could not square Locke's total rejection of innate knowledge with his retention of the concept of a law of nature.

It is known to be Mr. *Lock's* darling Notion, That there are no innate Ideas, and no innate Law, and consequently, according to him, the Law

---

[1] Collins to Locke, 15 March 1703/4. MS. Locke C. 7, f. 26.

of Nature is not innate; but he tells us, that the *Knowledge of it is attain'd by the light of Nature, or by our natural Faculties from natural Principles.* But I would ask him, Whence we have these natural Principles, from which by our natural Faculties, we attain to the Knowledge of the Law of Nature; for he denies all innate Principles (p. 60).

The test for innateness for Milner was the ready and prone assent of reason.

Now of such things, as so soon as they are alledged, all Men acknowledge them to be true or good, they require no Proof or farther Discourse to be assured of the Truth or Goodness of them, we need not fear to say, that they seem to have a good Title, to be receiv'd for common Notions or Catholick Truths written in the hearts of Men; which is all that the Lord *Herbert* contends for (p. 177).

Henry Lee (*Anti-Scepticism*, 1702) gave the usual expression to this belief. All men are born with a certain genius or capacity, a set of dispositions which are universally the same. An external object is required to serve as a stimulus for bringing forth the latent disposition, but the reason these truths or principles are called innate is that the soul is not indifferent to receiving and recognizing them. The soul is not a *tabula rasa* because it does not receive all impressions or truths with equal indifference. And the kind of truths it does receive are a result of the dispositions given to us by God. The classic statement of this position is found in Leibniz, who in his *Nouveaux Essais* urged against Locke that truths are innate in the sense that the figure of Hercules is in the marble potentially, waiting for the sculptor and even determining the way in which the sculptor proceeds. Ideas and truths are innate in us as 'une disposition, une aptitude, une préformation'. Like Lee, Leibniz had argued:

il ne me semble point qu'il s'ensuit que les occasions qui les font envisager, les font naistre. Et cette experience ne sçauroit determiner, si c'est par immission d'une espèce ou par l'impression des traces sur un tableau vuide, ou si c'est par le developpement de ce qui est déja en nous, que nous nous en appercevons. Il n'est pas extraordinaire qu'il y ait quelque chose en nostre esprit dont nous ne nous appercevions point toujours. La reminiscence fait voir, que nous avons souvent de la peine à nous souvenir de ce que nous sçavons, et à attraper ce qui est déja dans le clos et dans la possession de nostre entendement. Cela se trouvant vray dans les connoissances acquises, rien n'empeche qu'il ne soit vray aussi dans celles qui sont nées avec nous. Et même il y a encor plus de difficulté de s'appercevoir de ces dernieres, quand elles n'ont pas encor esté modifidées, et circonstanciées par des experiences, comme les acquises le sont, dont souvent les circonstances nous font souvenir.[1]

With this orientation, neither Leibniz nor Lee would consider Locke's example of children as a legitimate test case, since they are hardly capable of any thoughts. Whereas Leibniz was concerned with the merits and defects of Locke's epistemology itself, Lee was concerned with these doctrines only as they affected religion and morality. Leibniz was willing to take as the criterion of innate truths, the familiar 'ready and prone assent'. 'Mais l'usage fait, qu'on a coustume d'appeler nées avec nous les verités à qui on donne créance aussitost qu'on les entend . . .'[2] Distinguishing between derived or contingent, and necessary or primitive truths, Leibniz sought to make his meaning more clear to Locke. Contingent truths depend upon experience, but

les verités primitives (telles que le principe de la contradiction) ne viennent point des sens ou de l'experience et n'en sçauroient estre prouvées parfaitement, mais de la lumiere naturelle interne, et c'est ce que je veux, en disant qu'elles sont nées avec nous.[3]

But these distinctions were not only wasted on Locke, who found them unintelligible; they went far beyond anything that Lee and the other contemporary English critics of Locke envisaged. Like most of the other critics, Lee was concerned to defend the stable tradition. He was afraid of the consequences of what he took to be the relativity of moral laws implied in Locke's rejection of innate kowledge. He insisted that prior to the influence of all custom, there are certain moral dispositions implanted in man's nature by God.

'Tis so far from being true, that there are no Laws of *Nature* or *Practical* Propositions impress'd upon the Minds of all Men, that all

[1] 'Enchantillon de Reflexions sur le I Livre de l'Essay de l'Entendement de l'homme', 1698, Gerhardt, op. cit., bd. v, p. 20.
[2] Ibid., p. 21.
[3] Ibid., p. 22.

Human Laws whatever derive the main strength of their Obligation from them, and are either valid or invalid, as they are *agreeable* or *disagreeable* to them.[1]

The distinction between innate laws and natural laws was taken as entailing a relativity of morality. The *Esssay* was attacked from various quarters for this abandonment of the stable tradition. William Sherlock had preached from the pulpit the charge that Locke's book was atheistical because it rejected innate ideas.[2] Lee had even found a connexion between the rejection of innate ideas and the suggestion that matter might be able to think, arguing that the only justification he could find for Locke's devoting time to denying innate ideas and principles was that he meant to make the soul material and to follow Hobbes on idea-genesis. Locke's rejection of innate knowledge was labelled by many theologians as Socinian and atheistical, so that the publication of Sherlock's charge came as no new attack. But the clergy considered they had won a great triumph through Sherlock's publication.

> The Clergy triumph upon Dr. S's *Digression concerning Connate Ideas* in his late book. Those that I am acquainted with take all occasions to tell me of it: but if reducing 'em to silence be a mark of its being indefensible, I have had that advantage over 'em. Upon which I made this observation, that it is easier to defend nonsense in print than in discourse where they have time to invent disguises & artifices to impose on the Reader, & where they have the liberty to omitt speaking to what is material.[3]

---

[1] Lee, op. cit., p. 37.

[2] See Collins's remark in his letter to Locke, 13 June 1704. 'Dr. Sherlock in a book that will be publish'd in two or three days, hath printed some part of what he formerly preach'd against your Essay &c: & I presume intends more by his calling this a first part. What relates to you I have read over & since there are several new & extraordinary Arguments & Questions put to you I shall transcribe a little whereby you may judge of the rest.' (MS. Locke, C. 7, f. 45.)

[3] Collins to Locke, 20 June 1704. MS. Locke, C. 7, f. 47. Tyrrell commented on Sherlock as follows: 'I have not yet Read what Dr. Sherlock has written against your thoughts of Innate Ideas, but if that book be no better than others I have seen of the same Author's, I cannot from the character I have received of it, but think he had done much better to have confin'd himself to practical rather than polemick divinity . . . .' (Tyrrell to Locke, 4 July 1704. MS. Locke, C. 22, f. 169.) Robert South urged Locke to reply to Sherlock in forceful terms, so erroneous and damaging did he think the charge of atheism was. (South to Locke, 18 July 1704, MS. Locke, C. 18, ff. 175–6.)

The denial of innate ideas meant for Sherlock the banishment of 'Original Mind and Wisdom out of the World' and the making of 'Mind younger than Matter, later than the making of the World, and therefore not the Maker of it.'[1] If God be admitted, innate ideas follow, since ideas are necessary to God prior to the world. Man's mind is like that of God. Thus, our knowledge must also resemble God's knowledge.

For a Mind is, whether created or uncreated: and if created Minds are made after the Pattern of the Divine Mind, (and there is no other Pattern for Minds) Natural Ideas must be as essential to created Minds, as they are to the uncreated Mind; for there is no Notion of a Mind without them.[2]

Sherlock went on to offer other arguments in his own favour such as that ideas, not being in the objects external to the mind, must be in the mind and hence cannot come from without; or, that from the nature of a rational soul we can conclude the existence of ideas which are there. Knowledge for him comes from reflection upon knowledge given us by God. Like Lee, he denies that any man ever held the naïve doctrine of innateness: 'most of the Certain and Useful Notions we have, are Innate; and yet I doubt not but our Actual Knowledge is acquired, and possibly much in the same way that Mr. *Lock* represents it.'[3]

The motivation behind Sherlock's attack is found in one of his closing remarks in his 'Digression', where he expresses the fear that Locke's doctrine will provide solace for the atheists.

For after all, there is not a more formidable Objection against Religion, than to teach, That Mankind is made without any Connate Natural Impressions and Ideas of a God, and of Good and Evil: For if all the Knowledge we have of God, and of Good and Evil, be made by our selves, Atheists will easily conclude, that it is only the Effect of Education, and Superstitious fears (pp. 161–2).

Most of the critics of Book One were content to defend the dispositional version of the theory of innate knowledge,

[1] Sherlock, 'Digression', in his *A Discourse Concerning the Happiness of Good Men* (1704), p. 124.
[2] Ibid., p. 126.
[3] Ibid., p. 144.

believing that this satisfied all the needs of religion and circumvented many objections which had been raised. But a few stoutly refused to give up the naïve form of the doctrine. Robert South's sermon defending the naïve form was reprinted in 1697 unaltered. John Edwards, who attacked Locke's *Reasonableness of Christianity* for its unorthodox character, presents an interesting example of a late defender of this form of the doctrine. In one of his attacks against Locke, *The Socinian Creed* (1697), Edwards had objected to Locke's rejection of innate principles, calling attention to the fact that Socinus also denied innate knowledge. He insisted that innate principles are the foundation of religion and morality, as well as the standard of truth (p. 122). In a later work, *A Free Discourse Concerning Truth and Error* (1701), he develops his own positive form of the doctrine of innateness. There he divides ideas into two classes: those in God's and those in man's mind. 'The former made things to be True, the latter convey the notice of the Truth of them to us' (p. 27). Although the original pattern of truth is located in God,

yet He hath Copied it out into the Mind of Man, and hath imprinted the Figure of it on his Rational Nature. Humane Souls created after God's Image do in some manner contain in them This Transcript and Resemblance. There are in our Minds Natural Impressions & Inbred Notices of True and False, which are as it were Streams issuing forth from the Uncreated and Everlasting Spring of Truth. And these Notions are not Indifferent and Arbitrary, but Fixed and Indelible (pp. 27–28).

He proceeds to satisfy Locke's demand for a list of these principles, both speculative and practical, which he deems to be innate. Under speculative he lists the following: 'What is not cannot be known', 'Nothing can't possibly have any qualities or affections', 'a thing can't act without Existence', 'an Effect supposes a Cause', 'a thing cannot be and not be at the same time', 'the whole is bigger than its part' (p. 28). Under practical innate principles, Edwards lists the following: 'we ought to venerate, love, serve, and worship the Supreme Being', 'we must honour and obey our Parents', 'we must not injure and harm any Person, but render to every Man his due', 'we ought to deport ourselves towards others as we desire and expect they should act towards us' (pp. 29–30). Of the first class he says they are shown to be innate because they 'are assented to without the help of Ratiocination, without the least study, or dispute, or making of Deductions, or framing of Consequences' (p. 28). Without these principles we should attain to no truth and there would be no science or certainty. Of the second class, he says that 'These and other Natural Sentiments and Moral Principles, which are the basis of all Laws that respect the Moral Actions of Men, are those *Ideas* we speak of, which every Rational Person agrees to without any help of arguing' (p. 30). He appeals to Whichcote, who asserted in one of his sermons: 'Had there not been a Law written in the heart of Man, a Law without him had been to no purpose: for had we not principles that are concreated, i.e., did we not know something, no Man could prove anything.'[1] Whichcote had developed the doctrine at more length in the same sermon. 'The truth of first inscription is connate to man, it is the light of God's creation, and it flows from the principles of which man doth consist in his very first make.'[2] Whichcote went on to use the familiar language of the laws engraven in the heart, listing the usual moral principles as examples. Edwards found inspiration in this sermon of Whichcote. The phrase 'the law written in the Heart' means, Edwards said, 'that the same Truths and Duties which are commanded by the Moral Law or Decalogue, are primitively engraven on their Consciences' (pp. 31–32). St. Paul 'proves the existence and reality of these Inherent Signatures and Impresses of Truth and Goodness on the Soul from the office and known acts of Conscience, namely *accusing* or *excusing*, that is, its checking or applauding them according as their Actions are' (p. 32). He speaks of these principles being 'riveted into the very essence and specifick nature of Man', and of those notions 'which we came into the World with' (p. 33). All pretence at an allegorical interpretation of the doctrine is discarded. The doctrine is asserted in its

---

[1] Cf. *Select Sermons of Dr. Whichcot* (1698), sermon on John vii. 46, p. 8.
[2] Whichcote, ibid., p. 7.

naïve form, the form that Locke had challenged and sought to
refute. Writing after Locke's extended polemic, Edwards's
defence of the doctrine did not differ from that of his many
predecessors in the first part of the century.

> That all men were born with these Ideas, and had them even in the
> State of Infancy and Childhood appears from this, that at the *first asking*
> them about them, or at the very *first proposal* of the General Principles
> of Truth to them, when they come to any maturity of years, and make
> use of Speech, they freely give their assent to them, and acknowledge
> them for Truth (p. 37).

It is nonsense, he claims, to expect the child to be able to use
these notions from the very first day, since it takes him some
time to use his rational soul. The fact that some nations do
not agree on the alleged innate principles is no argument
against their innateness but rather proof of that nation's de-
pravity.

§ 3—*Conclusion*

Isaac Watts wrote in 1726 in his *Logick: Or, The Right Use
of Reason*:

> There has been a great Controversy, about the *Origin of Ideas*, (viz)
> whether any of our Ideas are *innate* or no, i.e., born with us, and naturally
> belonging to our Minds. Mr. *Locke* utterly denies it; others as positively
> affirm it (p. 28).

The debate had not been concluded by the time of Locke's
death, but the general movement towards a naturalistic religion
had made his criticisms more acceptable. By far the majority of
his critics, however, preferred to stand by the dispositional
variety of the theory. In the minds of these critics of Locke's
polemic against innate knowledge, the alternative was clear:
innate ideas and principles, or relativity of morals. This alternative haunted all the men who read Locke's polemic in the
seventeenth century, except those whose interests were in
the new forms of natural religion which were growing in popularity towards the end of the century. In the minds of these
sympathizers with deism and Unitarianism, rationality was
substituted for innateness as a basis for morality and religion.

For the traditionalists, however, the denial of a connatural ground for moral rules and laws opened the way for scepticism and atheism. Sherlock was even perceptive enough to recognize that the question of innate ideas could not be settled on the basis of experience. All that observation can prove is

That our Knowledge increases gradually, and that the external Impressions, which are made on us by external Objects, are helps to us in understanding the Natures and Ideas of Things; and that we have no Knowledge of any Ideas, which we never had any Hints or Intimations of from without: But our Observation and Experience, that is, what we feel within us, cannot prove, whether the Mind, upon these external Notices, finds these Ideas in it self, or forms them anew; for which way soever it be, the Workings of our Minds . . . must be so near the same, that our Experience can't certainly distinguish them. . . .[1]

It was not a question of empirical verification for Sherlock, whether he or Locke was correct on this issue. The important point was that in his opinion religion and morality could not survive or escape an extreme relativism (a relativism which several critics thought they saw in the *Essay* on other grounds as well) without constant appeal to characters imprinted upon the mind. Religion and morality dictated the outlines of theory of knowledge. Locke was seeking to show that these two areas could be separated and that the separation was not injurious to religion or morality. Collins was prepared to reject Sherlock's criticisms entirely as missing the point of Locke's argument, as in fact Sherlock and the other critics did. A man of Sherlock's position, imbued with the values of traditional morality and religion, could hardly be expected to appreciate the innovations which Locke and his followers were introducing.

There were very few men in the seventeenth century who were able to view Locke's epistemology objectively, to consider its consistency and validity apart from its implications for religion. Norris, one of the first critics of the *Essay*, stands almost alone in this respect. In his 'Cursory Reflections', Norris sought to show that Locke's discussion of innate knowledge was both inconsequential, because it failed to prove what he claimed, and inconsistent, because the denial of innate ideas

[1] Sherlock, op. cit., pp. 154-5.

conflicted with other principles in the *Essay*. Norris argued, in favour of the latter point, that although Locke denied in Book One that any propositions have universal consent, he later admits such propositions when he recognizes self-evident propositions. The self-evident propositions which Locke speaks about and accepts are the same as those receiving universal consent, because Locke calls 'self-evident' those propositions which receive the 'ready and prone assent' of men. We have seen that the appeal to quick assent to certain propositions crucial for morality and religion was frequent in the early part of the century and reappears among the many critics of Locke. Norris apparently considered such quick assent to be synonymous with universal consent. Like many defenders of the two versions of innate knowledge, Norris insisted that the examples of children and idiots were ill chosen, since such persons are not capable of thinking of such propositions. 'Now I always thought that Universality of Consent had been sufficiently secured by the Consent of all, and the Dissent of none that were capable of either' (p. 5). Since children and idiots are not even capable of assenting to or dissenting from such propositions, they have no bearing on the issue. 'And how then does the want of their *Suffrage* destroy universal Consent, when all Persons that think at all about such Propositions, think after one and the same way?' (p. 6). Norris concludes, then, that 'the most therefore that this author can mean by want of Universal Consent, is that every individual Person does not *actually Assent*'. The question then comes to be, whether lack of actual assent on the part of every individual is evidence that there are no innate truths. Norris points out that this is Locke's belief, for in book i, ch. i, no. 5, Locke asserts: 'it seeming to me near a contradiction to say, that there are truths imprinted on the soul, which it perceives or understands not', and 'to imprint anything on the mind, without the mind's perceiving it, seems to me hardly intelligible'. Norris, in other words, takes as crucial to Locke's argument the doctrine that the mind is not always thinking. Norris himself did not wish to champion the Leibnizian position of 'petites perceptions', but (and this is characteristic of his method of analysis) only to show that Locke recognized ideas which make an impression on us without our being aware of them. In book ii, ch. i, no. 6, Locke says: 'But all that are born into the world, being surrounded with bodies that perpetually and diversely affect them, a variety of ideas, whether care be taken of it or not, are imprinted on the minds of children.' Again, while discussing perception, Locke recognizes what Norris thinks he rejects while discussing innate principles:

How often may a man observe in himself, that whilst his mind is intently employed in the contemplation of some objects, and curiously surveying some ideas that are there, it takes no notice of impressions of sounding bodies made upon the organ of hearing, with the same alteration that uses to be for the producing of the idea of sound? (Bk. ii, ch. ix, no. 4.)

Later, in the chapter on memory, Locke wrote:

The other way of retention is, the power to revive again in our minds those ideas which, after imprinting, have disappeared, or have been as it were laid aside out of sight. . . . For, the narrow mind of man not being capable of having many ideas under view and consideration at once, it was necessary to have a repository to lay up those ideas which, at another time, it might have use of. (Bk. ii, ch. x, no. 2.)

Locke apparently sought to correct the literal interpretation of this doctrine of memory, for in the second edition he argued that the laying up of ideas in the mind meant no more than a power 'to revive perceptions which it has once had, with this additional perception annexed to them, *that it has had them before*'. Ideas were defined by Locke as actual objects of awareness. We cannot have ideas of which we are unconscious, since this violates our very definition. If those who claimed innate ideas had meant only that at some period in man's growth he will come to accept certain ideas about God, and moral goodness and evil, which none of Locke's critics would admit, then Locke's doctrine would not have been so disturbing.

It was left to an anonymous writer of the early eighteenth century to seek to synthesize the opposing views of the seventeenth century over this crucial problem of innate knowledge. In *A Philosophick Essay concerning Ideas* (1705), the author of this brief but penetrating and clarifying pamphlet sought to show that if we start out from the assumption that thought and idea are the same thing, we are led to the conclusion that 'there can be no Mind without some Idea' (p. 9). Thus, 'so soon as the Mind was Created, as it was of Necessity Created Thinking, so was it likewise with some Idea. (And this is what we are to understand when we speak of an Innate or Connate Idea.)' (Ibid.) This author was pushing Locke's reduction of ideas to powers, and Locke's claim that there can be no ideas without conscious awareness of them, to their logical conclusion, where ideas are nothing distinct from thoughts. 'All this seems to be so plain and obvious, that I cannot but wonder, how anyone, who allows this Notion of Ideas, can assert that the Soul of Man is but a *Rasa Tabula*... unless he at the same time does deny, that it is the very Essence of the Soul to think' (p. 10). What Leenhof claimed in 1688 is advanced by this writer as the inevitable conclusion to Locke's definition of 'idea'. It can be doubted whether Locke meant to equate thought and idea so closely, but the author of this tract is correct in suggesting that this is implied by Locke's doctrine. Even this definition of innateness, clever as it is, would not contradict Locke's position; but, if taken seriously, it might have offered a ground for reconciling both sides of the debate, that of the traditional moralists and that of the innovators of reason whose spokesman Locke became by tacit agreement. Had Locke entered into more discussions with these various contemporary critics, he might have been able to convince the old guard that he was just as much concerned to find a firm and unshakeable foundation for morality and religion as they were. The real issue was not over the reality or unreality of innate ideas and principles. Locke showed that the traditional arguments invoked in favour of the doctrine of innateness could not stand up to careful scrutiny. Sherlock pointed out that the issue was not empirical. The vital issue between Locke and his critics on this question was the grounds and foundations of morality and religion. The epistemological question concerning the genesis of our ideas was not an isolated theoretical problem for Locke or for his contemporaries. It was a question integral to the practical problems of life.

Deism and rational theology in general gained the ascendancy early in the eighteenth century, so that Locke's rejection of innate knowledge was only infrequently questioned after 1704. Even in 1703, Pierre Bayle was able to write: 'Je vous avouë qu'il m'a semblé victorieux, & qu'il faut donner à son combat la gloire du *debellatum est*.'[1] Henry Layton, in *Observations upon a Treatise Intituled, A Discourse concerning the Happiness of Good Men* (1704), argued against Sherlock that the denial of innate ideas does not deny the existence of God (pp. 38–39). Taking 'ideas' as 'images', he argued that there are no ideas in God's mind and that all ideas come from without the mind (p. 40). John Harris, writing a dictionary of terms, *Lexicon Technicum* (1704), followed Locke closely in defining 'ideas' as 'whatsoever the Mind perceives in itself, or stands there for the immediate Object of any Phantasm, Notion, Species, Thought, or Understanding', and gives the usual definition of 'innate principles'. In the second edition (called the 'second volume') in 1710, Locke's entire doctrine of ideas is extensively summarized, and Harris explicitly states that the doctrine of innateness has been conclusively refuted by Locke. Similarly, under 'idea', Chambers, *Cyclopaedia: Or, An Universal Dictionary of Arts and Sciences* (1728), says that 'our great Mr. Locke seems to have put this Matter [of innate ideas] out of dispute'. Under 'innate idea' he writes further that such ideas or principles 'are certain primary Notes or Characters, supposed to be stamped on the Mind of Man when it first receives its Being, and which it brings into the World with it; but the Doctrine of Innate Ideas is abundantly confuted by Mr. *Locke*'. Wollaston wrote in 1722 of the doctrine of innateness:

They, who contenting themselves with superficial and transient views deduce the difference between good and evil from the *common sense* of mankind, and certain *Principles* that are born with us, put the matter upon a very *infirm* foot. For it is much to be suspected there are no such *innate* maxims as they pretend, but that the impressions of education are

---

[1] Bayle to Coste, 27 December 1703, in *Œuvres Diverses* (1728), t. iv, p. 834.

mistaken for them: and besides that, the sentiments of mankind are not so *uniform* and *constant*, as that we may safely trust such an important distinction upon them.[1]

But adherents of the doctrine still spoke out against Locke. William Carroll, in a fantastic book, *Spinoza Reviv'd* (1709), charging Locke with advocating a Spinozistic universe of one material substance, mocks Locke for his ignorance in denying innate ideas of God (p. 101). LeClerc is criticized for accepting Locke's rejection of innate ideas. The doctrine of no innate ideas or principles is, Carroll says, 'one of the grand *Principles* of our *Modern Atheists*. And tho' 'tis thus positively asserted, yet our Philosopher neither does, nor can *know* what he says when he thus pronounces *Magisterially*, that we have no *Innate Idea* of *God*' (p. 162, footnote). A much more sober thinker than Carroll, Isaac Watts, *Philosophical Essays on Various Subjects* (1733), agrees that 'those Writers who hold innate Ideas in this Sense [the naïve sense] seem to lye under a great Mistake' (p. 99). But he does not wish to abandon the doctrine of innateness entirely. He suggests that the term can be applied to the natural and necessary connexion which he believed subsisted between brain traces and the origin of ideas connected with those traces, as well as to those maxims which cannot be doubted once the mind is confronted with them (pp. 104–5).

> Therefore I take the Mind or Soul of Man not to be so perfectly in-different to receive all Impressions, as a *Rasa Tabula*, or *white Paper*; and 'tis so framed by its Maker as not to be equally disposed to all sorts of Perceptions, nor to embrace all Propositions, with an Indifferency to judge them true or false (pp. 105–6).

In the same way Watts thinks it is impossible for man to deny the ethical proposition, 'He that made me should govern me', suggesting that this and similar propositions are innate. In short, the moral-sense doctrine, which Watts accepted, is described as a doctrine of innateness. The familiar arguments for innate knowledge were also reasserted in the eighteenth

---

[1] *The Religion of Nature Delineated*, p. 17.

century by an anonymous writer in *A Dissertation on Deistical and Arian Corruption* (1742).

> But yet we must allow that the Soul of every Man has the Knowledge, the Law and Love of God *naturally* wrote *within*, and so interwoven, as I may say, into its very Being, that it cannot be a *rational* Soul without it; so that this internal, or *innate* Light is *essential* to every *reasonable* Soul, as a *reasonable* and Moral Being (p. 28).

We can neither make truth, since it is eternal, nor receive it from the material world, since the concept of truth does not apply to that world. Hence, 'all the Ideas, or inward Characters, of Divine Truth and Holiness, must be Innate' (p. 29). The writer admits that man's awareness of these principles has been dulled by the Fall; but he concludes:

> Upon the whole then, the Doctrine of *innate Ideas* is such a *certain* and *necessary* Truth, that every Man that has but the least Insight into the Nature of the *human Soul*, cannot but see that the contrary Doctrine of Man's having *no* Light but what comes into the Mind from *Sensation*, or sensible Ideas, is a *new* Doctrine, suggested by Satan, to make Men Infidels, or practical Atheists (p. 29).

The doctrine was anything but new in 1742. It had a long history in the seventeenth century but only reached its clearest and most detailed exposition in Parker, Burthogge, and Locke. But the force of this doctrine was still being felt in the middle of the eighteenth century. It would not be too much to suggest that without the careful attacks by these writers, the new movements in religion would have had a much harder struggle for acceptance. So long as the belief in innateness persisted, religion could not be turned into the naturalistic doctrines of the deists, into a rational theology. But for those who found this transformation of the traditional religion anathema, the rejection of innate knowledge did appear as a suggestion of Satan. Religion and morality had been shaken, tradition questioned.

EPISTEMOLOGICAL SCEPTICISM

THE reaction to Locke's denial of innate knowledge was based almost entirely, as we have seen, upon the dangerous consequences such a position boded for religion and especially for morality. A few critics, like Norris, objected to Book One of the *Essay* on the grounds that the thorough empiricism implied by it and continued in the rest of the work would not account for all our knowledge and all our ideas, citing the non-sensible idea of God, and mathematics, as evidence. Most of the critics went on to show how the positive epistemological features of the *Essay* were just as unacceptable as the rejection of innate knowledge. Later in this study, I shall be concerned with the way in which these doctrines of the *Essay* were believed to lead to religious scepticism and disbelief. But before we pursue that aspect of the seventeenth- and early-eighteenth-century reaction to Locke's epistemology, we must examine the charge of epistemological scepticism which was made by many critics quite apart from a charge of religious scepticism. Not all the critics examined in this chapter were detached from religion; very few could be said to have made their criticisms of Locke in abstraction from religion altogether, but the majority of them were content to point out first the epistemological scepticism inherent in the *Essay*. They could then go on to show the ways in which this scepticism led to religious and moral scepticism.

§ 1—*Empiricism and Rationalism*

While the greater number of Locke's non-theological critics hastened to call attention to the difficulties of establishing the reality of knowledge, to the problems of the meaning and function of ideas, and to the idealism entailed by the definition of knowledge in the *Essay*, a few, notably Lee and Sergeant in England and Leibniz on the Continent, went to the very roots of Locke's empirical contentions and criticized what they took to be their essential weakness. The point involved in all three of these attacks is rather more subtle than the points raised by the other non-theological critics. Traditional religion was immediately suspicious of any movement which purported to dispense with non-empirical factors in the attainment or formulation of knowledge. Locke was clearly aligned on the side of the new science: his friends and his interests belonged there rather than with the familiar obscurities of orthodoxy. But the three men mentioned above saw in the *Essay* a concise expression of this empirical or inductive character of the new science, which demanded a direct attack. Of the three, Lee was the only one who showed any tendency to misread Locke as a sensationalist, i.e. as holding that all knowledge comes from our external sensations. Lee did not allow reflection as a source of knowledge, since he viewed this function of the mind as synonymous with awareness or consciousness. But, of course, Locke would not be guilty of a narrow sensationalism merely on the ground of a rejection of reflection or internal sensation as a source of knowledge. What concerned Lee most was the failure on Locke's part to derive knowledge from general principles. It is this question, whether knowledge can be derived from ideas of sensation and reflection without any appeal to rational postulates (a question Leibniz poses in the same form), which Lee believed Locke had answered incorrectly, and one which Lee believed to be fundamental to all theories of knowledge.

If all Knowledge comes by our *Senses* or *Reflexion*, which is his Maxim, then there can be no *certain* Knowledge of the Truth of any *general* Proposition whatever; because our Senses can reach but to *particulars*, and Reflexion no farther . . . There can be no Knowledge at all of *Substances*, not so much as of their *Existence*; because nothing can be known, according to that Principle, but what affects our *Senses*, and Substances, to be sure, don't; but only their Modes, Properties and Qualities. And tho this *abstracting* Faculty be the peculiar Privilege which he intirely reserves for *Mankind* above *Brutes*, yet at long run this amounts to no more than the Faculty of *speaking* or *using Signs* of their Conceptions.... For if Men, according to his avow'd Principle, do never exercise their *rational* Faculties by inferring any thing from *general* Maxims, tho own'd by all Mankind, but only by Induction, Exemplification or Enumeration of *particulars*, there will remain nothing to distinguish Men from Brutes, but only the Faculty of *speaking*, in most Men, or of making *artificial Signs* of Conceptions.[1]

Lee did not pretend that actual knowledge was derived by careful deductions from maxims or principles of reason. Appeal to maxims will not convince anyone of the truth of some particular belief which they may learn from their senses.[2] Maxims are defined as 'Propositions, whose parts . . . consist of such general Words as imply the Relation between them is natural or immutable.'[3] These maxims are alternatively referred to as axioms, *aeternae Veritates*, self-evident truths, innate or natural truths, or common principles of reason. Locke's conviction that such principles have been used as the actual source of knowledge is unfounded, Lee claims, since the use for which these are employed is one of justification: less obvious or less certain truths can be resolved into these firmly established principles and thereby be seen to be valid and certain. Understanding is never enlarged by maxims, but knowledge can be rendered more acceptable by their use. Thus, Lee does not wish to claim that the traditional maxims are integral to all knowledge, presupposed by all thought, but only that they serve a very useful purpose in organizing knowledge and in discovering which particular propositions can be trusted as sound. Even sensation, he suggests, could make all the necessary discoveries; but recourse to maxims saves time and effort. Moreover, the ability to derive knowledge from general principles is that ability which, in Lee's opinion, marks men off from brutes.

Locke had not stressed as much as his system demanded the role of reason in obtaining knowledge. His rejection of innate knowledge led many to believe that he did not recog-

---

[1] *Anti-Scepticism*, p. 67.
[2] Ibid., p. 272.   [3] Ibid.

nize the function of the rational faculty in knowledge. His prejudice against the use of maxims in knowledge only added to the general suspicion under which his epistemology fell. Lee was trying to reinstate reason in the structure of knowledge. The same sort of criticism of Locke's empirical inductive procedures came from Leibniz; but unlike Lee, Leibniz had rooted his criticism in a careful doctrine of necessary, as opposed to contingent, truths. In the preface to his *Nouveaux Essais,* he called attention to the disagreement between himself and Locke on the issue of innate knowledge, linking this to the further question of whether all truth is dependent upon induction, i.e. the enumeration of examples, or whether it does not have its foundations in some other source. His criticism of Locke's empiricism echoes that of Lee. 'Les sens quoyque necessaires pour toutes nos connoissances actuelles ne sont point suffisans pour nous les donner toutes, puisque les sens ne donnent jammais que des exemples, c'est à dire des verités particulieres ou individuelles.'[1] Mathematics and geometry are areas of knowledge in which we find truths independent of experience, but Leibniz argued as well that theology and jurisprudence contain many necessary truths. As Lee also held, the distinction between empirical and rational sources of knowledge accounts for the difference between men and animals: 'les bestes sont purement empiriques et ne font que se regler sur les exemples, car elles n'arrivent jamais à former des propositions necessaires autant qu'on en peut juger; au lieu que les hommes sont capables des sciences demonstratives'.[2] The simple listings or enumerations which animals were supposed to make 'sont purement comme celles des simples empiriques qui pretendent que ce qui est arrivé quelquesfois, arrivera encor dans un cas où ce qui les frappe est pareil, sans estre capables de juger, si les mêmes raisons subsistent'.[3] Reason alone is

capable d'etablir des regles seures et de suppleer ce qui manque à celles qui ne l'estoient point, en y inserant leur exceptions; et de trouver enfin

[1] Gerhardt, op. cit., bd. v, p. 43.
[2] Ibid., pp. 43–44.
[3] Ibid., p. 44.

des liaisons certaines dans la force des consequences necessaires, ce qui donne souvent le moyen de prevoir l'evenement sans avoir besoin d'experimenter les liaisons sensibles des images.[1]

The theme of the role of truths of reason in knowledge, of the necessary augmentation of empirical knowledge by rational principles, continues throughout the rest of Leibniz's *Nouveaux Essais*. In effect, Lee's criticism found an extended though unconscious elaboration in this work. The same type of criticism is found in Sergeant's *Solid Philosophy Asserted* (1697), although it is there buried under Sergeant's metaphysical verbiage. Besides having written one of the longest attacks against Locke of any of his contemporaries, Sergeant was an exponent and stout defender of the syllogistic method, his *The Method to Science* (1696) being an elaborate defence of this method of reasoning. The term 'science' in this work is used loosely to indicate any body of organized knowledge which can be demonstrated from principles by means of deductions. These two, principles and deductions, constitute the framework of knowledge around which any specific branch of human investigation can be arranged.

For, our Notions being Clear'd, First Principles establish'd, the true Form of a Syllogism manifested, Proper Middle Terms found, and the Necessity of the Consequence evidenced; all those Conclusions may be Deduced with *Demonstrative Evidence*, which ly within our Ken, or which we can have occasion to enquire after (p. [12], Preface Dedicatory).

Whether the subject-matter be physics, morality, or religion, Sergeant was convinced that the truths of that discipline could be demonstrated by the syllogism. Hence logical certainty was the earmark of genuine knowledge. The chief aim of science in this broad sense was 'to beget *Virtue*; and not onely to raise us to Higher Contemplation, but also to comfort, and strengthen *Divine Faith* in us, and to make it *Lively* and *Operative*' (p. [26], Preface). Only certain truth could achieve this end. The way of ideas, practised by the Cartesians and by Locke, could never lead to this desired result

---

[1] Gerhardt, op. cit.

because it begins analysis at the wrong end, with ideas instead of with things. Moreover, as Sir Kenelm Digby had argued earlier in the century, it is only when we add reason to sensation that knowledge is possible. For both Digby and Sergeant, certain basic principles constitute the foundation upon which reason seeks to interpret the reports of the senses. Empiricism cannot yield valid knowledge of the world independently of certain rational principles. To this extent, Sergeant criticizes empiricism from what can be called a Kantian point of view. But there were two basically different kinds of principles employed by Sergeant to augment what has been called 'pure empiricism': metaphysical assumptions and principles of reason.

Indicating that his own metaphysics lies in the Aristotelian-Thomistic tradition, Sergeant resorts to explanations in terms of this metaphysics at the slightest provocation. One entire section of his *The Method to Science* is devoted to elucidating the various ways in which Aristotle's ten categories are divided and to deducing certain particular truths about the nature of man, of living beings, and of being *per se* from these categories. Nothing brings out the difference between Sergeant's and Locke's methodology so strongly as does the presence of metaphysics throughout the former's writings. Where Sergeant cannot offer an explanation based upon experience, he does not hesitate to introduce a metaphysical explanation, and even his apparently empirical explanations are usually grounded in a metaphysical doctrine. As Locke commented in the margins of his copy of *Solid Philosophy Asserted*, 'The author has found a short way to solid philosophie by haveing nothing to doe that does not agree with our systems' (Locke, *Notes*, no. 72, p. 352).[1] Locke's philosophizing was not restricted by such devotion to tradition. He has fairly well separated his epistemology from his metaphysics. If he cannot find an

---

[1] As in the case of the Locke marginalia in Burnet's *Third Remarks*, so here the numbering refers to the succession of Locke notes in Sergeant's *Solid Philosophy Asserted*, while the pagination refers to their location in Sergeant's text. The Locke marginalia appear here with the kind permission of St. John's College, Cambridge.

empirical explanation, he usually admits the limitations of
human knowledge, as in the case of explaining why and how
parts of bodies cohere. Locke was seeking to interpret nature,
as Bacon had enjoined, rather by a careful attention to nature
than by anticipating her with metaphysical explanations.
Where natural causes were not evident, Locke usually ceased
inquiry, although there are some striking exceptions in the
Essay. Such limitations of human knowledge were unnecessary
for Sergeant and resulted, he felt, in confusions. In fact,
Sergeant credited many confusions in human knowledge to
one's seeking natural causes for various effects when the true
reasons or causes were 'only owing to *Trans-natural* ones, or
from these *Altissimae Causae*, which only Metaphysicks give
us; . . . Let any one ask a Naturalist, why Rotundity does
formally make a Thing *Round*, and you will see what a Plunge
he will be put to, not finding in all Nature a Proper Reason
for it'.[1] Locke was very clear about the needed separation
between natural philosophy and metaphysics.

> Transnatural causes in natural philosophie are not natural causes and
> consequently supernatural i.e. immediate effects of divine power open-
> ing out of the course of natural causes & effects: a sort of philosophizing
> which J. S. very much explodes (Locke, *Notes*, no. 43, p. 248).

In the margins of his copy of Sergeant's book, Locke took
time to write more than one comment against this theorizing.

The rationalistic method of gaining knowledge was too far
removed from the reality of things, too indirect, and too
private for Sergeant. The way of ideas was rationalistic
without having recourse to general principles, in that from an
analysis of ideas it attempted to derive conclusions about
reality. But Locke was also too much like the experimental
or inductive scientists who attempted to proceed entirely by
observation unaided by any basic principles. The rationalism
of the way of ideas was inherent in the methodology itself,
while the professed aim of Locke's application of this methodology was experimental. By denying the value of general
principles of reason, of maxims, Locke provoked Sergeant's

[1] *Solid Philosophy Asserted*, pp. 248, 249.

criticism on two counts: the method was fanciful and unreal when it relied upon ideas for knowledge, but useless and weak in refusing to augment observation by maxims. Asserting that the aim of natural science was to obtain universal conclusions, Sergeant asks: 'what one Universal Conclusion in Natural Philosophy . . . has been Demonstrated by *Experiments*, since the time that Great man, Sir *Francis Bacon*, writ his *Natural History?*'[1] It is impossible, Sergeant declares, to deduce universal conclusions from particular observations without the addition of some general metaphysical principles. The task of assigning 'the True Natural *Cause* for that Effect, and explicating it right, must be Decided by way of *Reason*; that is, by demonstrating first whose *Principles* of Natural Philosophy are *True* and *Solid*'.[2] He never does, of course, demonstrate that his metaphysics is the only true one. The only condition for such a metaphysics which he mentions, and this only obliquely, is that the true system must explain the essences of things and their causes. He apparently believed that a metaphysics which would not offer an explanation for certain problems such as why the parts of matter cohere, or how material effluvia get into the brain and cause thought, should be condemned from the start. Nor did he go beyond this to specify the rules for a proper metaphysics. His own books, however, disclose a strong faith that his system is the only true system. As Locke was led to remark while reading *Solid Philosophy Asserted*, 'J. S. speaks every where as if *Truth & Science* had personally appeard to him & by word of mouth actually commissioned him to be their sole Defender & Propagator' (Locke, *Notes*, no. 39, p. 239).

Metaphysical principles, however, are only one type of supplement to empiricism for Sergeant. In addition, there must be principles of reason. The laws of identity and contradiction in traditional logic are the most frequently cited examples. Sergeant insists in many places that knowledge must be capable of being reduced to such principles of reason,

---

[1] *The Method to Science*, p. [58] of Preface.
[2] Ibid., pp. 59–60.

which principles are intuitively true. It is generally recognized that an empiricism which rejects principles of reason
or presuppositions of thought cannot provide an adequate
foundation for knowledge. An empirical epistemology can be
constructed, without explicitly or implicitly assuming a
metaphysical point of view, but it is impossible to develop
such a system without implying principles of reason. It was the
custom in the seventeenth century to refer to such principles
of reason as 'maxims', and in many cases knowledge was
demonstrated as being deduced from maxims in the same
fashion as any syllogistic inference. As Locke commented in
the *Essay*:

> It having been the common received opinion amongst men of letters,
> that *maxims* were the foundation of all knowledge; and that the sciences
> were each of them built upon certain *praecognita*, from whence the
> understanding was to take its rise, and by which it was to conduct itself
> in its inquiries into the matters belonging to that science, the beaten road
> of the Schools has been, to lay down in the beginning one or more
> *general propositions*, as foundations whereon to build the knowledge that
> was to be had of that subject. (Bk. iv, ch. xii, no. 1.)

It was this use of maxims against which Locke was, in the
main, arguing in the *Essay*; he offered two additional warnings
concerning maxims: that they must not be transferred from
one field to another, and that they must not be accepted
uncritically. But one of the merits of Sergeant's discussion is
that he did not advocate the use of maxims in this way. Taking
as an example the maxim, 'yellow is yellow', Sergeant argued
that this is presupposed in all thought and discourse concerning colour, 'For, if any part of that Discourse makes
Yellow *not to be Yellow* . . . 'tis concluded to be most evidently
False; or, if it agrees with it, to be *True*.'[1] Discourse, judging,
and action all presuppose such principles. When a man loses
some object and looks for it, saying, '*I am sure it must be
somewhere or other*', Sergeant maintains that such a man
'guides himself all the while by this foreknown General

----

[1] *Solid Philosophy Asserted*, p. 368.

Maxim, "*Every particular Body in the World must be in some place*"' (p. 370). Sergeant rejects innate ideas just as stoutly as Locke, so the term 'foreknown' does not mean innateness. This term is best translated by the other term which he himself uses, 'foregranted'. Such principles which are foregranted may not always be explicit in our thinking ⸱and acting, but they are present as guides nevertheless. 'To apprehend more clearly the usefulness of these two Principles [those of identity and contradiction], let us suppose a Man *quite Devested* of them, and to have neither of them in his Judgment, and then reflect what he is good for' (p. 369). Locke agrees with Sergeant that a man devoid of the principles of identity and contradiction would be incapable of knowledge, but not for the reasons offered by Sergeant.

A man *divest'd*, i.e., quite bereft or incapable of knowing them to be true, is incapable of all knowledg for he is incapable of knowing the same to be the same & different Ideas to be different. But the same would happen to one that knows not that a Mangastan is a Mangastan and not a Turnep. (Locke, *Notes*, no. 82, p. 369.)

Knowledge for Locke presupposes the ability to recognize difference and sameness, but it does not entail an awareness of general principles. Such ability is intuitive. Locke was concerned to deny the principles of identity and contradiction as innate speculative principles in Book One for the same reason as he denies them in Book Four: they never function in obtaining human knowledge. He does agree that in discourse or argumentation these principles have to be agreed upon, having in mind perhaps Aristotle's observation concerning the difficulty of discoursing with those who reject these principles; but the use of maxims in discourse for Locke is '*to stop the Mouths of Wranglers*'. Sergeant interpreted this admission as a recognition of the value of maxims in gaining knowledge, for how could principles 'have this strange Virtue *to stop the Mouths* of such Unreasonable Men,' but because their Evidence is *Greater* than any *others*, or than Particular Self-evident Propositions are'? (pp. 367–8). Locke, however, is careful to clarify his meaning in the marginal notes. 'Not because their evidence is greater than any more particular self-evident proposition but because serving in all cases they are more inculcated and used than the other.' (Locke, *Notes*, no. 80, p. 368.) Principles have practical use in debates as a means of ending arguments; Locke was not concerned to deny this. What he wished to deny is their use in knowledge. In response to the assertion by Sergeant that 'it is impossible we can make an Ordinary, much less any Speculative, Discourse, but the Discoursers must agree in something that is either *Foreknown* or (at least) *Foregranted*; . . .' Locke underlined the word 'Discoursers' in the text of his copy of *Solid Philosophy Asserted*, and added in the margin: 'He means Disputants, but Mr. L speaks not of Disputation but Knowledg.' (Ibid., no. 81, p. 368.)

Sergeant presented his views on maxims directly to Locke in 1696 in a letter accompanying his *The Method to Science*, summarizing his position for Locke.

The most substantiall Difference between us (as far as I yet observe) is about the Necessity and Usefulness of Identicall Propositions, on which I mainly build; and to which (in my iudgment) all Truths must either be reduc'd, or they will, if scann'd by Speculative and Acute Logicians, be left destitute of their Deepest and Firmest Ground. For since you have so solidly confuted *Innate Ideas*, it must follow of course that Truths must be taken from the *Things without us*; and consequently must be *first built on*, and *finally resolved* into their *Metaphysical Verity* or their *being what they are*, which is an Identicall Proposition, and can be nothing else: nor can we *Speak* or *say* anything of their Natures or Essences *as such* . . . or express them at all but by such an Identicall Speech, as upon triall you will find. Again, we must either come at last to Self-evidence, or no Dispute can ever come to an end; nor can any Propositions, but such as these, possibly lay any claim to Self-evidence, since all else can bear Explicating on the making them plainer, and clearer which these cannot.[1]

Sergeant apparently failed in his attempt to convince Locke that every system of thought has to presuppose certain general maxims or principles as underlying the assertions made in

[1] MS. Locke, C. 18, f. 134.

that system. One reason for his failure in this respect is undoubtedly his own confusion and oscillation between metaphysical and rational principles. Since the metaphysical principles are used by Sergeant as starting points for knowledge, such a confusion of these with principles of reason clouds the insight that all knowledge contains certain pre-suppositions. Locke could easily agree with Sergeant in the above-quoted letter when he says that self-evidence is the basis for all certainty, since Locke himself made intuitive self-evidence the foundation of knowledge in his system. But whereas Sergeant restricted self-evidence to identical propositions, Locke found that the human mind can intuit self-evidence of a more complex nature, thereby dispensing with the one major argument in Sergeant's favour. Even in his letter to Locke, Sergeant strove to find some metaphysical support for his case by arguing that truth must be found in the things themselves and that truth of things is ultimately grounded upon their metaphysical verity. But in *Solid Philosophy Asserted*, where he put his case with Locke specifically in mind, the distinction between metaphysical and logical supplementation to empiricism is often obscured. In the midst of his discussion of maxims, Sergeant asserts that the fundamental error of the methodology of the ideists is that 'they rate the *Clearness* of their *Ideas* from the fresh, fair, and lively Appearances they make to the *Fancy*. Whereas only the Definition, by explicating the true Essence of a Thing, shews us Distinctly the true *Spiritual Notion* of it' (pp. 371–2). Notions can never be wrong since they owe their truth to God, although Sergeant admits that we may mistake what our words signify to others. However, 'if I, mistaking, or not mistaking, have such a *Meaning* of it in my *Mind* . . . that Meaning is truly *in me*' (p. 374). Locke is just in his criticism of Sergeant at this point.

Where are those definitions that explicate the true essences of things? & (excepting mathematical) how many of them has J. S.? He would obleige the world by a list of them if it were of noe more but those things he has talk'd of in his books & pretends to know. . . . He that has a

meaning to any word has it no doubt whilst he has it. But he that varys
the meaning of his terms or knows not precisely what he means by them
(as noe thing is more ordinary) fills his discourse with obscure & confused Ideas. (Locke, *Notes*, nos. 84, 85, pp. 372, 374.)

Generally, however, Sergeant is clear as to the function of
principles of reason. Taking identical propositions as the form
in which all such principles can best be stated, Sergeant
suggests that Locke's distaste for such propositions stems
from a misunderstanding of how they are used. They are not
set up as first bits of knowledge from which other knowledge
is deduced but rather lie at the bottom of our reasoning on all
things, to which all other knowledge can be reduced. If these
principles of reason were false, or if we were not '*pre-imbu'd*
with them, we could have *no Truth*, nor *any Knowledge* at all'
(p. 382). Locke misunderstood these attempts, insisting that
'Knowledge has its bottom only in the perception of the agreement or diversity of any two Ideas & is neither founded on
nor can be reduced to Identical propositions.' (Locke, *Notes*,
no. 92, p. 382.) But Sergeant sought to drive home his point
by calling attention to the fact that if Locke denies the usual
maxims he must substitute other principles in their place.
Sergeant finds such a basic principle in Locke's assertion
that 'all knowledge of the certainty of principles and consequently the way to improve our knowledge is to get, and fix
in our minds, clear, distinct, and complete ideas'. However,
if this is Locke's substitute, Sergeant argues that 'we must
be oblig'd to quit all our *Self-evident Maxims*, as of *little Use*,
upon which our selves and all the Learned part of the World,
have proceeded hitherto' (p. 406). Locke's comment, 'who
is it obleig'd him to quit them?' (Locke, *Notes*, no. 101, p. 406),
suggests that he did not mean to deny maxims altogether, just
as he previously admitted the necessity of such principles as
a means of enabling men to recognize the conditions of knowledge. But if he does not mean to reject maxims, while still
denying their use in knowledge, he would not seem to allow
them to retain much significance. In an earlier note, Locke
repeats his assurance that he does not intend men to give up

general maxims: 'who says they should be laid aside?' (Ibid., no. 86; p. 374.)

Thus it is clear that Locke did not reject maxims entirely, but it is not clear what use in epistemology he believed them to have. While being partial to the inductive procedures of the sciences contemporary with him, he by no means overlooked the necessity of rational faculties in acquiring knowledge from experience. Nor did he recognize induction alone as the primary source of knowledge, for intuition and demonstration have a prominent role in his analysis. In the concept of substance he in effect postulates a general principle or category of knowledge which functions to unify the experienced qualitative events. He was not satisfied with sets of qualities furnished by experience, although he admitted that we can have no clear idea of the nature of substances except as this combination of qualities. A compulsion of reason, a rational postulate, forces him to add to the empirical qualities an unknown substratum, the abode of the real essence. Similarly, an examination of Locke's arguments in favour of the distinction between primary and secondary qualities, on the basis of the reality of the former and the ideality of the latter, reveals that the answer given for the legitimacy of such a distinction is not empirical. On the basis of sense-experience and the introspective reflections of the mind, we cannot conclude that some sensations are *real* while others are not. Locke's arguments to this effect are based upon the conviction that solidity, extension, figure, motion, and rest are utterly inseparable from bodies, 'in what estate soever' they be, for these qualities characterize physical reality. This concept of reality was not derived from empirical observation but constituted the presupposition of the corpuscular hypothesis.

Locke's critics who wrote from the vantage point of the older rational systems did not challenge his concept of reality as such, although some held that his distinction between primary and secondary qualities was ill founded and of little use. But Lee, Sergeant, and Leibniz all objected to the ostensible objective of the *Essay*, to found all knowledge upon experience. These men wrote to show that if this dictum is taken in its literal sense as denying all contributions of the rational faculties and all function of general principles of reason presupposed by empirical knowledge, it is an obviously false dictum. While writing in reply to Lowde and Burnet, Locke had several occasions to point out that in denying innate ideas and principles he was not denying that man has certain rational faculties and capacities which aid his acquisition of knowledge. There was, in fact, a general tendency throughout the seventeenth century and the early years of the eighteenth to interpret Locke as advocating a simple sensationalism: so dominant and new was his formulation of the empiricism of the way of ideas that it overshadowed, in the minds of his critics, the careful analyses of knowledge and probability, of the degrees and extent of human knowledge, expounded in Book Four. While Leibniz invoked principles of reason as a means of organizing knowledge into a system from which certain truths could be deduced, and while Lee restricted the role of maxims in knowledge to the resolution of dubious truths into these certain and accepted principles, Sergeant saw, more clearly than either, the presuppositional character of principles of reason. Locke very likely would have agreed with Sergeant's position on this point had he fully understood it, for we have seen that he did not rule out maxims completely and that he recognized the necessity of man's being able to distinguish objects from one another. Had he taken the arguments of his objectors more seriously he might have been able to make explicit the exact roles of empirical and rational procedures in his system.

§ 2—*The Nature of Ideas*

Locke's empiricism was attacked because it was deemed insufficient in accounting for knowledge and in explaining its foundation. Lee, Leibniz, and Sergeant were concerned with laying bare what they took to be the necessary rational presuppositions of any theory of knowledge. All three were

committed to a theory of knowledge which in effect removed
analysis and investigation from experience and gave it an
a priori foundation in general principles. They were willing
to allow Locke his empiricism provided that he recognized
the role of general principles as a supplement to observational
knowledge. In their emphasis upon principles of reason as
sources of knowledge these men were removing themselves
in some degree from the realm of experience to the realm of
reason. The curious aspect of the situation is that two of the
three who attacked Locke in this manner, Lee and Sergeant,
also charged him with idealism because of his preoccupation
with ideas instead of with things. Locke, they believed, had
retreated too far from reality by basing all knowledge upon
ideas. Many critics of the *Essay* were profoundly disturbed
by his usage of the term 'idea': some of the misunderstandings
which arose between Locke and his critics came about undoubtedly because of the reader's unfamiliarity with this term
as it occurred in Locke's epistemology.

Henry Lee admitted that he had not always been able to
follow the language of the *Essay* since it was 'writ in a kind
of new Language'.[1] Lee's struggles to understand the distinction between real and nominal essences were occasioned
by what for him were the new words and phrases.

And so far as I can yet perceive, if my Author be put out of his Ideal
Trot, and can but be prevail'd with to condescend to ordinary Folks
Language, all the Dust he has rais'd in this whole Matter will fall, and
that it will clearly appear he is quite out of the way or only introducing
a new way of talking.[2]

It was not only the term 'idea' which troubled Lee: the
entire *Essay* was written in an unfamiliar language. He summarized his distrust of this language as follows:

So that when the matter comes to the Push all this Pudder and Confusion arises from these new inchanting Words, *Ideas* and Essence. For
suppose, that instead of his Phrase of complex *Ideas* of Substances, one
shou'd say, several Qualities and Properties united or combin'd, instead
of simple *Ideas*, single Qualities; instead of Essence, all the Properties,

---

[1] *Anti-Scepticism*, p. 1, preface. Cf. p. 48.   [2] Ibid., p. 260.

Qualities, or Accidents by which one individual Substance is distinguishable from another; instead of abstract *Idea*, one shou'd put *Genus* or *Species* . . . then all this Smoke will vanish, we shall both see one another and plainly discover that our Knowledge of Substances and their Modes . . . is not only real and certain, but is the All we have or can attain; and that all other is meer whimsy, is a new Name for Nothing.[1]

This distrust of and unfamiliarity with the language of ideas was expressed by many other readers. In each case, the reader professed to hold up common speech as the proper alternative. Peter Browne, writing against Toland's *Christianity not Mysterious*, singled out Toland's use of the way of ideas as a foundation for his radical version of religion and complained:

And the talking of Idea's, and running endless divisions upon them, is a cheap and easie way, some Men nowadays have taken up, of appearing wise and learned to the world. Whereas the bottom of it all is no more than this, That Men of nice heads have agreed to speak of plain things in a peculiar dialect of their own; which if they were stript of those terms of Art, and put into plain language, have nothing in them more than what is obvious to the common sense and reason of all men.[2]

Referring to the same work by Toland, Stillingfleet censured the terminology of the way of ideas.

But none are so bold in attacking the *Mysteries of the Christian Faith*: as the Smatterers in *Ideas*, and new Terms of Philosophy, without any true Understanding of them. For these *Ideas* are become but another sort of Canting with such men; and they would reason as well upon *Genus* and *Species*, or upon *Occult Qualities*, and *Substantial Forms*, but only that they are *Terms* out of *Fashion*.[3]

In his answer to Locke's second letter of defence against his attacks,[4] the bishop repeated his charge that the falsity and inadequacies of Locke's epistemology were attributable in large measure to his terminology.

As to the *Term* of *Ideas*, I have no Objection to the use of the word it self; provided it be used in a common Sense, and no Weight be laid upon it more than it can bear; for I am for no new affected *Terms* which

---

[1] *Anti-Scepticism*, p. 261.
[2] *A Letter in Answer to . . . Christianity not Mysterious* (1697), pp. 2–3.
[3] *A Discourse in Vindication of the . . . Trinity* (1697), p. 273.
[4] *Mr. Locke's Reply to the . . . Bishop of Worcester's Answer to his Letter* (1697).

are apt to carry Mens Minds out of the way; they are like *Ignes fatui* which seem to give light, but lead those that follow them into Bogs.[1]

Later, in the same answer, he blames the lack of general principles and rigid demonstrations upon the newness of the language, showing his own fondness for the methods of Sergeant.

> But your Way of *Certainty by Ideas* is so wholly New, that here we have no *general Principles*; no *Criterion*, no *Antecedents and Consequents*; no *Syllogistical Methods* of *Demonstration*; and yet we are told of a better Way of Certainty to be attained, meerly by the help of *Ideas*.[2]

Timothy Goodwin, the biographer of Stillingfleet, also stressed the newness of Locke's terminology, citing it as one factor leading to the popularity of the *Essay*.

> This Essay abounding with a Set of new Philosophical Terms, as if some wonderful Improvement of Knowledge was to have been hoped for from it, and being written with a graceful Air, and liveliness of Spirit, and elegancy of Style and politeness of Expression, a smartness in Reasoning, and an ingenious improvement of his Arguments to the best advantage, by a closeness of Reference, and patness of Similitudes and Allusions, no wonder a new Scheme of Notions, and a profess'd Design of promoting true Understanding, and a right Apprehension of Things, set off with these uncommon Advantages, should easily recommend it self to the Affections of the Studious, especially the younger part of them.[3]

Another (anonymous) writer of the seventeenth century, besides stating that Locke was inconsistent, a sceptic, and a materialist, agreed with Stillingfleet that Locke had introduced a new vocabulary into the language.[4] John Milner (*An Account of Mr. Lock's Religion*, 1700) objects that the frequent use of the term 'idea' confuses the reader, suggesting that 'Mr. *Lock* and others, had done better, if they had not amus'd the World so much with the term *Idea* as they have done' (p. 14). Like Lee and Browne, Milner contrasts this language with the ordinary language which he prefers, arguing that

[1] *The Bishop of Worcester's Answer to Mr. Locke's Second Letter* (1698), p. 71.
[2] Ibid., p. 120.
[3] *The Life and Character of . . . The Late Dr. Edw. Stillingfleet* (1710), pp. 86–87.
[4] B., F. *A Free but Modest Censure* (1698), p. 6.

'Mr. *Lock* had made his *Essay* more easie and intelligible to all sorts of Readers, if he had made use of other Terms, and not fill'd every Page almost with the mention of *Ideas*' (p. 15). George Hickes, who accused Locke of borrowing from the scholastics, urged that 'there is not one sound Notion in it [the *Essay*], under his affected *new Terms*, to improve Human Understanding (I say, to improve, not to Poyson it) which the School *Logicks*, and *Metaphysicks*, which are Subordinate to one another, have not taught under the *old*'.[1]

The very newness of the language employed by Locke startled some, convinced others that he was merely using another ruse to attempt to persuade the reader of the novelties to be found within, and led still different readers to distrust the entire position. Traditional language, they thought, provided sufficient material for the expression of any new opinions which might occur. To such critics as these, the suggestion that part of the blame for faulty philosophy or for inadequate analysis lay in the rigid and unquestioned language of the past could be no more than pretence. When Book Three, with its concern for linguistic analysis, was taken seriously by Locke's contemporaries, little understanding of his objective was shown. In most cases, this part of the *Essay* was completely ignored.[2] But the new uses of old terms which were an essential feature of Locke's work served many as the initial clue that something was contained in this book which was not in harmony with orthodox doctrines. Sergeant had written his *Solid Philosophy Asserted* in an effort to counteract the scepticism into which he believed Descartes's and Locke's new way of talking led. He undoubtedly summarized the opinion of many of Locke's critics when he concluded the preface of his *Transnatural Philosophy* (1700) by remarking:

In a word, since *Ideas* are both *Unintelligible*, and altogether *Useless*, & (I fear) *ill Use* is made of them, contrary to the Intention of their

---

[1] Carroll, William. *Spinoza Reviv'd* (1709), p. [34] of 'Prelim. Discourse' by Hickes.

[2] The important doctrine of real and nominal essence of Book Three was much discussed, together with the doctrine of substance. Cf. below, pp. 126 et seq.

Authors; it seems but fitting that the *Way of Ideas* should be *lay'd aside*; nay, that the very *Word* which has got such a *Vogue*, should be no longer heard of, unless a good reason may be given why we should use *such Words* as *no Man understands*.

But Sergeant was not so much troubled by the newness of the terminology of the *Essay* as he was by the essential errors in the method of ideas. He seems to have seriously endeavoured to determine precisely what the ideists meant by 'idea', but he found that the Cartesians were not united over the question of the nature of ideas, and discovered, so he thought, that Locke meant by the term only similitudes of things. But whatever the exact intention behind the new term in philosophy, Sergeant was convinced that its use could lead only to scepticism. Like several other contemporary critics, Sergeant found that the doctrines implied by the new terms were themselves inadequate and erroneous.

Sergeant was not alone in trying to overcome the difficulties of understanding the new terminology. John Norris, in his 'Cursory Reflections', raised the crucial question concerning the key term 'idea', namely, 'what sort of entities are ideas?' Norris, like Sergeant, could not be satisfied with Locke's reluctance to deal with such ontological problems, and was even less pleased with Locke's inclusive definition of ideas as 'whatsoever the mind perceives in itself, or is the immediate object of perception'. He wanted to know what kind of things these ideas are in essence: 'Are they in the first place Real Beings or not?' (p. 22). He was certain that they were real beings for Locke, in the sense that they have 'Real Properties, and [are] really different one from another, and representing things really different' in nature. (Ibid.) But, 'are they Substances, or are they Modifications of Substances?' (p. 23). Norris argued that Locke could not have meant them to be modifications of substances, since modifications cannot be 'representative' of substances, as ideas must be for Locke. Thus, 'if an Idea be a Modification only it cannot subsist by it self, but must be the Modification of some Substance or other, whereof also there may be an Idea; which Idea being (as is supposed) only a Mode, must have another Substance, and so on without end'. (Ibid.) Thus Locke would be driven to say ideas are substances, substances and modes being exclusive alternatives for Norris. Norris's question then becomes, 'are they Material Substances or Immaterial?' That they cannot be material is proved, he believed, in the following way:

> If he says they are *Material* Substances or Corporeal Emanations from sensible Objects, I would desire him to weigh with himself, and try if he can answer, what is alledged by M. *Malebranch* against the Possibility of such Emanations. Particularly, let him tell me how this can consist with the *Impenetrability* of Bodies, which must needs hinder these Corporeal Effluvias from possessing the same *Ubi* or Point, which yet must be supposed, if these be the Representers of Objects, Since there is no assignable Point where the same, and where multitudes of Objects may not be seen (p. 24).

Norris pressed Locke even more closely by asking how and where such material effluvia can be received. He did not think we could receive them upon the soul since this is an incorporeal substance which cannot receive any 'stamp' or 'impression'. Since he conceives of the brain as a fluid, he does not understand how it could retain any of these effluvia if it did receive them, since 'The least jog of a Mans Head must needs obliterate such slight and Aerial Traces, as the Wind does the Figures that are written upon the Sand' (p. 25). Moreover, the great number of such impressions coming to the brain must soon fill the brain beyond capacity. Even if we 'could get over all this', the greatest difficulty, Norris insisted, still remains: 'How will such Corporeal Effluvias be able to represent immaterial and intellectual Objects?' (Ibid.) At best, they will be able 'to represent Material Objects, and not all of them neither, but only those whose Emanations they are'. (Ibid.) The only alternative which Norris can see for Locke is that he must mean by 'ideas' immaterial substances. Norris himself agrees with this interpretation, for he believes they are all in essence immaterial, although not all of them are immaterial in their representation. However, this position is not free from difficulties. 'How shall Bodies send forth such

Immaterial Species? They can emit nothing but what is Corporeal, like themselves' (p. 26). Thus, Norris believed he had driven Locke into the corner from which he could only emerge an Occasionalist.

> The short of this Argument is, If our Ideas are derived from sensible Objects, then they are Material Beings, because Matter can send forth nothing but Matter. But they are not Material Beings, for the Reasons alledg'd above. Therefore they are not derived from Sensible Objects. Which I think has the force of Demonstration (pp. 26–27).

In his later work, *An Essay Towards the Theory of the Ideal or Intelligible World* (1701–4), Norris argues that if Locke means that material objects send ideas to the mind, then he has 'derived our Ideas from a false Original' (vol. ii, p. 37), but if all he means is that 'sensible Objects do by the Impression which they make upon our outward Senses serve to excite Ideas in our Minds', then there is nothing very dangerous or original in Locke's doctrine. But he repeats his charge that Locke has left to one side the most important question concerning the nature of ideas. Locke had, of course, expressly indicated in his Introduction that he was not concerned to explain how perception takes place once the material particle has reached the organ of sense, for he found himself totally incapable of offering any explanation of the process which converts material particles into immaterial apprehension. In his 1693 'Remarks upon Some of Mr. Norris's Books' (first published posthumously in 1720 by Pierre Desmaizeaux), Locke reiterated this belief and added as a reason for the inexplicableness of the transposition that 'no man can give any account of any alteration made in any simple substance whatsoever; all the alteration we can conceive, being only of the alteration of compounded substances; and that only by a transposition of parts'.[1] In this short tract, as in the longer one on the 'Examination of P. Malebranche's Opinion' (first published in 1706 by Anthony Collins and Peter King), Locke sought to show that the occasionalist explanation did not account for the important question of the nature of ideas, and

---

[1] Section no. 2, in *Works*, vol. x, p. 248.

suggested as well that an examination of optics would seem to show that we see all things in the bottom of our eyes and not in God.[1] But although Locke was capable of writing coolly against Norris and Malebranche, he was more than a little annoyed that Norris should have spent so much time in his 'Cursory Reflections' over this question of the nature of ideas. In the early, unpublished draft of this reply to Norris, Locke had observed:

> Tis a hard case that this man of Reflections will not suffer a poor neighbour of his to know his owne designe in writing, or pursue that designe according to his owne fashion or abilities perhaps I was lazy & thought the *plain historical method* I had proposed to my self was enough for me perhaps I had other business & could afford noe more of my time to these speculations, nay possibly I found that discovery beyond my reach & being one of those that doe not pretend to know all things am not ashamed to confesse my ignorance in this & a great many other & therefore shall acknowledg it as a great favour from the Reflector to instruct me better in *the nature of Ideas*.[2]

He could not see in Norris's questionings the pure speculative interests which Norris claimed to be following. He thought he detected there the traces of a pervasive egoism: 'There are some happy Genius's who thinke they either are not or ought not to be ignorant of any thing. The unlimited possessions which these sons of light by the luckinesse of their birth enjoy in the intellectuall world justly deserve our admiration.'[3] If not attempts to show off his learning against the shallowness of Locke's thought, then the series of questions concerning the nature of ideas is, Locke argued, useless and without significance.

> I must confesse it a marke of my poverty not to be provided with Ragousts to entertain him according to his relish on all those subjects for there is [never an one of those materiale or immateriale Emanations] or Effluvias not I perceive a leg or a wing of any of those dotrell Ideas that imitate everything whether you would hash them up as *material* effluvias or serve up as immaterial, *immaterial as to their substance or Immaterial as to their representation* but mang'd by good cookry might make

---

[1] 'Examination of P. Malebranche's Opinion', section no. 11; in *Works*, vol. ix, pp. 217-18.
[2] MS. Locke, C. 28, f. 109. [3] Ibid., f. 110.

most a considerable dish, as you may see p. 21–31 where out of his
aboundant liberality & in consideration of my unprovided kitchin has
furnished out to him self a large entertainment according to his owne
pallate & thither I send any one who has a minde to feast himself upon
Ideas.[1]

Norris was clearly a victim of his own set of categories in
seeking to push Locke into the occasionalist position. The
substance–accident ontology was applied to Locke's empirical
epistemology, an ontology which Locke rejected as far as ideas
were concerned. He did not conceive of ideas as real beings,
in Norris's sense, independent of the mind. The discussion
in the *Essay* does not proceed without a large element of
ambiguity about the term 'idea', but it should be clear that
Norris's ontology is inapplicable to ideas. Anthony Collins
understood Locke's intentions on this issue of the nature of
ideas, pointing out the irrelevance of most of Norris's criticism.

I only observe that how curious soever some may think these en-
quirys are, as they carry no opposition to the design of the Essay, so
neither are they pertinent to the Authors design, for how does the
knowing the nature of Ideas concern one who only considers 'em as
objects of the Understanding? & how does the question whether the
senses are the real or occasional causes (for it is granted that wee can
know nothing without em) of our Ideas contradict a matter of fact about
the Original of our Ideas, that may be true, whether the senses be either
the real or occasional causes of 'em. Malebranch & his following as well
as those that account for the mode of Human Understanding after the
4 other ways assigned by him do agree that wee cannot have Ideas of
sense without our senses, & so agree to as much as the Author of H.U.
affirms or is necessary to his design.[2]

Likewise, the anonymous writer of 1705, to whom I have
referred in the previous chapter, saw that the kind of criticism
levelled by Norris was misplaced. Just as this writer sought to
bring harmony into the disputes over innate ideas, so he tried
to unite the opposing camps over the meaning of the term
'idea'. He opens his remarkably clear-sighted tract with a
succinct summary of the various definitions of 'ideas' then
current.

[1] Ibid., ff. 110–11. The passage in brackets was crossed out.
[2] Collins to Locke, MS. Locke, C. 7, f. 28. Letter of 15 March 1703/4.

There is Hardly any Topick we shall meet with that the Learned have differ'd more about than this of Ideas; like Men blundering in the dark, they feel after them to find them; some catch at them under *one* Appearance, some under *another*; some make them to be *Material*, others *Spiritual*; some will have them to be *Effluvia*, from the Bodies they Represent, others Totally Distinct *Essences*; some hold them to be *Modes*, others *Substances*; some assert them *All* to be *Innate*; others *None*: So that one would think there must needs be a very great Intricacy in that which has given Rise, not only to such a *Variety* but also such a *Contradiction* of Opinions.[1]

The writer suggests two reasons for the confusions on this subject, the first of which is the failure to explain meanings sufficiently. He describes the second cause of confusion as follows:

That in considering the *Mind*, some men do not sufficiently abstract their Thoughts from *Matter*, but make use of such Terms as can properly relate to *Matter* only, and apply them to the *Mind* in the same Sense as they are spoken of *Matter*, such as *Images* and *Signatures*, *Marks*, and *Impressions*, *Characters* and *Notes* of *Things*, and *Seeds of Thoughts* and *Knowledge* (p. 5).

The anonymous writer of 1705 then proceeds by laying down certain definitions as a preliminary to expounding his thoughts on the problem. 'By an Idea, I mean the Representation of something in the Mind. (This Definition I think all sides are agreed in thus far, but whether this Representation be only a Modification of the Mind, or be a Distinct Being, or Substance United to the Mind, is a Question)' (p. 6). He cites 'Marlebranch' as holding the latter 'curious hypothesis'. Mind is defined, according to the standard conception, as a thinking thing possessed of perception, understanding, &c. From these and several other definitions, the author of this tract proceeds to deduce, in an orderly and valid fashion, certain conclusions which he thinks should bring light into the many disputes over the question of ideas. Like Locke, he insists that thoughts and ideas are identical and that hence there can be no unconscious thoughts. To the question raised by Sherlock, 'what becomes of these ideas when they go out of the mind?', the

[1] *A Philosophick Essay concerning Ideas* (1705), p. 4.

author very cleverly replies that this is an improper question to ask unless ideas be real beings independent of minds.

But this Question can be nowise proper for those who make Thought and Idea to be the same; for according to this Notion they are not *Real Beings* but only *Modifications of the Mind*, or so many several *Modes of Thinking* upon the several Objects presented to the Mind; or if you please, it is the Mind it self operating after *such* and *such* a Manner, just as the Roundness of a Body, and its Motion are nothing but the Body it self figur'd and translated after such and such a Sort (p. 13).

Moreover, the writer sees that once we have identified ideas and thoughts, it is incorrect to speak of ideas as coming from without, since they 'are wholly owing to the Mind, and are indeed nothing else but *the natural Operations of the Mind upon the several Objects presented to it*' (p. 20).

Had Locke seen sufficiently clearly these implications of his position, he could have written a reply to clarify the difference between his own epistemological analysis and that which used the older metaphysical categories of substance and accident. He so quietly dispensed with the traditional categories on this question that many of his critics did not appreciate the novelty which he was introducing. What was required in the *Essay* was not so much an elucidation of the meaning of 'idea', which Norris demanded, as a careful explanation of how the analysis of ideas in that work differed from the older methods and why Locke had found it expedient to depart from tradition in this instance. But I do not think anyone in the seventeenth century was capable of appreciating just what did differentiate Locke's epistemological analysis from that of his contemporaries and predecessors, although many saw that it did indeed differ. A polemic against the categories of substance, accident, real being, essence, and existence could not have been written by Locke, but not entirely because he himself adopted this terminology with slight modifications in later portions of the *Essay*: he did not fully understand the implications of his own analysis. Locke was the inheritor of two traditions: the one, the new science with its radically new categories, the other, the older scholastic tradition which he

in part ridiculed but did not entirely reject. He did succeed
moderately well in modifying the traditional categories of
substance, accident, and essence to make his acceptance of
them fairly consistent with his radical rejection of them in the
earlier portions of the *Essay*, although he was not clever
enough to escape the pitfalls of his own representative theory
of perception. It was undoubtedly this confusion of acceptance and rejection of the familiar traditions which raised
doubts and suspicions in the minds of his readers when he
based all knowledge upon ideas.

§ 3—*Idealism in Knowledge and Truth*

In an interesting section in his 'Examination of P. Malebranche's Opinion', Locke very clearly saw the implicit
immaterialism in Malebranche's analysis of ideas, an implication of the way of ideas already developed by Burthogge in his
Organum Vetus & Novum and given its classical expression
by Berkeley in the early years of the eighteenth century. On
Malebranche's principle of seeing all things in God, how,
Locke queries, can we know that there is any physical world
existing without?

> For we see nothing but the ideas that are in God; but body itself we
> neither do nor can possibly see at all; and how then can we know that
> there is any such thing existing as body, since we can by no means see or
> perceive it by our senses, which is all the way we can have of knowing
> any corporeal thing to exist?[1]

It will not do, Locke points out, to say dogmatically that upon
the occasion of objects being presented to us God causes us
to have their perception, for this conclusion is precisely what
awaits proof.

> But the sun being risen, and the horse brought within convenient dis-
> tance, and so being present to my eyes, God shows me their ideas in
> himself: and I say God shows me these ideas when he pleases, without
> the presence of any such bodies to my eyes. For when I think I see a star
> at such a distance from me; which truly I do not see, but the idea of it

---

[1] *Works*, vol. ix, p. 253.

which God shows me; I would have it proved to me that there is such a star existing a million of million of miles from me when I think I see it, more than when I dream of such a star. For until it be proved that there is a candle in the room by which I write this, the supposition of my seeing in God the pyramidical idea of its flame, upon occasion of the candle's being there, is begging what is in question.[1]

But what Locke here charged against the occasionalists, namely, that their doctrines led them into an idealism or phenomenalism by offering no way in which the reality of physical objects could be proved, was itself strongly urged against the doctrines of the *Essay* by some of its more formidable critics. William Carroll, in his *Dissertation* (1706), remarked:

That which his *Words* are the *Marks* of, are the *Ideas* in his own *Mind*: Nor can he apply them, as *Marks* immediately to *any thing else*, but the *Ideas* that he himself hath: For this would be to make them Signs of his own *Conceptions*, and yet apply them to other *Ideas*; which would be to make them *Signs*, and not *Signs* of his *Ideas* at the same time; and so in Effect, to have *no Signification at all*. Words being voluntary *Signs*, they cannot be voluntary *Signs* imposed by him on *things he knows not* (pp. 44–45).

John Witty, in *The First Principles of Modern Deism Confuted* (1707), likewise places his finger upon the crucial sceptical feature of Locke's epistemology. If knowledge is limited to simple and complex ideas,

we must give up all pretence to any real Certainty of all *matters of Fact* which we see not, or have not seen our selves; of all *Persons* or *Things* which exist, live, or are transacted out of our view; or which have existed, liv'd or were transacted out of our times; . . . (pp. 23–24).

Norris was the first critic to notice this epistemological scepticism inherent in the principles of the *Essay*, and objected in his 'Cursory Reflections' to the purely verbal or ideal definition of truth and knowledge as the agreement of ideas or the words standing for ideas. Norris insisted that if knowledge is defined in terms of agreement and disagreement, these relations must refer to real objects. It was undoubtedly because of this kind of criticism of the way of ideas that the

[1] Ibid., pp. 253–4.

anonymous writer of 1705 defined truth as 'the *Real Relation* *that there is between things as to their Agreement or Disagreement*', clearly distinguishing this from the idea of truth which 'is the Thought that we form concerning this Relation; the *former* is in the Object without, the *latter* is within us in the Mind'.[1]

Samuel Bold, in *Some Considerations On the Principal Objections* (1699), said that two main charges were brought against Locke's definition of knowledge: (1) 'That the Proposition is not true. In consequence of which, *the way of Ideas* is condemned as *no way at all to Certainty, or Knowledge*'; and (2) that the definition 'is inconsistent with, and of dangerous consequence to the *Articles of the Christian Faith*' (pp. 3–4). But an examination of the various criticisms made against the *Essay* in the seventeenth and early eighteenth centuries reveals that along with the first charge cited by Bold there went the more important claim that the definition of knowledge in the *Essay* led to epistemological scepticism. If a valid claim for epistemological scepticism had not been made, it is doubtful whether the second charge which Bold distinguished would ever have been raised. In his defence of Locke, Bold failed to comprehend the significance of this additional charge. He championed the verbal definition of propositions given by Locke and accepted completely the Lockean definition of knowledge, arguing throughout his tract along strictly coherence-theory lines. Bold claimed that no one questioned the definition of the truth of propositions as the correlation of words with ideas; but we have seen that both Norris and Carroll singled out precisely this feature of the *Essay* for criticism. Bold was of course correct in arguing that we cannot know that a given proposition is true or false unless we do perceive the relation between the ideas which it expresses in words, unless 'certainty, or knowledge of the truth of Propositions, may be had without *perception*, or without perceiving the truth of what is expressed' (p. 5). Bold was correct in arguing that even self-evident propositions demand a per-

[1] Op. cit., p. 21.

ception or awareness of the connexion of the terms of the propositions. What Bold did not see was that the apprehension of self-evident propositions was not of the same kind as the apprehension of existential propositions; for, although it is true that in both cases the awareness of the order of terms and of their relations must be had and compared with the corresponding ideas before we can apprehend the truth or falsity involved, existential propositions carry an important rider along with them without which they become useless or else mere components of a coherent system. It was largely against the rationalist thinkers who maintained that existential knowledge could be deduced from maxims and general principles of reason that Bold wrote; but Bold himself, and Locke with him, would be guilty of somewhat the same errors as he complains against if he could not show that the propositions of perception have a real referent existing in the world.

Henry Lee saw these pitfalls of the way of ideas clearly, defining truth, like the anonymous writer of 1705 and like Norris in the previous century, as the 'Conjunction or Disjunction of things according to the real Relation those things have to each other.'[1] Locke's definition can give no certainty of existence since it is restricted to the realm of ideas. In the case of particular propositions, affirmative or negative, there can be no certainty, since, unless we assume the existence of the subjects of such propositions, we have an empty assertion. But to make this assumption is to go beyond our ideas. The 'ideal' principles of Locke lead to scepticism 'because they will neither allow us to suppose, nor can prove the real Existence of things without us'.[2] Throughout his long commentary on the *Essay*, Lee sought to prove (1) that 'Our Knowledge is of something else, besides of our own Ideas'; (2) that if it is only of our own ideas, knowledge is entirely useless; and (3) that such a definition as Locke gives 'involves us in endless Scepticism or Doubtfulness of the Truth of all Propositions whatever.'[3] The basic presupposition of the

---

[1] *Anti-Scepticism*, p. 264.   [2] Ibid., preface.
[3] Ibid., p. 235. There is an error in the pagination at this point, the pages 235

corpuscular hypothesis is that perception takes place through a causal process which passes from object to sense organ, the object end of the process having certain definite characteristics which constitute its 'reality'. But Lee found weak and invalid the arguments produced by Locke in support of his belief in the reality of knowledge. What good is it, he asked, 'to know that the Ideas of White, Red, Round, and Square, disagree, if there be really no Bodies without me that have those Powers to reflect Light differently, or have any such Figures?'[1] Lee was quite willing to admit that 'we can know nothing but our own Thoughts', in the sense that without taking notice of outward effects, knowledge is impossible. The terms 'thought', 'perception', or 'operation' did not trouble Lee, but the term 'idea' held for him the power of a new entity capable of keeping knowledge restricted within this realm of ideas. By employing the term 'thought' in Locke's definition rather than 'idea', Lee believed we were less liable to overlook the importance of the external referent in our definition. It was upon the suppositions of common sense, i.e. (1) that our 'senses and other faculties are true', and (2) that God is infinitely wise, powerful, and good and hence cannot be deceived Himself or allow man to be deceived, that Lee sought to base his own system, failing to understand that these suppositions themselves were on no better (and perhaps on a worse) footing than Locke's careful attempts to defend the common-sense belief.[2] Lee was not to be shaken out of his traditional beliefs and assumptions, even when the doctrines of the ideists had revealed the epistemological and ontological difficulties inherent in establishing the validity of any existential claim. Like the defenders of the two forms of the doctrine of innate knowledge, Lee was tenaciously attached to tradition. In this case, the tradition was not religious and moral, but for the most part independent of these areas of thought. Past thinkers had based their specula-

and 236 being repeated. The reference here is to the second occurrence and corresponds with the signature, kkk.

[1] *Anti-Scepticism*, p. 237.
[2] Ibid., p. 247. Cf. pp. 267-8.

tions upon the conviction of an external world existing independent of man. Locke's formulation of knowledge in terms of ideas made Lee aware of the objections to Locke's own system, but he did not see that they had equal application to his own.

Sergeant was another critic who clung to tradition in the face of the many challenges the *Essay* offered, but in many ways Sergeant saw more clearly than did Lee the epistemological difficulties of the way of ideas. It was the entire method of ideas as a means to knowledge which he attacked; and, although the Aristotelian-Thomistic tradition which he offered as an alternative did not circumvent the dangers of epistemological scepticism, or did so only by bold unquestioned assumptions, Sergeant's extended attack upon the way of ideas laid bare some crucial difficulties which Locke might have been able to patch up had he found the time and inclination to reply seriously to him. Sergeant had disputed with the Cartesians, as with Locke, over the criterion of certainty being centred in clear and distinct ideas; for this approach seemed to him, as to Norris and Lee, to be placing the criterion of truth within the knowing mind rather than in the objects known. He never found a satisfactory answer to the question of the nature of ideas, but he was convinced that they functioned to deny the mind direct access to things by restricting it to some kind of third entity. Cognition was thus made to consist in a triadic relation involving the knowing mind, the object or referent, and the ideas by means of which the mind came to know things. Sergeant wished to reduce the process of knowing to a dyadic relation consisting only of the knowing mind and the object known. The 'notion' was his attempted way of defending such a direct realist position. In making more precise Sergeant's concept of the notion, one of the first tasks is to elicit the distinction between a notion and an idea. His twofold analysis of man into a corporeal and a spiritual part is the basis for this further distinction. Corresponding to the two aspects of man are two separate faculties: the fancy and the understanding. Both faculties must operate in every act of knowledge; but, since the faculties are distinct, 'the Immediate *Objects* peculiar to those Different Faculties, must likewise be as widely Different from one another, as are those Powers to which they belong; and consequently, be as vastly Opposite, as the Natures of *Body* and *Spirit* can distance them'. In other words, to every 'Thought or Act of Knowledge we have . . . there must be two sorts of Interiour Objects concur; whereof, the one is *Corporeal*, the other of a *Spiritual* Nature.'[1] It is this distinction between the object of the fancy (the idea or the phantasm) and the object of the understanding (the notion) which differentiates man from the beasts on the one hand, who have only material phantasms, and the angels on the other, who have only spiritual notions. The phantasms are material copies of the external objects, while the notions are meanings and hence intellectual. Phantasms are causally related to physical objects and to notions, serving as a necessary middle term between the external world and the mind. Without material phantasms, there would be no notions; but, whereas the phantasm is a crude duplication of the physical object (or some aspect of it), the notion has become refined to the point at which there is no significant difference between it and the physical object. Hence, by restricting the method of knowledge to such spiritual 'notions', Sergeant believed himself able to avoid the dualism which he found in the epistemologies of Descartes and Locke. He sought thereby to maintain a kind of direct or naïve realism.

He explains that the words 'notion', 'simple apprehension', 'conception', and 'meaning' are all synonymous terms. He calls the immediate objects of the mind 'notions' because 'they are the Parts or Elements of Knowledge', which when put together constitute cognition. 'They are call'd "*Simple Apprehensions*", to distinguish them from *Judgments*, which are compounded of *more* Notions, and belong to the *second* Operation of our Understanding.'[2] Apprehension on this

---

[1] *Solid Philosophy Asserted*, p. [25] of the Preface.
[2] *The Method to Science*, p. 3.

simple level does not take place until the impressions of the senses have been communicated to the soul. The apprehension is simple because it involves no judgement. Sergeant does not work out a semiotic theory whereby what is communicated to the mind becomes a meaning-sign, but he does say that 'meaning' is synonymous with 'notion'; notions affect the mind, 'which only can *mean* or *intend*'. It is mainly in this sense that he defines notions as simple apprehensions, but apparently he meant to use the term in a still wider sense, as conceptions, because the mind conceives or breeds these notions as 'the *Embryo's* of Knowledge'. When the impressions of sense reach the mind, the conception which takes place amounts to a simple apprehension of a sign conveying meaning to the mind. The only difference between notions in the mind and the things of which they are notions is that the former have a different manner of existing. To avoid the epistemological dualism which he found in the ideists' method, Sergeant refused to convert the simply apprehended meanings into media of knowledge which communicate the natures of things external to the observer. The meanings *are* the things themselves. We intend or mean not some idea but the thing itself when we assert something about the world. The things themselves exist in our mind in the form of notions. There is no difficulty in this view, Sergeant hastens to add, when we recognize that 'the same *Ens* or Thing may have diverse *Manners* of Existing; one Corporeal, the other Intellectual or Spiritual; since the Thing . . . abstracts even from Existence it *self*' (Ibid.). There is nothing contained in the notion or the meaning apprehended by the mind which signifies that the thing exists or does not exist. The only notion which entails existence is that of God. A word or sign in cognition implies a meaning, but existence is not contained in that meaning. The fact that the thing external to the mind has a corporeal existence while the notion of it in the mind has an immaterial existence does not mean that we do not know the thing directly in experience, since what is essential to the thing is contained in the notion of that thing and is precisely the thing itself in these respects. Thus, Sergeant has drained off all aspects of objects except their meanings, and then argued that those objects thus bereft exist in the mind. It is in this sense, and this sense only, that his epistemology can be said to be direct realism; the mind is in immediate contact with the essential natures of objects, since by definition the form of the object contains its essence, and the form is transmitted to the mind. To the extent that notions are signs, conveyors of meaning, Sergeant's epistemology is just as dualistic as Locke's.

Sergeant assumes from the beginning that we do have knowledge of things. All men agree, he believes, with this assumption. The question then is not whether we have knowledge of an external world, but *how* we gain this knowledge. If such knowledge is indirect, as the Cartesian method implies, our 'knowledge' cannot always be certain or sound. Thus, the only way in which we can have trustworthy knowledge of the world is by direct contact with that world. Sergeant's implicit objective is to justify direct realism and to show how direct knowledge of the world is possible. By means of his concept of a 'notion' he seeks to argue that knowledge goes on in terms of meanings which reveal the full and direct nature of objects. He recognized two levels of the genesis of meaning, however: the primary level where meanings are given to the mind directly by external objects (a physiological genesis), and the secondary level where meanings are inherited and passed on or refined through usage (an ethnological genesis). The important level from the epistemological point of view is, of course, the physiological. None of Sergeant's arguments in support of his position on the nature of notions proves his thesis, since the most they show is that meanings exist in our minds. Had he offered some convincing proofs for the physiological genesis of notions from material phantasms, he could have placed his direct realism on stronger ground. But notice the nature of his explanation. External bodies are said to give off effluvia which are literal aspects of the object and which enter the pores of the various sense organs. The material and the spiritual parts of man come together at some point, such as at Descartes's pineal gland. Following scholastic tradition, Sergeant terms it the 'seat of knowledge'. Every effect which alters the material part of man at this point (the brain or nearby regions) also creates an effect in the spiritual part. This effect is the union of matter and form. The material effluvia do not enter the form or spiritual part. Rather, a Spinozistic parallelism takes place in which the alterations in the spiritual part correspond with and duplicate therein the alterations in the material section.

> Those *Effluviums* sent out from Bodies, have the *very Natures* of those Bodies in them, or rather are themselves Lesser Bodies of the *Self-same* Nature, ... which are cut off by Natural Agents from the great Lump; and, therefore, by Application of themselves, they imprint the *very Body it self*, or a Body of that Nature, on that material part which is the *Seat of Knowledge*. Whence the Soul being, at the same time, affected after *her* manner (or *Knowingly*) as that part was affected, she has also the *very Nature* of that Body (as far as the Sense exhibits it) put in her by that conformable Impression, when she has a *Notion* of it.[1]

This physiological account is really a metaphysical explanation devised to support his correspondence theory of truth. It fails to give an adequate metaphysical, let alone an empirical, account of how meanings enter the mind directly from objects. As Locke satirically remarked, 'And now let the reader consider whether by reading what he finds from hither [where Sergeant's explanation begins] he has not got a perfect clear knowledge how material things get into the imateriall soule.' (Locke, *Notes*, no. 24, p. 76.)

Forced in the direction of a more immediate realism by the objectionable features of the ideists' theory, Sergeant saw he had to maintain that the process of knowing consists in our having the very predicates and accidents of objects within our minds. He insisted that his notions or meanings differed fundamentally from Locke's ideas, but this conviction was attributable to his interpreting all ideas in the *Essay* as resemblances in the crude sense. His notions were not like

---

[1] *Solid Philosophy Asserted*, p. 69.

objects; they were the objects themselves as they exist im-
materially in the mind. The term 'idea', in fact, could signify
nothing else for Sergeant than a resemblance of physical
objects; otherwise, parallel with his attempted definition of
'notion', it must be the very thing itself. Hence, since ideas
were so carefully separated from things by both Descartes and
Locke, the only way they could be representative and thus
conveyors of the natures of objects was to be similitudes of
things. Only under these conditions, Sergeant thought, can
an examination of ideas yield a knowledge of the natures of
objects. But is this a sufficient condition? Sergeant points out
that 'had I known such things *formerly*, then a Resemblance
of them might, in that case, revive, and call into my mind the
knowledge of them', as a picture revives and calls to mind
a distant friend.[1] But he fails to understand how we can have
our first knowledge of things by means of copies or resemblances, since a prerequisite for recognizing a picture as a
picture of something in the world is to have some prior knowledge of the thing pictured. Secondary knowledge of nature
may be obtained by the way of ideas, but this way presupposes
a primary knowledge obtained in some more direct manner.
Even on the secondary level, cognition by means of ideas
encounters difficulties. If the ideas which represent objects
are only like those objects in some respects, our knowledge
will obviously be limited so that we can never have a complete
knowledge of objects. If, on the other hand, an idea is like the
thing in all respects, 'then 'tis *in no Respect unlike it*; and, by
Consequence, *in no Respect Different from it*, (for that *Difference* would be an *Unlikeness*;) and, if it be *in no respect Different*, it follows, out of the very Terms, that it is the *very same*,
in the Mind, and *out* of the Mind; . . .'[2] Sergeant did not wish
to say that two patches of red of exactly the same shade are
really identical. What he maintains is that there is a sameness
in all respects save number. The fact that the one, the idea or
notion of this shade of red, exists in the understanding in-
tellectually, while the other, the patch of colour, exists outside

---

[1] *Solid Philosophy Asserted*, p. 20.   [2] Ibid., p. 36.

the understanding corporeally, shows that they are not identical. Notion and object do differ in this respect. Locke was aware of the importance, for Sergeant's position, of establishing an essential but non-numerical identity between notion and object, but he did not understand what it is for 'a material thing to exist spiritualy'. (Locke, *Notes*, no. 17, p. 59.) Moreover, he disagreed entirely with the argument employed by Sergeant to show that exact likeness results in sameness. After following Sergeant's many arguments to the effect that if x and y are alike they must be the same, Locke remarks: 'I cannot but wonder to hear a man soe often repeat. What if he were not a Dictator in philosophie? would be Nonsense, viz., *that a like is the same.*' (Ibid., no. 18, p. 61.) If this argument were true, Sergeant would be committed to the conclusion that in knowing God (or any object), '*the soul becomes god*' or its object. (Ibid., no. 14, p. 40.) In an attempt to persuade Stillingfleet that the new way of ideas was nothing new and that, on the definitions of 'idea' used in the *Essay*, even Stillingfleet has to admit to such entities, Locke satirized Sergeant's doctrine of notions.

Not thinking your lordship therefore yet so perfect a convert of Mr. J. S.'s, that you are persuaded, that as often as you think of your cathedral church, or of Des Cartes's vortices, that the very cathedral church at Worcester, or the motion of those vortices, itself exists in your understanding; when one of them never existed but in that one place at Worcester, and the other never existed any where in *rerum natura*.[1]

Such a position as Sergeant tried to maintain blurs the distinction between object and knower, a distinction which Locke wished to keep precise. But Sergeant saw no objection to such a position. Like Sir Kenelm Digby, he belongs to that tradition in epistemology which explains knowing in the Aristotelian fashion as an absorption of the form of objects by the mind, the form constituting the essential features of the object which is known. That which is cognized directly by the mind is the spiritual apprehension; but this apprehension is the same as the object external to the mind, which

---

[1] Locke's *Reply to the ... Bishop of Worcester's Answer to his Second Letter* in *Works*, vol. iv, pp. 390-1.

is corporeal, because every essential aspect of the physical object is contained in the spiritual notion. However, it is contained there by definition or assumption and not on the 'evidence of experience. When the postulational nature of the argument is\ recognized, Sergeant's direct realist position degenerates into a Lockean dualism.

When Locke objects to the principle that 'a like is the same', or when he expresses inability to understand what is meant by saying a material thing exists spiritually, he is calling attention to the fact that Sergeant's epistemological position is not as direct as Sergeant would have his readers believe. There is for Sergeant an epistemological object which is distinct, in certain well-defined ways, from the ontological object. The latter cannot be known without the former. But it is Sergeant's contention that his epistemological object is translucent, so that in cognition the mind knows the ontological object without any third mediating factor. The epistemological object on Sergeant's system purports to be just the ontological object translated into intelligible terms. A mind which is spiritual simply cannot cognize a material object without some such translation taking place. The greater the alteration the less direct the cognition. Unlike Locke, who sought to develop a theory of knowledge within experience, Sergeant went beyond experience in order to defend his belief in direct realism. Accordingly, he resorted to the Aristotelian-Thomistic position for support, since it makes the minimum amount of change in translating the material phantasm into spiritual form or notion. The only change which that position allows is that which is necessary to enable a material object to be known by a mind. Locke's fault, and the fault of all ideists, from Sergeant's perspective, is that their translation of the material particles which strike the senses goes beyond this minimum alteration.

As Sergeant interprets the ideas of the ideists throughout his writings, the medium of knowledge for these men is not the thing known but only a copy or resemblance of the thing. However correct such an interpretation of some of the

Cartesians may be, it is obviously false when applied to Locke. The very first marginal note in his copy of *Solid Philosophy Asserted* calls attention to this error. 'Where is it Mr. Locke says ideas are the similitudes of things? He expresly says most of them are not similitudes.' (Locke, *Notes*, no. 1, p. [vi].) It is important to notice that in this note Locke does not deny that some ideas are similitudes of things in the literal sense in which Sergeant interprets all ideas as being so. In his *A Letter to the Right Reverend Edward, Lord Bishop of Worcester* (1697), Locke reminds Stillingfleet of a similar qualification already expressed in the *Essay*: 'not that they are all of them the images or representations of what does exist; the contrary whereof, in all but the primary qualities of bodies, hath been already shown'.[1] Again writing to Stillingfleet, Locke is careful to assure his lordship, in reply to charges of scepticism, that he has everywhere affirmed 'that the simple ideas, of primary qualities, are the images or representations of what does exist without us'.[2] Likewise, after Sergeant has repeated the assertion that the word 'idea' is used by Locke in the sense of resemblance, similitude, or image, Locke places in the margins the questioning word 'where?' (Locke, *Notes*, no. 9, p. 23.) When Sergeant, in discussing secondary qualities, expresses an inability to conceive 'why the ideas of secondary qualities should have nothing existing like the bodies', Locke calls attention to the fact that 'idea' is never given a blanket definition in the *Essay* as resemblance. 'Blewnesse or heat in the minde are the Ideas there whether they be like any thing in the object or noe. But he will have Mr. Locke to mean *resemblances* by *Ideas*, though Mr. L says expresly that he does not.' (Ibid., no. 31, p. 137.) The essential, defining characteristic of ideas for Locke is that they are in the mind in some sense of the phrase. He does not mean by 'idea' any object of the mind, if we mean by the term 'object' an ontological object. In other words, the very definition of idea given at the beginning of the *Essay* embodies

[1] Bk. ii, ch. xxx, no. 2; quoted by Locke in *Letter*, in *Works*, vol. iv, p. 75.
[2] *Letter*, ibid.

an epistemological dualism. The phrase 'whatever is the object of the mind when the mind thinks' uses the word 'object' in an epistemological sense. At most, only some of these objects are exact copies of their ontological referents. But if all ideas are not even resemblances of things, Locke's transition from material particles to intellectual objects is rendered even more difficult than before, since now the epistemological objects are in some cases entirely unlike the ontological objects. There is a difficulty concerning just what is meant by any idea being *like* a quality which belongs to a material object; but when Locke so clearly makes a distinction between primary and secondary qualities on the basis of the latter being unlike anything in the object, it is hard to understand how Sergeant could have misinterpreted Locke as saying all ideas are resemblances. It is especially difficult to understand this misconception when a recognition of the nature of secondary qualities would have made Sergeant's case against Locke even stronger: for ideas which are unlike anything in nature would seem to be more un-solid than 'meer resemblances'.

Despite this important misunderstanding of Locke's use of 'ideas', Sergeant was able to point out one of the crucial difficulties of the dualistic epistemology set forth in the *Essay*. Whether ideas are copies of things or not, if all knowledge is dependent upon ideas, it seems impossible to escape from the circle to establish the reality of knowledge. Sergeant could have called attention to the fact, as Descartes did, that even if we grant the difference between the idea of the sun during the day and the idea of the sun in our recollection, there is no reason for concluding that the former idea represents more correctly the physical object called the sun. Descartes escaped this difficulty by means of a metaphysical assumption concerning causality; but, since Locke denied this view of causality (at least on the sensory level), he could not use this route of retreat. Interpreting Locke's ideas to mean resemblances (thereby anticipating a growing tendency among Locke's critics of the early eighteenth century), Sergeant was content to rest his case against this aspect of the representative theory of perception on the ground that Locke could provide no means of discovering the correctness of the representation. Epistemological scepticism was inherent in the fundamental methodology of the ideists.

The question which Lord Herbert of Cherbury solved by the assumption of a conformity between faculty and object; which Hobbes sought to circumvent by reducing the physical and the mental world to motion; and which Descartes and Henry Lee resolved by appeal to a good God, turned out, in the hands of Locke, to be incapable of solution without going outside a strict empiricism. The idealism or phenomenalism inherent in a consistent and thorough application of the way of ideas, a kind of scepticism which Burthogge and Berkeley found consistent with religion, was avoided by Locke's reluctance to relinquish the common-sense beliefs of ordinary experience. Just why Burthogge's application of the way of ideas did not bring down precisely the same sort of criticism as Locke's much milder version evoked will remain forever a mystery, but it is clear that Locke did not wish to commit himself to that sort of phenomenalistic analysis. Although he continually stressed the ambiguities and invalidity of any attempt at formulating a concept of substance which went beyond the nominal essence or collection of sensible qualities, he found some inner compulsion to retain that much of the older tradition in metaphysics which posits a substance and a real essence in objects. He did not wish to merge the object with the idea. He was forced, by his own convictions and by his attachment to the two traditions in theory of knowledge, to accept an epistemological and ontological dualism with its attendant difficulties in accounting for knowledge of the world of objects. Even his own recognition of these difficulties did not deter his critics from attaching to the *Essay* the label of 'idealist' and 'sceptical'.

Controversy with his critics being foresworn, the epistemological difficulties of scepticism remained precisely in the same unsatisfactory stage as that found in the fourth book of the

Essay. Discussion did not clarify the problems. Thus, for the men of the seventeenth and early eighteenth centuries, with the epistemological scepticism of the *Essay* firmly established by several capable critics, the stage was set for the unveiling of the religious scepticism implicit in the acceptance of the epistemological doctrines of that work.

RELIGIOUS SCEPTICISM

HAD Locke's *Essay* been written during a period in which religious controversy was less rampant (were this conceivable), it is doubtful whether the doctrines advanced in that work could have aroused much reaction. Although the non-theological criticisms which we have examined in the previous chapter showed an appreciation of the epistemological doctrines in themselves, each of the critics there discussed, with the exception of Leibniz, had an ulterior purpose behind his arguments. Each wrote in defence of religion and was concerned to break down popular acclaim for the *Essay* in both the purely theoretical and the practical spheres. The publication of the *Essay*, coming especially at a time when new radical sects of natural religion were emerging, led to its becoming the centre of much religious discussion; for the parallels between the empiricism of Locke's epistemology and the naturalistic doctrines in religion, with their appeal to reason, could not have been overlooked by his contemporaries. In many respects, Locke expounded the epistemology and even ontology of the deistic movement. His own sympathies were strongly in support of the new religious theories advanced by Thomas Firmin, his friends, and associates. The extent to which Locke wrote with the express purpose of giving support to deism cannot, unfortunately, be established. We have seen how prevalent was the doctrine of innate knowledge among his contemporaries and have found reasons for thinking that Locke wrote the first book of his *Essay* to refute this view of his fellow countrymen. Since we know from his own statement that his reflections upon the problems of the *Essay* were stimulated by certain difficulties in religion and morality, and since we know where his own sympathies lay in respect to religious beliefs, it does not seem extravagant to suggest that the positive doctrines of that work were also written with the religious problems in mind. It would be a gross overstatement to claim that Locke was unaware of the implications for religion of many of his epistemological doctrines, for a man so well versed in the controversies of his day could not fail to grasp the revolutionary character of many of these doctrines for religion. I am sensible of Locke's many asseverations to Stillingfleet that he wrote with none of these controversies in mind. For example, in his *Letter* to Stillingfleet he writes:

> There is in the world a great and fierce contest about nature and grace: it would be very hard for me, if I must be brought in as a party on either side, because a disputant, in that controversy, should think the clear and distinct apprehensions of nature and grace come not unto our minds by the simple ideas of sensation and reflection. If this be so, I may be reckoned among the objectors against all sorts and points of orthodoxy, whenever any one pleases: I may be called to account as one heterodox, in the points of free-grace, free-will, predestination, original sin, justification by faith, transubstantiation, the pope's supremacy, and what not?[1]

Locke was drawn into the debate over the nature of the Trinity in part through a misunderstanding aroused by Toland's use of clear and distinct ideas, but it was nevertheless true that Locke's epistemological doctrines were appearing more and more in the writings of the new men of religion, as the century came to an end. It is difficult to consider Locke completely sincere in his repetitious assertions of his noninvolvement in such important religious doctrines as that of the Trinity or the role of reason and faith in religion. It would be most strange if a man of Locke's learning sincerely believed he could write in the seventeenth century about such doctrines as the method to and sources of knowledge, the nature of substance and essence, the empirical foundations of all knowledge, and escape an assessment of these doctrines from the theologians, since these were all doctrines of direct relevance to religion. Modern critics are given to seeing in Locke's

---

[1] In *Works*, vol. iv, p. 68.

Essay a treatise on theory of knowledge and metaphysics, written independently of his social context, a context which concerned itself chiefly with the obscure questions of church dogma. It is misleading to read the *Essay* in this manner. I would suggest that Locke was being facetious and argumentative in protesting to Stillingfleet so extensively his innocence and aloofness from these religious disputes. Locke did, without a doubt, make certain outstanding contributions to the problem of knowledge; and I would not wish to suggest that these aspects of the *Essay* were an accidental product of his own religious speculations. What I am suggesting is that the *Essay* had at least some of its major origins in the theological discussions of the seventeenth century, and that no one of the doctrines advanced in that work can legitimately be considered in abstraction from this context. Nevertheless, I am not essentially concerned here with assessing and uncovering the motives which lay behind the writing of the *Essay concerning Human Understanding*. My objective is rather to present the role this work played in the minds and discussions of Locke's contemporaries. In this light, the epistemological doctrines of his system can be seen to have challenging implications.

Apart from the negative polemic of the first book, and the general scepticism entailed by the representative theory of perception and the definition of knowledge in Books Two and Four, the clergy found the *Essay* objectionable primarily for its reduction of knowledge to ideas, for its doctrine of real and nominal essences, its doctrine of substance as unknowable, and the suggestion that God could annex to matter a power of thinking. Not all of these objectionable doctrines are epistemological in character, although all but the last are immediate consequences of Locke's cognitive orientation. His contemporaries regarded all these doctrines as results of the basic epistemological scepticism of his empiricism. The inevitable consequence of accepting any of these doctrines was, in the minds of the seventeenth- and eighteenth-century orthodox men of religion, religious scepticism and disbelief.

§ 1—*The Role of Ideas in Religious Knowledge*

G. R. Cragg has claimed that with the publication of
Toland's *Christianity not Mysterious* (1696) 'the deistic
controversy began in earnest'.[1] Such a claim may lay too
much stress upon one book, but there can be no doubt that
Toland's work aroused an enormous reaction which led most
of the prominent religious figures in England to reconsider
their own beliefs and either to attack or to defend the new
movement, which by then was growing in strength. The very
title of Toland's book epitomized the general attitude of the
deistic and other naturalistic sects: the claim that nothing
about the Christian religion was above reason. The attack was
directed upon such doctrines as that of the Trinity and transubstantiation, but Toland's main concern was with bringing to the front the basic dispute over the reasonableness
or mysteriousness of this religion. Locke's own work in this
field, *The Reasonableness of Christianity*, had appeared in 1695
and elicited several prolix rebuttals.[2] But the appeal of Locke
in that work was made not from the epistemological principles
set forth in his *Essay*, but from the standpoint of common
sense and simplicity. The significance of Toland's *Christianity
not Mysterious* for this study lies in the way in which he took
Locke's epistemological doctrines as the basis from which to
explain his own radical religious beliefs. The appearance of
Locke's principles in this context did much to focus attention
upon the role of Locke's epistemology in religious knowledge.

Toland pointed out in the preface to his book that the preliminary dissertation upon reason was not of such importance
that the rest of the book could not be understood without
understanding these principles. He inserted this discussion to
'prevent the foreseen Wranglings of certain Men, who study
more to protract and perplex than to terminate a Contro-

---

[1] *From Puritanism to the Age of Reason* (1950), p. 139. Cf. Abbey and Overton,
The English Church in the Eighteenth Century, vol. i, p. 182.

[2] The most vehement of these were those of John Edwards, the same man
who in 1701 maintained the naïve form of innateness in opposition to Locke.
Cf. his *Some Thoughts Concerning the Several Causes and Occasions of Atheism*
(1695) and *Socinianism Unmask'd* (1696).

versy' (p. xviii). But in a work which took as its main tenet
the belief that 'Reason is the only Foundation of all Certitude;
and that nothing reveal'd, whether as to its Manner or Existence, is more exempted from its Disquisitions, than the
ordinary Phenomena of Nature' (p. 6), it was not a mere
digression to consider the nature and province of human
reason. The way of ideas played a prominent role in this
discussion.

Every one experiences in himself a Power or Faculty of forming
various Ideas or Perceptions of Things; Of affirming or denying, according as he sees them to agree or disagree: And so of loving and desiring
what seems good unto him; and of hating and avoiding what he thinks
evil. The right Use of all these Faculties is what we call Common Sense,
or Reason in general. But the bare Act of receiving Ideas into the Mind,
whether by the Intromission of the Senses, as Colours, Figures, Sounds,
Smells, &c. or by the Soul's considering its own Operations about what it
thus gets from without, as Knowing, Doubting, Affirming, Denying, &c.
this bare Act, I say, of receiving such Ideas into the Mind, is not
strictly Reason, because the Soul herein is purely passive. (Pp. 9–10).

Reason is later defined as 'that Faculty every one has of Judging
of his Idea's according to their Agreement or Disagreement'
(p. 57). Ideas are divided into simple and complex, and the
Lockean definition of knowledge is reproduced almost verbatim.
Toland also draws the distinction between intuitive or self-
evident knowledge and demonstrative or mediate knowledge,
insisting as Locke had done that each step of a demonstration
must be itself self-evident. He limits the term 'reason' more
properly to mediate knowledge, making the ideas of sense and
reflection 'the common Stock of all our Knowledg; nor can
we possibly have Ideas any other way without new Organs
or Faculties' (pp. 14–15). The representative character of
Locke's epistemology is fully recognized and accepted
(pp. 16–17) and the distinction between primary and secondary
qualities reappears.

The Reason then why I believe the Idea of a Rose to be evident, is the
true Representation it gives me of that Flower. I know it is true, because
the Rose must contain all the Properties which its Idea exhibits, either

really, as the Bulk and Form, or *occasionally*, as the Colour, Taste, and Smell. And I cannot doubt of this, because the Properties must belong to the exemplary Cause, or to Nothing, or be the Figments of my own Brain: But Nothing can have no Properties; and I cannot make one single Idea at my Pleasure, nor avoid receiving some when Objects work on my Senses: Therefore I conclude the Properties of the Rose are not the Creatures of my Fancy, but belong to the exemplary Cause, that is, the Object (p. 18).

Faithful representation by ideas of their objects is required by Toland for his basic principle of evidence, which he defines as '*the exact Conformity of our Ideas or Thoughts with their Objects, or the Things we think upon*' (p. 16). So long as we consult the reports contained in our ideas, we shall never err. Thus, the way of ideas, with its representative capacity assured as valid, becomes the sole guide for all truth and knowledge. The criterion of clear and distinct ideas enables us to set the limits to reason: '*what is evidently repugnant to clear and distinct Idea's, or to our Common Notions, is contrary to Reason*' (p. 23). However, counter to the charges made by some of Toland's critics, clarity and distinctness did not constitute the sole criterion of certainty or intelligibility for him. With Locke's doctrine of real and nominal essence in mind, he argued '*That nothing can be said to be a Mystery, because we have not an adequate Idea of it, or a distinct View of all its Properties at once; for then every thing would be a Mystery*' (p. 75). The restrictions inherent in human knowledge do not place any unnecessary limits to knowledge: '*knowing nothing of Bodies but their Properties, God has wisely provided we should understand no more of these than are useful and necessary for us; which is all our present Condition needs*' (p. 76). The doctrine of real and nominal essences is developed at length by Toland, where we find the first open reference to Locke. 'As we know not all the Properties of things, so we can never conceive the *Essence* of any Substance in the World. To avoid ambiguity, I distinguish, after an excellent modern Philosopher, the *Nominal* from the *Real Essence* of a thing' (p. 83). Like Locke, Toland used the doctrine of a twofold essence, not by way of excluding all reference to a trans-empirical reality, but as a means of accepting the doctrine of real essence without having to admit a mysterious element actively necessary in our knowledge.

It follows now very plainly, that *nothing can be said to be a Mystery, because we are ignorant of its real Essence, since it is not more knowable in one thing than in another, and is never conceiv'd or included in the Ideas we have of things, or the Names we give 'em* (p. 85).

Clarity and distinctness are made consistent with inadequacy and obscurity in virtue of the doctrine that, though limited in scope, man's knowledge is nevertheless sufficient for his needs. But though we lack a precise knowledge of the real essence of material or immaterial substances, we are not thereby given licence to deny their reality.

There is nothing more evident than the Modes or Properties of *BODY*, as to be extended, solid, divisible, smooth, rough, soft, hard, &c. But we know as little of the internal Constitution, which is the Support of these sensible Qualities, as we do of that wherein the Operations of the *SOUL* reside. And, as the great Man I just now mention'd observes, *we may as well deny the Existence of* Body, *because we have not an Idea of its real Essence, as call the Being of the* Soul *in question for the same reason* (p. 87).

Immediately after the publication of Toland's book, a great outcry was made against it and its author. It was the subject of a court action in Dublin, where Toland was residing, and Toland was advised to leave the city. It was also the object of a censure issued by the Grand Jury of Middlesex.[1] All over England and Ireland replies to the doctrines of Toland began to appear. More than half of these directed a large portion of their attack against the epistemological principles invoked in the first part, the principles borrowed from Locke. Thomas Beverley, in *Christianity The Great Mystery* (1696), objected to the restriction of the term 'reason' to 'the singling out of that compare, and ballancing of the *Idea's* of the Mind, and Arguing from them . . .' (p. 13). Fear of the scepticism of the way of ideas was expressed by the same writer in a charge similar to that made by Sergeant one

[1] Cf. Gailhard's account of the edict, in his *The Epistle and Preface To the Book against the Blasphemous Socinian Heresie* (1698), p. 82.

year later: 'Any pretended *Idea's* that are not according to Things, are *Fantoms*, and not *Idea's*; all other Apprehensions, Conceptions, Notions, Conclusions, that Created Understandings can Form, are nothing, if taken out of the Understandings that Formed them; . . .' (p. 17). An anonymous critic writing in 1697 *Reflexions upon Mr. Toland's Book*,[1] insisted that clear and distinct ideas can, in reference to revealed truth, only tell us that things are possible. The only ground we have for believing, for example, in the flood, is that God tells us about it (pp. 4–5). 'Now I have as little Prejudice against *clear Ideas* as I have against an *infallible judge*; but I am afraid that in many cases these are as hard to be found as the other' (p. 13). The question of what constitutes being 'above reason' was bound up with the criterion of clarity and distinctness as a basis for knowledge.

It was, however, in the hands of Peter Browne and the bishop of Worcester that these epistemological principles invoked by Toland found their ablest opponents. Browne, in *A Letter in Answer to a Book Entituled, Christianity not Mysterious* (1697), admitted that Toland was correct in saying that Christianity was not mysterious, since it was meant for the plainest men in the world; but he insisted that this assertion does not mean that there are no mysteries in Christianity. He agreed that there is nothing contrary to reason in the Gospels and nothing above reason, in the sense of being beyond our comprehension. 'But if by *not being above reason*, be meant that there is nothing spoke of in it, but what we have as compleat and perfect knowledge of, as we have of any object of our Senses, it is absolutely false; . . .' (p. 8). Toland's doctrine of evidence as the only ground of persuasion is criticized as overlooking the basis of authority in religious knowledge: 'all natural Truths which do not necessarily require Revelation, need no other ground of perswasion, but *Evidence* and *Authority*' (p. 19). Browne agrees that '*Clear and distinct Idea's are the foundation of all our knowledge and assent*', but insists that it is false to say '*we can believe nothing*

[1] First published in *The Occasional Paper*, as no. 3 (1697).

but what we have a clear and distinct Idea of' (pp. 27–28).
His point is that we believe some things of which we do not
have clear and distinct ideas, on the strength of some clear
and distinct ideas which we do have. He insists that, though
we do not have any clear and distinct idea of the things of the
other world, we are bound to believe in these things on the
authority of the Scriptures, which provide the base of clear
and distinct ideas. It was typical of Browne that while object-
ing to the doctrines of Toland and Locke, he nevertheless
showed a strong proclivity towards the doctrines he was
arguing against. Thus, he did not reject outright the doctrine
of clarity and distinctness as criteria for certain knowledge.
Toland and Locke had, of course, accepted the existence of
real substances despite the obscurity of our knowledge of
them—an assumption of no less weight than Browne's insistence upon Christian dogma. But this non-empirical assumption on the part of Toland and Locke was missed by Browne,
as well as by most other critics of the century. Browne went
on, by way of supporting his case for the necessity of accepting
notions lacking clarity and distinctness, to distinguish
between immediate ideas, *'a conception or notion of the thing
as it is in itself'*, and mediate ideas, *'a notion we form of any
thing in our Minds by Analogy or Similitude'* (p. 31). This
distinction was developed at great length in his later work,
The Procedure, Extent, and Limits of Human Understanding
(1728). Here it constitutes the necessary division between
knowledge and faith: 'we have no proper Idea's of the things
of another World, but frame to ourselves conceptions of them
from those things in this World whereof we have clear and
distinct Idea's'.[1] In this way, 'it is plain that though we may
be said to have *Ideas* of God and Divine things, yet they are
not *immediate or proper* ones, but a sort of composition we
make up from our Idea's of Worldly Objects; which at the
utmost amounts to no more than a *Type* or *Figure*, by which
something in another world is signified'.[2]

[1] *A Letter in Answer to . . . Christianity not Mysterious*, p. 32.
[2] Ibid., p. 41.

Browne went on to attack the doctrine of substance and essence in Toland's book, but more importantly, like many of his contemporaries, he attacked the way of ideas as it appeared in the service of religion, his main argument being that this way to knowledge did not do justice to religious beliefs. Scepticism and the limitation of knowledge to the natural or physical realm were the feared consequences of this method. Stillingfleet expressed the same reaction to Toland and Locke as did Browne, but his first attack unfortunately overemphasized the role of the criterion of clarity and distinctness in the two systems. The erection of all knowledge upon such a criterion excludes, he insisted,

all certainty of Faith or Reason, where we cannot have such *clear and distinct Ideas*. But if there are many things of which we may be certain, and yet can have no *clear and distinct Ideas* of them; if those *Ideas* we have, are too imperfect and obscure to form our Judgments by; if we cannot find out sufficient intermediate Ideas; then this cannot be the *Means* of *Certainty*, or the *Foundation* of *Reason*.[1]

After discussing the doctrine of substance, Stillingfleet concludes: 'For I take it, that the main Debate in point of Reason depends upon this, whether we can be certain of the Being of a Thing, of which we can have *no clear and distinct Idea*? If we may, then it can be no Objection in point of Revelation, that we can have no *clear and distinct Idea* of the Matter revealed; . . .'[2] But in the answer to Locke's *Reply to . . . the Bishop of Worcester's Answer to his Letter*, Stillingfleet shifted his attack to the more important and accurate charge that the certainty to be had by the way of ideas was inadequate for religious knowledge. He insisted that certainty by ideas refers to certainty by means of propositions and is to be distinguished from certainty by sense. Furthermore, he distinguishes these two ways of certainty from a third, certainty by reason, 'When from the Existence of some things evident to Sense, we inferr the Existence of another thing not evident to Sense.'[3] The latter is demonstrated by an example of the inference to substance from sensible qualities. Finally

---

[1] *A Discourse in Vindication of The . . . Trinity* (1697), p. 233.   [2] Ibid., p. 280.
[3] *The Bishop of Worcester's Answer to Mr. Locke's Second Letter* (1697), p. 11.

Stillingfleet distinguished a certainty by remembrance. In all cases he argued that some clear and distinct ideas are necessary for certainty, although the final knowledge we reach may involve obscure ideas. He expresses doubts concerning the ability of the way of ideas to furnish certainty of God's existence and certainty of the immateriality of the human soul. Like Berkeley, Stillingfleet suggested that there is no criterion provided by Locke for knowing when we have clear and distinct ideas. 'But suppose an *Idea* happen to be thought by some to be *clear and distinct*, and others should think the contrary to be so, what hopes of *Demonstration* by *clear* and *distinct Ideas* then?'[1]

Toland had, of course, gone beyond the bounds of Locke's principles in laying such stress upon clarity and distinctness as the criteria of certainty, but we have seen that even for him this was not the sole basis in terms of which certainty and rationality were weighed. Locke was quick to call Stillingfleet's attention to the subordinate role this criterion played in his own system.

Who your lordship here argues against, under the title of this new hypothesis about reason, I confess I do not know. For I do not remember that I have any where placed certainty only in clear and distinct ideas, but in the clear and visible connexion of any of our ideas, be those ideas what they will; as will appear to any one who will look into B. iv. c. 4, no. 18, and B. iv, c. 6, no. 3, of my Essay, . . .[2]

Locke admitted that the clearer and more distinct the ideas involved are, the more clear and distinct would be our reasoning about them, but he readily pointed out that he recognized that we may have certainty about obscure ideas:

by the clear ideas of thinking in me, I find the agreement of the clear idea of existence, and the obscure idea of a substance in me, because I perceive the necessary idea of thinking, and the relative idea of a support; which support, without having any clear and distinct idea of what it is, beyond this relative one of a support, I call substance.[3]

Locke was loud in his protestations that he had been falsely coupled with Toland. He accordingly sought to dissociate his

---

[1] Ibid., p. 141.
[2] *Letter to the . . . Bishop of Worcester*, in *Works*, vol. iv, p. 29.   [3] Ibid., p. 42.

way of ideas from that used by such men as Toland. But three major factors led Locke's contemporaries to find justice in Stillingfleet's insistence that, even though some men used his ideas to bad purposes, Locke should feel a duty and compulsion to explain his system and to show how it did not undermine the fundamental articles of the Christian religion: (1) the newness of the application of the way of ideas in the *Essay*, a factor which we have already examined; (2) the doctrine of substance and essence which was not distorted by Toland and which occupied the minds of so many men in the century; and (3) the many rephrasings of various parts of the *Essay* in the deistical tracts of the period, a factor which I shall examine at length in the next chapter. It is the second factor which we must now examine, bearing in mind that although Stillingfleet and others may have falsely supposed that Locke placed the criterion of certainty in clear and distinct ideas, their reaction against the doctrines of the *Essay* was motivated by the disbelief which they all shared in the fruitfulness of the way of ideas in religious knowledge. If the way of ideas placed its emphasis upon an empirical, naturalistic foundation for all knowledge, if the radical new sects in religion could draw support so easily from the *Essay*, and if the way of ideas pursued by Locke discounted (if not discarded) the doctrine of real substances, that book was open to suspicion from all the tradition-directed members of society.

§ 2—*The Doctrine of Substance*

As I have already remarked, Locke was the heir of two traditions which he tried to 'combine in the *Essay*. The phenomenalism of Burthogge's way of ideas found for the most part a consistent elaboration in the first twenty-two chapters of Book Two of the *Essay*. Even in the doctrine of substance expounded in chapter twenty-three, the phenomenalistic doctrine of Boyle and More concerning substance and the classification of physical objects into genera[1] is clearly in

---

[1] Boyle, R. *The Origine of Formes and Qualities*, pp. 59, 61–62; More, H. *The Immortality of the Soul*, pp. 11, 51.

evidence. The scholastic doctrine of substance had earlier
(bk. ii, ch. xiii, nos. 18–20) been ridiculed by Locke in terms
which would lead the reader to think he was encountering
another attack upon tradition. Such ridicule brought its own
share of criticism from Locke's readers, but it was the more
positive doctrine of substance as the underlying core of
physical and immaterial objects which aroused the more
heated debates. Locke was concerned to limit the discussion
of substance to the idea of substance which men can be said
to have. As with the problem of the physical genesis of perception, where he wished to avoid all questions of the physiological components of this sensitive act, so with the problem
of substance, he ostensibly proclaimed himself uninterested
in the problem of the ontological nature of substance, insisting
that the idea which we can have of substance is at most only
an obscure and indefinite conception. That he did not doubt
the ontological reality of substance as commonly conceived
in his century may be construed from his protestation to
Stillingfleet that he was not among those thinkers who wished
to read substance out of the world.[1] Moreover, it seems clear
enough from the *Essay* itself that Locke thought of substance
as the locus of the real essence and as the principle of individuation of physical and immaterial objects. But it is equally
clear, I think, that Locke was working towards a new conception of substance in keeping with the phenomenalism of
men like Burthogge, a doctrine which defines substance in
terms of the collection of qualities composing a given object.
However, the expansion of this latter novel conception proved
too difficult for Locke. He was not as indifferent to ontological questions as his statements sometimes imply. He was
concerned to explain the individual identity of objects and
found that he could not do so, to his satisfaction at least,
without some recourse to non-phenomenalistic categories,
although he was able to find satisfaction in accounting for
personal identity without appeal to such categories. When we
pass to this aspect of Locke's concept of substance, two

[1] *Letter to the . . . Bishop of Worcester*, in *Works*, vol. iv, pp. 6–7.

alternatives present themselves. Either we can interpret him in the most sympathetic manner possible as appealing to a mental category of substance as the unifying principle in the diversity of experience, or we can read him as holding reluctantly to a clear ontological doctrine of substance as a prerequisite for explaining knowledge and reality. The latter, the actual approach Locke took in controversy with the Bishop of Worcester, is very close to the traditional doctrine of substance.

The discussion of substance in the *Essay* was concerned with the epistemological problems related to our knowledge of substance, and not with the ontological nature of this important term. It was the epistemological restrictions defended by Locke that attracted the attention of his readers. But the reception of this aspect of Locke's doctrine was not entirely critical; the doctrine and the terminology employed by Locke appear in some of the theological tracts of the century. William Sherlock was probably one of the very first of the theologians openly to adopt the language and concepts of the *Essay*. Writing in 1690 to defend his particular version of the doctrine of the Trinity, Sherlock, the same man who was to attack Locke so vigorously in 1704 on the question of innate ideas, asserted that 'all Men must confess, that they have not a clear and comprehensive Notion of the Nature and Essential Properties of a Spirit'.[1] He went on to affirm that

It is agreed by all Men, who ever considered this matter, that the essences of things cannot be known, but only their properties and qualities: The World is divided into Matter, and Spirit, and we know no more, what the substance of Matter, than what the substance of Spirit is, though we think we know one, much better than the other: We know thus much of Matter, that it is an extended substance, which fills a space, and has distinct parts, which may be separated from each other, that it is susceptible of very different qualities, that it is hot or cold, hard or soft, &c. but what the substance of Matter is, we know not: And thus we know the essential properties of a Spirit; that it is a thinking substance, with the Faculties of Understanding and Will . . . but what the substance of a Spirit is, we know no more than what the substance of matter is.[2]

[1] *A Vindication of the Doctrine of the . . . Trinity* (1690), p. 4.
[2] Ibid., pp. 7-8.

Abstracted from its properties, neither matter nor spirit can have any meaning.

> For what the Essence and Substance of a Spirit is, when we distinguish it from Understanding and Will, which we call the Powers and Faculties of a Spirit; for my part, I know not, no more than I do, what the naked Essence and Substance of Matter is, stript of all its Qualities and Accidents. . . . And therefore as we frame the Notion of Bodies from their external and sensible Qualities, so we must frame the Notion of a Spirit from its intellectual Powers, of Will, and Understanding, &c.[1]

Even as late as 1697, Sherlock was appealing to this Lockean doctrine as a defence against some Socinian attackers.[2] There is never any open reference to Locke in Sherlock's early works, but it would seem clear that he exemplifies the immediate absorption of Lockean doctrines even by those who attacked Locke on other grounds. Sherlock's use of such principles, just like Toland's similar borrowings later, did not go unchallenged. Robert South, a believer in the naïve form of innateness, in his *Animadversions upon Dr. Sherlock's Book* (1693), attacked the theoretical structure upon which Sherlock's doctrine of the Trinity was built.[3] Setting up the familiar substance–accident ontology as a counter-division to Sherlock's matter–spirit dichotomy, South argued as follows against the Lockean doctrine of substance:

> Now, if by *knowing*, he means the knowledge of a thing, by a direct *Apprehension*, and *Intuition* of it, so as to have an exact Idea, or resemblance of it thereby imprinted upon the mind: I pretend not that the *Essences of things* are by any Human Intellect so known. But then, this is still but one way of knowledge; . . . But if on the other side, by *knowing a thing be meant*, the knowing it to be of such, or such a Nature, by such peculiar Properties, such peculiar Effects, and Operations, as discriminate it from other things, and that, to know it thus, be truly to know it: Then I affirm *That the Natures, or Essences of things may be truly and* (one way at least) *perfectly known* (p. 15).

South did not intend to acquiesce in the Lockean doctrine of nominal essence, whereas Sherlock apparently was ready to

[1] Ibid., pp. 73–74.
[2] Sherlock, *A Vindication of Dr. Sherlock's Sermon* (1697), pp. 29–30.
[3] This doctrine came to be styled 'Tri-Trinitarianism' because Sherlock sought to give each of the three figures in the traditional doctrine a separate and unique reality.

accept it without seeing the dangerous consequences for religion of such an acceptance. South was convinced that the real nature of an object is revealed through its effects. Accepting the traditional ontology, South argued that we can gain an adequate idea of the nature of substance from reflection and definitions. Sherlock's limitation of the idea of substance to that which can be derived from matter and sensation was thereby rejected. 'Essence' is that by which a thing is what it is and this is never hidden from us: it is provided by the metaphysical postulates of the system which South and his countrymen inherited. Any doctrine which denied these postulates not only disrupted tradition and hence came under the censure of orthodoxy; but, by making the real essence of substance unknowable, the Lockean doctrine exposed the doctrine of the Trinity to attacks. For if we cannot know the real nature of substance, how can we be expected to understand or even find intelligible the doctrine which proclaims that three distinct personalities inhere in the same substance?

Sherlock's peculiar version of the doctrine of the Trinity aroused many criticisms in the century, but very few besides South sought to undermine the doctrine of substance at its base. This early absorption of Lockean principles by the defenders of orthodoxy against the new radical sects of the day went unnoticed. Locke's name was not even mentioned in the controversy.[1] Sherlock's departure from orthodoxy was not as radical as that of Toland, though the disputes it aroused were no less vehement. But it was not until Toland's employment of it that Locke's doctrine of substance was brought out into the open and proclaimed inimical to traditional religion. For all of the critics of Toland's work who looked to the theoretical structure of his position, the complaint against the doctrine of substance was the same; by denying man a

---

[1] That Sherlock was familiar with the *Essay* is attested by the fact that in one of his replies to South, he cites Locke as an authority for the doctrine of personal identity, another doctrine which Sherlock borrowed and adapted from Locke. (Cf. his *A Defence of Dr. Sherlock's Notion* (1694), p. 6.) So far as I know, Locke was never mentioned by Sherlock in relation to the doctrine of substance.

knowledge of the essence of substance, the doctrine of the
Trinity was endangered. Oliver Hill (*A Rod for the Back of
Fools*, 1702) interpreted Toland as arguing that Christianity
is not mysterious because all things are equally mysterious in
their real essence. 'A rare way it is to prove that there is no
Mystery, by making every thing a Mystery to Mankind; and
to make Reason capable to apprehend Mysteries, by shewing
it knows nothing' (p. 19). Hill had no doubts concerning our
knowledge of the real essences of things. 'That Mankind hath
some knowledge of the true Essence of things, and adequate
Ideas, appears to me very plain from *Adam* in *Paradise*,
giving names to all the Beasts according to their Nature.'
(Ibid.) The same line of attack is found in the anonymous reply
to Toland, *Reflexions upon Mr. Toland's Book* (1697).[1] Peter
Browne (*A Letter in Answer to a Book Entituled, Christianity
not Mysterious*, 1697) did not find the distinction between real
and nominal essence quite so disturbing as did some other
writers, but only because, by reducing it to a common-sense
recognition of the limitations of human knowledge, he took
most of the sting out of Locke's doctrine. He argued that
it is absurd to say there are two essences in one thing, con-
fessing that he does not think the doctrine in its original
application (he recognized Toland's borrowing) meant to
assert such absurdities.

If it had been said in plain language, that there is something in natural
things *we do apprehend*, and something *we do not*; which is all that's
meant in that distinction: This wou'd have been Philosophy for the
Vulgar; and therefore to make a Mystery of it, it must be call'd the
Nominal and *Real Essence* of a thing: though it carry a flat contradiction in
Physicks, and a monstrous consequence in *Morality*, and lays a foundation for Eternal Scepticism (p. 110).

But Locke was not merely saying that we know some things
about natural objects and are ignorant of others: he was cast-
ing doubt upon man's ability to grasp the real essence of those
objects. It was this challenge to tradition which disturbed his
contemporaries.

[1] Cf. pp. 27–28, no. 3 of *The Occasional Paper*.

The longest and most sustained attack against Locke's concept of substance came from Stillingfleet's pen. Briefly, Stillingfleet wrote to show that the idea of substance does not come from sense or reflection; that the new way of reasoning introduced by Locke had almost discarded substance from the world; and that Locke was wrong in claiming that nothing is meant by the term 'substance' except a supposition of 'I know not what'.[1] He argues that, although we cannot have a clear idea of substance, we can still have some more definite conception than Locke allows. Such a conception is formed from the general idea of substance 'which the mind doth form, not by *meer comparing those Ideas it has got by Sense or Reflection*; but by forming distinct general Notions of things from particular *Ideas*' (p. 235). Like Locke he argues that this general idea of substance is a rational idea demanded by consideration of the modes and accidents, but he objects to Locke's founding this supposition upon such a tenuous basis as a necessity of thought, insisting that the idea is founded upon 'true reason'. The way of ideas is attacked generally as not being able to provide an idea of a spiritual substance which could, with complete certainty, exclude all possibility of matter being given a power of thought. Against the doctrine of real and nominal essence he argued that either we can know from the idea-effects that real beings do exist as their cause, or it is impossible 'to have any certainty at all of any thing without ourselves' (p. 256). Stillingfleet held to the former alternative, claiming that although we may not 'comprehend the *internal Frame*, or *Constitution* of things, nor in which manner they do flow from the Substance; yet by them we certainly know that there are such *Essences*, and that they are distinguished from each other by their *Powers* and *Properties*' (p. 257). He was, in other words, content with the assertion, necessitated by his religious metaphysics, that there are real essences.

In his *Letter to the Right Reverend Edward, Lord Bishop of Worcester* (1697), Locke was anxious to deny Stillingfleet's

[1] *A Discourse in Vindication of the Doctrine of the Trinity*, pp. 233–4.

charge that he had discarded substance, claiming that Book
Two, Chapter Twenty-three was designed precisely to show
that he recognized the ontological reality of this entity.[1] In
this letter he tried to dissociate the idea of substance from
substance itself, insisting that his discussion had been concerned with showing the obscurity of the idea, and even that
Stillingfleet's conception was no more definite than his own.
'Nay, as long as there is any simple idea or sensible quality
left, according to my way of arguing, substance cannot be
discarded; because all simple ideas, all sensible qualities,
carry with them a supposition of a substratum to exist in,
and of a substance wherein they inhere.'[2] But it was this very
supposition to which Locke appealed that seemed to Stillingfleet to poise the doctrine of substance upon so precarious a
foundation. In his reply to Locke's letter, Stillingfleet pointed
out that the issue between them was not whether Locke
recognized substance as an ontological ingredient in the
world, but whether from his principles we can obtain any
certainty of reason about substance. If not, we cannot say
what it is that distinguishes one person from another. Moreover, he objected to Locke's entire doctrine of personal
identity, since Locke made the identity of persons completely
distinct from any relation to substance.[3] Finally, 'if *Nature*
and *Person* be *abstract*, and *complex Ideas*, as you say, and such
are only Acts of the Mind, I do not see how it is possible for
you to reconcile these Notions with the Articles of the *Trinity*
and *Incarnation*'.[4] Even if Locke does admit a belief in real
substance, his principles will not allow us to gain knowledge
of its nature. Arbitrary classification is substituted for natural
or real sorting by God. Stillingfleet's description of our idea
of substance is, of course, identical with Locke's except that
he prefers to call it a necessary or rational idea, 'because it is
a Repugnance to our first conception of Things that Modes or

---

[1] In *Works*, vol. iv, p. 5. Cf. p. 18.   [2] Ibid., p. 7.
[3] Mathew Tindal had in 1695 invoked both Locke's doctrine of substance and
his doctrine of identity in his interpretation of the Trinity. Cf. his *Reflexions on
the XXVIII Propositions touching the Doctrine of the Trinity*, pp. 22–24.
[4] *Answer to Mr. Locke's Second Letter* (1698), p. 55.

Accidents should subsist by themselves'.[1] The repugnance for him, the necessity of thought compelling us to posit or think of something over and above the sensible qualities, was derived from 'Reason and Consideration of the true Nature of things.'[2] Locke's contention in the face of all such assertions was simply that he had found no one as yet who could show how such knowledge of natural kinds was derived. But one of the main merits of Stillingfleet's criticism was to show that Locke could not derive even the obscure idea of substance, which he claimed, from his own principles. On Locke's avowed principle of deriving all knowledge from ideas of sensation and reflection, we can have no idea of substance except as a complication or collection of simple qualities. Locke admitted to Stillingfleet that the idea of substance was never meant to arise out of sensation or reflection alone, but was a manufactured idea constructed by the mind from the general notion of substance abstracted from each particular idea of substance, and from the relative idea of a support. But Locke nowhere explains in terms of his general empirical scheme for all ideas, merely from a consideration of the sensible ideas of qualities collected into wholes, how the mind can derive the non-empirical concept of a real ontological substance supporting these qualities. The transcendence of his own empirical phenomenalism was made possible only by a bold rationalism grafted on to his earlier attempts at constructing an empirical epistemology. Locke's idea of substance as an addition to the sensible qualities, as the locus of the real essence, is not derivable from simple ideas of sense but is an hypothesis of reason. That the impetus for forming the concept arose in part from experience is, as Aaron has suggested, very probable; for sensible qualities are experienced in unity, not as isolated factors. 'There is an awareness of ideas as going together. The mind has not ideas of isolated qualities, but of qualities together in one unity. Now here, surely, is the empirical basis of the concept of

[1] *Answer to Mr. Locke's Letter* (1697), p. 14.
[2] *A Discourse in Vindication of the Doctrine of the Trinity*, p. 258.

thing.'[1] It was to account for such concomitance of qualities that Locke seems to have formulated his non-phenomenalist concept of substance, but it hardly seems correct to say that this concomitance supplies the empirical basis for the concept. At most, it provides an empirical foundation for a phenomenalist concept of 'thing' or 'substance', since the togetherness refers to qualities and nothing more. Where is the empirical justification for going beyond the association of qualities to seek a non-empirical explanation of this phenomenon? As Stillingfleet queried: 'How came we to know that these *Accidents* were such feeble things? What *simple Ideas* inform'd you of it? If none, then it is to be hoped there is some other way to attain *Knowledge* and *Certainty* in this matter.'[2]

In book ii, ch. xxiii, Locke calls the primary qualities 'accidents' and insists that the mind feels constrained to think a substratum for them to inhere in. But in book ii, ch. viii he claims that the primary qualities are combined into atoms or particles to constitute the real qualities of physical objects. Locke was unable to remain satisfied with this phenomenalist definition. He felt the need of a unifying principle for the primary qualities themselves, a principle or category to unite the various atoms comprising a given object into one whole. But if the primary qualities are the irreducible elements of the physical world, and if they form spatial relations between themselves, where is substance to be located? If atoms are material particles which cannot be penetrated, in what sort of stuff could they inhere or be combined, save a material stuff? If, on the other hand, substance is not material, what else could it be save a mental category enabling us to view experience as unified? Locke was perhaps working towards some such Kantian position, but the force of the traditional categories was, even for him, too strong to permit such a radical departure. He was convinced of the necessity of something over and above 'the extension, figure, solidity, motion, thinking, or other observable idea' of objects, but he maintained that we can form no determinate idea of this unifying

---

[1] Aaron, op. cit., p. 171.   [2] *Answer to Mr. Locke's Letter*, p. 17.

factor.[1] Stillingfleet held the troublesome aspect of this
doctrine to be Locke's candid recognition of the indeterminate character of our idea of this rational conception.
Nothing in Locke's empiricism, nothing in the doctrine of
ideas as expressed in the early portions of Book Two, permits
the introduction of this complex idea of substance. Just as
Stillingfleet claimed, the supposition is made by our reason
without any legitimate empirical grounds in sensation or
reflection. Stillingfleet was correct too in calling attention to
the pernicious character of Locke's recognition of the indeterminate character of our knowledge in this respect, for
a certainty of real substance was, as he argued against Locke,
required for the defence of important religious doctrines.
Locke did not succeed in showing how his principles were
consistent with these doctrines. He made his general system
harmonious with Christianity, however, by a *tour de force*, by
resorting to postulates of reason. It was to Stillingfleet's
credit to have seen the crucial split in Locke's avowed procedures; but their controversy, so pregnant with possibilities
of clarifying the position, terminated without his eliciting
from Locke anything more than rephrasings of his doctrines
and a constant plea to be dissociated from the Deists and the
Socinian thinkers.

The Toland–Stillingfleet controversy concerning the nature
and role of substance in religious knowledge did not constitute
the sole attack upon the doctrine of substance. Pierre Bayle
in France criticized the doctrine from the perspective of its
incompatibility with the immateriality of mind or spirit.
Bayle credits the indeterminate character of our knowledge
of substance in Locke's *Essay* to the difficulty of conceiving
how mind and matter interact: 'la dificulté de concilier
l'immaterialité des âmes humaines avec leur situation dans des
corps organisez a contraint d'habiles gens à soutenir . . . que
ce qui constituë la substance d'un esprit, & la substance d'un
corps nous est entierement inconu . . . .'[2] He interpreted

---

[1] *Letter to the . . . Bishop of Worcester*, in *Works*, vol. iv, p. 7.
[2] *Reponse aux Questions d'un Provincial* (1704–7), t. iv, p. 219.

Locke as saying that extension, impenetrability, and motion are properties of matter or material substance but not the essence of that substance, showing his recognition of the non-phenomenalistic doctrine of substance in the *Essay*. These properties of matter subsist in an unknown subject, a doctrine which Bayle holds as equivalent to saying that impenetrability and extension are accidents of matter and not its defining characteristics. But such a position is incongruous with the doctrine of transubstantiation, for Locke's doctrine thus understood claims that matter, considered as essential and substantial, is able to exist without extension. The same argument applies to thought in reference to mind, mind being able to exist without thought if thought is only an accidental property distinct from the essential nature of mind. Moreover, if our knowledge of the real essence is so obscure and incomplete as Locke claims, we cannot say that mind cannot be extended or that matter cannot think. The most that we can say is that experience reveals that the one is susceptible of thought, the other of extension. We may perhaps say in addition, Bayle suggests, that there is something in the substance of matter which makes it more susceptible to extension than to thought, and likewise that there is something in spirit more receptive to thought than to extension, but we could not explain this tendency. Thus, 'on ne pourra plus conclurre que si une substance pense elle est immaterielle', an inference which Bayle, like many other men of the period, wished to assert with the utmost force.[1] Finally, Bayle believed that the doctrine of substance in the *Essay* could lead only to 'l'ancien Chaos des Scholastiques, à l'éduction des formes, à la distinction reelle entre la substance & ses accidens, & à tels autres dogmes absolument inexplicables'.[2]

Locke found his defender against Bayle in LeClerc, who, in his long review of the fifth edition of the *Essay* in his *Bibliothèque Choisie*, sought to show that Bayle had misinterpreted Locke's doctrine of substance. For LeClerc, Bayle was a man 'peu propre à pénetrer & à développer une matière;

[1] Ibid., p. 222.   [2] Ibid., p. 223.

mais très-propre à faire des difficultez sans fin, contre ce
qu'il n'entendoit pas'.[1] But LeClerc failed to appreciate the
acuteness of Bayle's insights. The criticism of substance
in Bayle's *Reponse* is, like Stillingfleet's criticism, religiously
oriented and designed to show the sceptical consequences of
following out the doctrine of the *Essay* in all its implications;
and like Stillingfleet, Bayle hit upon a crucial difficulty in the
doctrine. The difficulty can be formulated as an alternative:
either Locke must keep his doctrine of substance restricted
to the phenomenalistic level and reduce substance to a collection of qualities, or he has to be interpreted as claiming
(what seems clearly to have been his intention) that substance
is something over and above the known properties. He did
not, it is true, wish to hold that substance can exist without
its accidents, without its primary qualities; but, however
essential these qualities may be for the real essence of substance, the non-phenomenalistic concept of substance entails
the admission that the real essence comprises more than these
qualities. Thus, Bayle was correct in seeing in the doctrine
of the *Essay* the problem of relating the accidental qualities
of material and immaterial substance to the real, hidden
essence. LeClerc objected to Bayle's interpretation, which
split substance into essence and accidents, on the ground
that 'ce que nous appellons la Matiere, ou le Corps, est aussi
essentiellement composé de l'Etendue & de la Divisibilité,
que de cette Substance inconnue, qui leur sert de sujet'.[2]
Locke's doctrine was that the known qualities flow from or
can be deduced from the hidden part of the real essence: but
it is never clear from the *Essay* whether he really did mean
to say that the accidental qualities are a part of that essence.
In his letter, occasioned by the bishop of Worcester's *A
Discourse in Vindication of the Doctrine of the Trinity*, Locke
speaks of the real essences themselves as being the 'internal
constitution, or frame, or modification' of substances, but he
does not clarify, either here or in a later reply, the relation

---

[1] *Bibliothèque Choisie*, t. 12, 1707, art. iii, p. 105.
[2] Ibid., p. 107.

between this internal constitution and the known primary qualities.[1] He did not wish to say that substance can exist without its major properties of extension or thought, but the limitations of human knowledge prevented any specification of this relation.

Physical objects as well as immaterial minds were for Locke divided into perceivable and imperceivable components. The real essence of either is to some extent at least hidden away in the unknowable but necessary substratum. Had Locke pursued this distinction between real and nominal essence, or between that aspect of the object which is sensible and that which is not, to the point where he would convince himself that the only profitable knowledge is that requiring a knowledge of the real essence, he would have been driven into the most stultifying of sceptical positions. Metaphysics would then have blurred the clear empirical direction of most parts of the *Essay*. But Locke did not allow himself to become trapped in this morass. The distinction between real and nominal essence, between unsensed substance and sensible qualities, was theoretically important for him, but, practically, of relative unimportance. Human knowledge is limited, but its limitations are not such as to hamper action or hinder man in attaining happiness. The doctrine of substance, in other words, entails only a theoretical scepticism. But it was precisely this dichotomy of theoretical and practical and his greater concern with the practical which led many of his readers to find more scepticism in the *Essay* than Locke could have ever seen or admitted. While the majority of his critics found the doctrines theoretically offensive because of the importance of their relevance to theology and the foundations of morality, Locke could only reaffirm, in the face of their charges of scepticism, his essential and good-natured common-sense convictions in the usefulness of knowledge. We find in this attitude, I believe, another piece of evidence in support of interpreting Locke as concerned with solving epistemological problems for the sake of practical difficulties encountered in

[1] In *Works*, vol. iv, p. 82.

reflections upon moral and religious issues. Where the solutions of such difficulties carried the discussion into the intricacies of theoretical implications, Locke was always prone to drop the discussion and assert his own convictions. Three notable instances of this attitude are found in his discussion of the physical basis of perception and of the reality of our representative knowledge, and in the non-phenomenalistic concept of substance. At every juncture, it is the theoretical aspects of his epistemological doctrines which are left insufficiently discussed and developed and which are taken up by his contemporary readers for criticism. Not a little of his reluctance to enter into free and open debate with his critics on these issues can be put down to his disinterestedness in and perhaps inability to discuss these important theoretical issues.

Stillingfleet and Bayle discerned crucial theoretical fissures in the doctrine of substance. Sergeant's and William Carroll's criticisms against substance were less acute although representative of the general reaction. Sergeant saw in the doctrine of substance a threat to natural science. He equates 'substance' with 'thing'. Hence, if Locke is correct about the unknowableness of substance, 'we must bid Adieu to all Philosophy, which is the *Knowledge of Things* . . . .'[1] But Sergeant's conception of a 'thing' is not Locke's. Substance in general is defined as 'a capacity to exist' and individual substances are nothing more than all of the accidents taken collectively. 'This Discourse is built on this Principle, that all our *Ideas* or Notions (and amongst them the Notion of *Substance* or *Thing*) are but so many *Conceptions* of the Thing; or which . . . is the same, the *Thing thus* or thus *conceiv'd*. . . .'[2] Even though man can never know all of these accidents and hence can never know the actual substance in its entirety, Sergeant's position entails an entirely different definition of substance from that employed by Locke. Substance is the most essential part of objects for Locke, but by no means that object in its completeness. Existence and substance are practically identical

---

[1] *Solid Philosophy Asserted*, p. 238.   [2] Ibid., p. 240.

for Sergeant. Hence, it is impossible not to know the meaning
of the term substance.

> For, every one must needs know what it is *to be*; since without know-
> ing *this*, we could not understand anything another *says*, not what our
> selves *think*; for all this is perform'd by *Affirming* or *Denying*, express'd
> by '*is*' or '*is not*', which speak *Actual Being*, or *not Being*.[1]

When we descend to the level of individual substances,
Sergeant admits that there is a great deal of confusion in our
knowledge through the complexity and number of modes
which go to make up the individual substance. But there is
only one notion which is the notion of substance proper: that
which is capable of being. The essential nature of substance
is made actual only by its modes, and thus the modes are the
how while the substance itself is the *what*. The *quiddity* for
Sergeant is not a complex substratum containing the hidden
essence of the thing: it is only the possibility of being something. Sergeant does not specify the *what* any more than did
Locke or Stillingfleet, but his failure to do so was a result of
his belief that substance is nothing more than the *capacity* of
being this or that. Sergeant denied that substance as supporter
of accidents is the primary meaning of the term, although he
did recognize this as one meaning then in use. Locke's
doctrine of substance, then, was faulty from his point of view
because it used a secondary meaning of the term and made
substance unknowable. However, Sergeant's own definition
does not fare much better when examined. As Locke wisely
remarked of the definition of substance as a capacity to exist:
'All which amounts to noe more but this, that Substance is
some thing which is what Mr. L says.' (Locke, *Notes*, no. 40,
p. 241.) Besides, Locke did not see how Sergeant could make
a distinction between accidents and substances on this
definition.

> If the Idea of Substance be capacity to exist then Accidents are sub-
> stances for they are capable to exist. If it be as J. S. puts it here & also
> wher a thing capable to exist, then his Idea of *substance* or *thing*, will be
> this, that a Thing is a Thing capable to exist. Which as much clears the

---

[1] Ibid., pp. 240–1.

point as if he should say an [accident] is an accident capable to exist. Or a man is a man capable to exist. (Ibid., no. 41, p. 244.)

To Sergeant's charge that the *Essay* makes objects unintelligible because their essence is unknowable, Locke responds with the terse but taunting comment: 'We may know that they exist though we can not explain all their properties & qualities.' (Ibid., no. 45, p. 250.) Sergeant's attack upon the doctrine of substance might have made Locke explain in more detail just how we can know that bodies in their substantial natures exist without knowing all their properties. Unfortunately, it did not have this effect. What we have in place of such a possible explanation is a reaffirmation of the main lines of the *Essay* on this point. There were several different views of substance current at the end of the seventeenth century, views which were frequently confused. The *Essay* itself embodied two such concepts of substance, and neither their connexion nor their distinction is made clear by Locke. In the writings of Sergeant and Locke we find a representative of the Aristotelian concept of potentiality as the defining characteristic of substance, and a representative of the scholastic concept of substance as the supporter of qualities, but the nature of the substratum for Locke is unknown. Neither Locke nor Sergeant recognized the difference in each other's concept on this issue, and neither man saw the full implications of the position he defended. Sergeant's position on the definition of physical objects comes very close to a phenomenalistic definition in which the object as it exists actually is nothing more than the sum of all its qualities. Since he accepts the Aristotelian doctrine of causality in which all actual events must have arisen from a potential condition, he includes in his definition the idea of the capacity to exist. Locke, with his decidedly dualistic bent, could not find in this description an adequate account of physical objects. A substance, substratum, or matter (these words are used interchangeably by both Locke and Sergeant) which is nothing more than a mere capacity of being, violated the most essential aspect of physical objects for Locke. 'Matter is a solid substance & not a power', a solid substance defined by impenetrability. (Ibid., no. 87, p. 375.) Impenetrability and extension for Sergeant were just attributes of body. Matter for him was the power of bodies to become altered. Thus, he criticized Descartes for making extension the only notion of body, and Locke for making extension and solidity (as he thought) the nature of body. Both men, in Sergeant's eyes, omitted the essential nature of bodies, namely, potentiality. Such an omission was tantamount to a failure to consider matter at all. Misled by the difference in their conceptions of matter, Sergeant read Locke as making this omission and charged him with failing to consider the nature of matter. One of Locke's longest notes concerns itself with clarifying this misinterpretation, while criticizing the false conception of matter which he found in Sergeant.

Here J. S. falls under the same rebuke which he bestows on Mr. Locke for a misunderstood expression & not for any mistake in his meaning, for that by body he means an extended solid substance & not the modes of Extension & Solidity without substance may be seen, B. II, C. XIII, § 12, B. III, C. X, § 15. There argueing against Cartes's use of the word Body he thought it sufficient to mention those modes which in the proper use of the word Body are different from that sole mode which Des Cartes uses it for, without mentioning of substance. And therefore to use his own expression Meer power is noe more the notion of matter than an Hors-shoe is a pancake. (Ibid., no. 87, pp. 375-6.)

Sergeant, Stillingfleet, and Browne found inadequate the doctrine of substance Locke advanced because of its stress upon the arbitrariness of the formation of the concept of substance, and because of man's inability to know its real nature or essence. All three were writing from a religious perspective and saw the dangers of such a doctrine for the dogmas they were dedicated to defend. Distrust of the positive doctrines of the *Essay* was growing as the seventeenth century drew to a close. Theologians were beginning to charge Locke with maliciously seeking to undermine religion, instead, as Stillingfleet had only urged, of offering principles which were inconsistent with tradition. The concentrated attacks upon his book of which Locke had complained to Molyneux and

Burnet[1] were becoming more contentious. Locke was being aligned more and more with the members of the radical non-conformist religious sects. One of the more vehement of such attacks against Locke's doctrine of substance appeared after his death, in the writings of William Carroll. In a series of tracts Carroll strove to show that Locke's doctrine of substance was an expansion of Spinoza's pantheism, of the doctrine that there is only one substance in the world and that this is material. Writing in 1705 against Samuel Clarke's Boyle lectures,[2] Carroll calls attention to Clarke's acceptance of the Lockean doctrine of the nature of substance.

> Tho' this *Sceptical Hypothesis* is absolutely false, and borrow'd from Mr. *L.* as other things in these Sermons are; yet it shews us, that as Mr. *C. neither has nor can have*, any Idea of the *Substance* of *God*, so likewise, *he neither has, nor can have*, any Idea of the *Substance* of *Matter*.[3]

Clarke had written expressly to refute all atheistical systems such as those of Hobbes and Spinoza, but Carroll argues that in order to refute these men, Clarke has to show that the substance of God is not the substance of matter. With the essence of substance unknowable, neither Clarke nor Locke can meet this charge. 'This *Atheistical shopkeeper* [Spinoza] is the First that ever reduced *Atheism* into a *System*, and Mr. *Locke* is the Second; with this Difference, that the latter has only copied the former as to the main . . .'[4] Locke, Carroll believed, was intent on showing that all things in the world differ not as to substance but only in a bare difference of modifications of substance.

> I need not to quote more out of him, for by far the greatest part of his three last Books are imployed in depriving us of the means to difference, or distinguish, or prove, that there is more than One real Substance, and to establish *Spinoza's Sceptical Hypothesis*, whose *Basis* is this, *We neither have*, nor can have, the Idea of *Substance by Sensation or Reflection*.[5]

Carroll's longest attack upon the Lockean doctrine of substance is found in his *Dissertation upon the Tenth Chapter of*

---

[1] Cf. above, pp. 7–10.
[2] *A Demonstration of the Being and Attributes of God.*
[3] *Remarks upon Mr. Clarke's Sermons* (1705), p. 5.
[4] Ibid., p. 9.   [5] Ibid., pp. 10-11.

the Fourth Book of Mr. Locke's Essay (1706). In this work, he charges Locke with striving to hide his chief aim by drawing out his work to four books, but Carroll asserts that one can see that amidst this 'Wood of Words' Locke has

carefully divested of their ordinary settled Significations, the most important Terms imploy'd by him, such as *God, Spirit, Man, Matter, Substance, Essence, Sort, &c,* and afterwards by using those Terms as Signs or Marks of Ideas, different from those whereof the common Custom of the *English* Language made them Signs, that is, in a Sense wherein the Readers were not accustomed to take them; he really establish'd *Spinoza's* Hypothesis, and made some Readers believe, that he establish'd the Truth quite opposite to it, but which indeed, he really and fundamentally subverted (p. 2).

He discerned two uses of 'substance' in the *Essay*: substance in a singular sense, as a supposed something, and in a plural sense, as a collection of modifications. The first use is designed to support his doctrine of one single substance. When Locke argues (bk. ii, ch. xiii, no. 18) that many people seek to apply the confused notion of substance to God, to finite beings, and to material objects, Carroll claims that they either apply it in the same sense to all three or else in three distinct meanings. Carroll states that one can easily see that by using the term 'substance' in the singular, Locke is seeking to establish his Spinozistic thesis.

If it be in the same *Sense* or *Signification* that the Word *Substance*, is taken, and stands for the same *Idea*, when 'tis said, That *God is a Substance*, that a *finite Spirit is a Substance* and that *Body is so*; it will thence follow, That *God, finite Spirits*, and *Body*, agreeing in the same *common Nature* of *Substance, differ not any otherwise, than in a bare different Modification of that Substance*; . . . (pp. 28–29).

With the real essence of substance unknowable, Locke is committed to the doctrine that so far as man can know with certainty, material and immaterial substance may be the same substantially, differing only accidentally. The charge of materialism against Locke was commonly made by his contemporaries on the ground of his suggestion that God might be able to add to matter a power of thinking. Carroll arrived at the same conclusion in a different way, by an analysis of the doctrine of substance. Carroll was fully aware that Locke wished to commit himself to talking only about the idea of substance and not directly about substance itself, but he pointed out quite validly that Locke proceeds, in Book Four, to demonstrate the real existence of God and to deny that he intends to make the substance of God material. But, Carroll argued, on Locke's principles, all our knowledge of God should be restricted to modifications and could never extend to His real nature.

For instance, he says in the Section, we examine, that *Matter*, cannot *think*, that a *Cogitative Being* cannot be *Matter*, and the like; whereby the sober Reader is apt to think he separates two real distinct Substances one from another; and that he removes all Matter whatever from God, when he says in the Close of this Section, *it necessarily follows, that the first eternal Being, cannot be Matter*; whilst Mr. L. in the preceding Assertions, separates one from the other, but two different Collections of Modifications only; and in his Conclusion, removes nothing else from being his first eternal Being, but one of those Collections of Modifications, as we have seen before (p. 109).

Not only had Locke denied innate ideas, by means of which Carroll believed man to gain his knowledge of God, but Locke had reduced the nature of God to matter.

Locke had, of course, excepted our knowledge of God from his general dictum concerning the unknowableness of substance, believing that he had firmly established the immateriality of God, in accordance with the demands of religion. Carroll was much too extravagant in his charge that Locke had borrowed his doctrine of substance from Spinoza or that Locke consciously meant to establish anything like the Spinozistic universe; but like many other critics contemporary with Locke, Carroll had detected the tendencies inherent in the general doctrine which Locke sought to defend. Scepticism as to the nature of God, His incarnation, the relation of the incarnate God to the two other persons in the Trinity, and scepticism concerning the nature of the human soul, were inextricable ingredients in this doctrine. Both the phenomenalistic and the non-phenomenalistic concept of substance gave rise, in the minds of Locke's contemporaries, to doubts and uncertainties about basic religious dogmas, although it was the latter which caused most of the stir. But in the phenomenalistic concept, Locke was not far removed from Hume's view of the self as the collection of functions and properties known through experience. As early as 1710, Berkeley drew these conclusions from the *Essay* in his analysis of substance as applied to physical objects.[1] Isaac Watts continued this tendency by arguing that grammatical usage of our terms had led men in the past to ascribe to objects a substance over and above the sensible qualities.

> It must be confest, when we say, *Spirit is a thinking Substance*, and *Matter is an extended solid Substance*, we are sometimes ready to imagine that *Extension* and *Solidity* are but meer *Modes* and *Properties* of a certain unknown *Substance* or Subject which supports them, and which we call *Body*. . . . But I rather think this to be a meer Mistake, which we are led into by the *grammatical* Form and Use of Words; and our *logical* Way of thinking by *Substances* and *Modes*, as well as our *grammatical* Way of talking by *Substantives* and *Adjectives*, delude us into this supposition.[2]

In his *Philosophical Essays* (1733) he explicitly credits Locke with having swept such invalid concepts from our philosophy: 'Mr. *Locke* has happily refuted that unreasonable Notion of *Substance* in general, which makes it to be some real thing in Nature, different from all the united Qualities, the supposed Properties and Powers of Body and Spirit. . . .' (p. 47). The so-called properties of matter and spirit are sufficient in themselves for the concept of substance. 'Why then may we not suppose that *solid Extension* and a *Thinking Power* may be the very Substances themselves, tho' the Names *grammatically* taken may seem to denote *Property* and *Quality*?' (pp. 53–54). Moreover, like Carroll, Watts saw the dangers of materialism in Locke's non-phenomenalist concept, arguing that if we allow a further unknown support or substance, this supposition can lead, as it does in Locke, to the supposition of matter being able to think in virtue of the same common substance

---

[1] *A Treatise Concerning the Principles of Human Knowledge* (1710).
[2] *Logick* (1726), p. 13, footnote.

underlying matter and thought. Despite Locke's protestations
in his letter occasioned by Stillingfleet's attack, Watts was
able to discredit the non-phenomenalistic concept of substance
in the *Essay* as an inconsistency due to Locke's not having
fully grasped the direction of his own thought. But there were
men in the service of religion who, even in the middle of the
eighteenth century, insisted upon this aspect of the doctrine
of substance as expressive of the true meaning Locke wished
to attach to the term. Andrew Baxter was one such individual
who sought to counteract Watts's radical interpretation.

> Mr. *Locke* allows that the internal, unknown constitution of things
> is *something*; since their discoverable qualities are owned to depend
> on this; . . . This is taken notice of because sceptical men begin to sup-
> pose they have Mr. *Locke's* authority for insinuating that the unknown
> constitution of things is in itself nothing; and that *substance*, or what *he*
> calls *substratum* is but empty sound.[1]

Baxter, however, was not fully satisfied with the Lockean
doctrine, but saw in it the same tendency to separate the
properties of substances from their real essences as did
Bayle.[2]

§ 3—*The Controversy on Thinking Matter*

The doctrine of substance elaborated by Locke thus served
as the natural predecessor for the discussions of epistemology
and ontology by the philosophers and theologians of the
eighteenth century. This doctrine, as we have just seen, served
also to arouse the clergy of Locke's own day to varying reactions. Those of Stillingfleet, Bayle, and Sergeant concerned
chiefly the nature of the ontological distinction of real and
nominal essence and the definition of substance. In the minds of
these and the other theologians who criticized the doctrine, it
was the doctrine of the Trinity which functioned as the standard
in terms of which all doctrines of substance were measured;
for a theory of substance which failed to render justice to the

---

[1] *An Enquiry into the Nature of the Human Soul* (1733), p. 144, note r.
[2] Ibid., pp. 152–3.

complications of this Christian dogma could not be tolerated by the orthodox men of religion. But these same men also saw in Locke's twofold doctrine of substance, and especially in the non-phenomenalistic concept, a threat to the doctrine of the immateriality of the human soul. Locke's doctrine of substance, with its emphasis upon the hidden nature of the real essence of substance, both material and immaterial, opened the way, it was feared, for a Hobbesian materialistic universe. Seventeenth-century Cartesianism had stimulated many speculations, both in France and in England, upon the rationality of animals, whether brutes had souls or were mere machines. Locke must have been well acquainted with these discussions. There are frequent references throughout the *Essay* to rational parrots, the status of monsters, the lack of abstractive powers in brutes, &c., which clearly reflect interest in this problem.[1] Although his suggestion that God might be able to add to matter a power of thinking was only incidental to the development of his doctrine of substance, within the context of such discussions as those concerning the rationality of brutes and the necessary condition for immortality as consisting in the immateriality of the soul, it could not have failed to fan the flames of this particular controversy. The full origins of the controversy over the ability of matter to think have not as yet been satisfactorily uncovered. It very definitely seems to be an offshoot of the Cartesian discussions on the nature of animals' minds and their possible souls; but the discussion in England of the early part of the century suggests that its relation to the doctrine of immortality is no less important. It is in this latter relation that the controversy takes on a relevance to Locke's *Essay* and to his doctrine of substance.

The passage in book iv, ch. iii, no. 6 of the *Essay* wherein the suggestion is made that matter might be given the power of thinking by God is introduced as a digression, illustrating the limitations of human knowledge. Locke is there concerned to argue that however much human knowledge may be extended

[1] See bk. ii, ch. xi, nos. 11–13, ch. xxvii, no. 9; and bk. iv, ch. iv, nos. 14–16.

by diligence and care, knowledge 'would never reach to all we might desire to know concerning those ideas we have; nor be able to surmount all the difficulties, and resolve all the questions that might arise concerning any of them'. We have the ideas of a square, a circle, and equality, but Locke doubts whether we shall ever 'be able to find a circle equal to a square, and certainly know that it is so'. Similarly, 'we have the ideas of *matter* and of *thinking*, but possibly shall never be able to know whether any mere material being thinks or no', since it is beyond the powers of human knowledge to determine, by the analysis of our ideas, 'whether Omnipotency has not given to some systems of matter, fitly disposed, a power to perceive and think, or else joined and fixed to matter, so disposed, a thinking immaterial substance'. Locke's digression on this point is clearly directed towards the many discussions of the relation between matter and thought and the relation between immortality and immateriality current in his own day. He is not concerned to doubt the immateriality of the human soul, but only to argue that, since our knowledge does not permit us to have certainty on this matter, we should recognize our limitations and admit that immateriality is not necessary for the doctrine of the soul's immortality.

All the great ends of morality and religion are well enough secured without philosophical proofs of the soul's immateriality; since it is evident, that he who made us at the beginning to subsist here, sensible intelligent beings, and for several years continued us in such a state, can and will restore us to the like state of sensibility in another world, and make us capable there to receive the retribution he has designed to men, according to their doings in this life.

Thus, it is not of such great importance 'as some, over-zealous for or against the immateriality of the soul, have been forward to make the world believe', to demonstrate or establish beyond doubt that the soul is immaterial. 'He that considers how hardly sensation is, in our thoughts, reconcilable to extended matter; or existence to anything that has no extension at all, will confess that he is very far from certainly knowing what his soul is.' It is beyond doubt, Locke believed with Descartes, that there is something in us which thinks. It makes no difference whether, besides the property of thinking, this something has also the property of being solid and extended. As he remarked to Stillingfleet, 'the general idea of substance being the same every where, the modification of thinking, or the power of thinking joined to it, makes it a spirit, without considering what other modifications it has, as whether it has the modification of solidity or no'.[1] Similarly, 'The idea of matter is an extended solid substance; wherever there is such a substance, there is matter, and the essence of matter, whatever other qualities, not contained in that essence, it shall please God to superadd to it.'[2] Writing to Collins late in life, Locke sought to clarify the issue once again.

> But not to waste your time, in playing with the arguments of men, that examine not strictly the meaning of the words they use; I will show you the fallacy whereby they impose on themselves; for such talkers commonly cozen themselves, as well as others. Cogitation, say they, 'is not comprehended in the idea of extension and solidity'; for that is it which they mean, when they say, the 'idea of matter'; from whence they conclude right, that 'cogitation belongs not to extension or solidity; or is not included in either of them, or both together'; but this is not the consequence that they draw, but infer a conclusion that is not contained in the premises. . . . Extension and solidity, we have the ideas of; and see, that cogitation has no necessary connexion with them, nor has any consequential result from them; and therefore is not a proper affection of extension and solidity, nor doth naturally belong to them; but how doth it follow from hence, that it may not be made an affection of, or be annexed to that substance, which is vested with solidity and extension?[3]

The context for this digression of Locke's is to be found in the many treatises in England which dealt with the immortality and immateriality of the human soul. Of the works written about this question exclusively, those of Henry More, Walter Charleton, and Samuel Haworth are typical representatives of the more astute treatments of the subject prior

---

[1] *A Letter to the . . . Bishop of Worcester, Works,* vol. iv, p. 33.
[2] *Mr. Locke's Reply to . . . Worcester's Answer to his Second Letter,* ibid., p. 460.
[3] Locke to Collins, 21 March 1703/4, *Works,* vol. x, p. 284.

to 1690.[1] Richard Bentley's Boyle lectures of 1692 tended to summarize and epitomize this issue, for, like his many predecessors, Bentley directed his attack against the Epicureans and sought to demonstrate the existence of an immaterial, thinking soul. It is, he declared, the 'Opinion of every Atheist, and counterfeit Deist of these times, that believes there is no Substance but Matter.'[2] Thus, atheism was directly linked to the doctrine of materialism and to the suggestion that matter might be able to think. The opposing doctrine could only be the immateriality of the soul, for only by showing that thought and extension are incompatible and that the soul which thinks is immaterial did these men think they could properly refute materialism and establish the legitimacy of the theory of human immortality. Locke's doctrine which allowed God the power of annexing to matter the power of thought, played into the hands of the materialists and atheists. As Peter Browne observed while writing against Toland:

> Mr. *Lock's* Notion of the *Soul* is only that of a *thinking substance* without any regard either to the *materiality* or *immateriality* of it; though one wou'd think he inclines to the former, when he shews this to be the sense of the word *Spirit* both in Prophane and Divine Authors. However he says afterwards that the utmost *Proof* we can have for the immateriality of it will amount only to a *Probability*; and this much concerning it he thinks deducible from his Principles; and particularly from his supposition of a *System of matter*; and adds that he would gladly see a better proof of it either from the Bishop of *Worcester* or any one else.[3]

Browne professed to be able to give Locke the required proof, but he did not do so in this or, as far as I can determine, in any later work. In the minds of Browne, Stillingfleet, and many other theologians of the period, the immortality of the soul could not be accepted or demonstrated until the immateriality of the soul had first been established. Locke's readers could

---

[1] More, H. *The Immortality of the Soul* (1659); Charleton, W. *The Immortality of the Human Soul* (1657); Haworth, S. Ἀνθροπωλογία, *Or, A Philosophic Discourse Concerning Man* (1680).

[2] *Matter and Motion cannot Think*, 3rd edition, 1694, p. 14. This quotation only occurs in this edition.

[3] *A Letter in Answer to a Book Entituled, Christianity not Mysterious*, p. 106.

not understand his contention that immateriality was irrelevant to the doctrine of immortality.

Reaction to this digression on immateriality and immortality came soon after the *Essay*'s appearance, although no public objections appeared until later. Molyneux, in his copy of the first edition of the *Essay*, has a marginal note indicating the early disturbance Locke's digression occasioned. Writing on bk. iv, ch. x, nos. 9–13, he says:

> I have heard it objected by some, that our Author, in these Sections Concerning Gods Immateriality, seems to Contradict Himself in what he asserts pag. 270. § 6 Concerning the possibility of Matters Thinking. But I Conceive our Author herein is very Consistent with Himself. For in this Place he only Asserts (for the Reasons here alledged) that tis Impossible that an Infinite Omnipotent Cogitative Being should Be Material. But granting (for the Reasons here alledged) an Omnipotent Cogitative Immaterial Being; Then (For the Reasons in pag. 270. Sec. 6) it is Impossible for us, without Revelation, to Discover whether this Omnipotent Cogitative Immaterial Being has not given to Matter (fitly Disposed) a Power to perceive and Think. For granting, that he has so done, it will not thence follow, that tis possible, that this Infinite Cogitative Being may Himself be Material.[1]

The disputes which Locke's digression aroused mostly originated in the early eighteenth century, for, besides Browne and Stillingfleet, very few critics of the *Essay* in the seventeenth century noticed this important challenge to Christian dogma. Early in the eighteenth century, Henry Lee expressed the common fear, when he saw in Locke's self-drawn implications of the limitations of knowledge a tendency towards Hobbism. If God has the power of adding to matter the property of thought,

> Man may be only a Species of Machins; and that we call our Souls, may be nothing but the Contexture of several parts of our Bodies to perform those feats of Motion, which for an honourable kind of Distinction we call Thoughts, tho really they are only the Operations of Matter, qualified with the knack of thinking.[2]

[1] p. 315. Molyneux left numerous marginal summaries of Locke's arguments but only one or two critical observations of his own in these notes. His copy of the *Essay* is in the Bodleian Library.

[2] *Anti-Scepticism*, p. 246.

The most extended defence of the immateriality of the soul against Locke's suggestion was written by John Broughton, *Psychologia; Or, An Account of the Nature of the Rational Soul* (1703). Broughton began from the assumption that reason is the 'self-moving Power of the Soul', while spirit is 'the Principle of *Life* and *Sensation*', opposed to body which is the principle of '*Mechanism* and *Local Motion*' (pref., p. [5]). Spirit and body are separate from one another, spirit being utterly incapable of local motion, and body equally incapable of life and sensation. He agrees with Locke's contention

that 'tis possible to conceive a *Spirit* devested of the Operation of *Thought*, and barely, in his own *Term*, as an *unsolid Substance*; but it is sufficient that we place the Distinction upon the *Capacity* and *Incapacity* of *Thought*; for the other [of solid and unsolid] is no way serviceable to us; because we did not come by the Knowledge of *Spirit*, as really existing, by our *Idea* of something *unsolid*, but only by our Idea of something that thinks: So that our Idea of an *unsolid Substance*, is not form'd from the Contemplation of any thing without us, as that of *Solidity* is; but is a bare *Hypothesis* to solve the Phaenomenon of Thought (pref., pp. [6–7]).

The supposition that body can think reduces all phenomena to body and embraces corporealism and atheism. But the curious aspect of Broughton's discussion is that he accepts the Lockean definition of substance: '*That, to us, unknown Nature, upon which all that we know of the Nature of anything depends, as to its Being; and which is, as to its Essence in general, independent on every thing but God*' (p. 2). Similarly, his definition of 'attribute' could come from either Spinoza or Locke: '*all that belongs to a Substance, and is not the Substance it self*; or, *all of the Substance that falls under our Knowledge and Apprehension*' (p. 2).

Once having given these definitions, he proceeds to argue as if he ignored them, using in his argument the usual definition of substance as that which can exist by itself, and the definition of mode or attribute as that which cannot so exist. Like Stillingfleet, he urges that, for one who seeks to make all knowledge come from sensation and reflection, the idea of substance will turn out to be, as it was for Locke, an absurd idea (p. 8). Substance, Broughton insisted, becomes the object of our understanding neither by sensation nor by reflection. He claimed that we have some knowledge of substance in terms of its accidents, invoking the principle that there is a proportional difference in substance where there is a difference in attribute, in order to argue that we know of at least two distinct substances, i.e., material and immaterial. He could not envisage the theoretical possibility offered by Locke of matter being able to think.

> It seems then there is a *fit Disposition* requir'd on Matter's side, as well as an omnipotent Power from without, to make it *think*. If I shou'd ask this Great Thinker, in what Part of Matter, or under what Circumstances he ever found this Disposition, I cou'd not reasonably expect a prompt Answer. I am sure, that in his Ideas of *Matter* and *Thinking*, there is no such thing to be found: And therefore, if he is Master of the Secret, his *Knowledge* is far larger than his *Ideas*; whereas it is true, and the Subject of this very Section, *That our Knowledge is narrower than our Ideas* (p. 20).

Broughton called Locke's supposition of a thinking matter 'the most Modern objection . . . to evade the Necessity of owning an *Immaterial Substance* in Human Nature' (p. 52). He admitted that Locke proved that the first existent being could not have been material; but he held that Locke's supposition left the way open for the atheist's saying that the essentially cogitative matter may replace God. Once we grant the possibility of matter thinking, Broughton believed that all Locke's efforts to show that the first being could not be material are irrelevant. 'For when the Possibility of the Thing is once really granted in Principle, these Absurdities following upon it, will quickly resolve into so many unconceivable Ways of Omnipotence exerting it self' (p. 55). Like Stillingfleet, Broughton thought this particular doctrine of Locke's to be dangerous in the hands of those less perspicacious or those avowedly antagonistic to religion.

> But if they shou'd gain no real Advantage by this Concession, because still the Supposition of a God, Eternal, and the Creator of all things, seems to remain untouch'd; yet, as Mr. L very well observes, they *letting slide out of their Minds, or the Discourse, the Demonstration whereby*

*an eternal knowing Being was proved necessary to exist; wou'd argue all to
be Matter, and so deny a God;* The Danger of granting these Men what,
over and above, it is absurd to grant to any Man, is to me a good Warrant
why I shou'd . . . deny the general Possibility of *Matter's Thinking*
(p. 56).

Broughton was obviously motivated by the necessities of
belief to deny what Locke, from different motives, could
grasp as a theoretical possibility beyond the scope of human
knowledge.

Locke found his defender against Broughton in Samuel
Bold, who sought to counter Broughton's fears by repeating
in detail the steps of Locke's digression, explaining as Locke
had done that the supposition in question was a theoretical
possibility resulting from the limitations of human knowledge.[1] He, too, was ready to accept immortality without
immateriality. It was Locke's friend, Collins, who had given
Broughton's book to Bold and elicited Bold's defence.

To give you my opinion of the book it is to me a Discourse upon
nothing, or which is all one, on something that no body knows any thing
of, or if any one did, would know less from reading his book. I have
given it to Mr. Bold from whose better judgment you may have farther
satisfaction about it.[2]

Locke himself had looked into Broughton's book and con-
curred in Collins's judgement.

The other book, you mentioned, I have seen; and am so well satisfied,
by his 5th section, what a doughty 'squire he is like to prove in the rest,
that I think not to trouble myself to look farther into him. He has there
argued very weakly against his adversary, but very strongly against himself.[3]

But Locke was genuinely alarmed to learn from Collins that
Bold not only had written something against Broughton but
that he was going to publish his remarks. Locke urged Collins
to stop Bold from sending them to the press.[4] Locke and

---

[1] *A Discourse Concerning the Resurrection of the Same Body* (1705).
[2] Collins to Locke, 30 June, 1703. MS. Locke, C. 7, f. 2.
[3] Locke to Collins, 9 July 1703, in *Works*, vol. x, p. 266.
[4] Cf. Locke to Collins, 21 February 1703/4 and 24 February 1703/4, in
Works, vol. x, pp. 276, 278.

Bold, however, were not the only figures in the period who were defending the position which Broughton had attacked. Broughton, in fact, was writing not only to refute Locke's suggestion of matter being given a power of thought; he wrote as well against William Coward's *Second Thoughts Concerning Human Soul* (1702), in which Coward not only took up the suggestion made by Locke, but actually maintained that the human soul is just such a power of life and movement super-added to the physical body. Whether or not Coward was actually directly influenced in this belief by Locke cannot be determined; but it is curious that a few years after Locke's suggestion had caught the attention of the critics, a serious writer should champion the precise view suggested in the *Essay*. It is, however, indicative of Locke's own views that neither he nor his friend Collins found the arguments of Coward's later work, *The Grand Essay* (1704), convincing. Thus it is clear that Locke did not mean to accept the view as actual fact which he had suggested in his digression as a possibility.[1]

Coward was opposed to analysing man into a material and an immaterial component. The soul of man, he maintained, is the life of man. There is no such thing as a spiritual substance. Moreover, the attempt to adhere to the traditional doctrine of an immaterial soul leads, he asserted paradoxically, into atheism and scepticism. Succinctly stated, his startling doctrine claimed that

all those Operations of Reason, Motion, &c. may be and are perform'd by an extraordinary or supereminent Power; First at the Creation implanted by God, in Matter or Material Man . . . which Power ceases to be, when the Body dies, and will not be renew'd again, or Reimplanted in the same Matter, until the Day of the Resurrection; . . .[2]

Thus, Coward actually defined the soul as a power inherent

---

[1] Cf. Collins to Locke, 16 February 1703/4. 'Dr. Coward has publish'd a Book to show that no such thing as Immaterial substance exists in nature & that all matter has originally a principle of selfmotion in it. his arguments are very far from proving either & are too mean to give you any account of.' MS. Locke, C. 7, f. 16. Also, Locke to Collins, 28 February 1703/4, where Locke indicates that he had seen some of Coward's earlier works. (In *Works*, vol. x, p. 279.)

[2] *Second Thoughts*, pp. 22–23.

M

in matter. Man became a kind of thinking matter. He did not find it at all strange that God '*should make Matter capable of performing all Acts of Ratiocination or Reasoning*'.[1] Likewise, he did not see why we should not credit rationality to brutes.[2] He even cited Hobbes as authority, with full recognition of the condemnation such authority would bring down upon him. But he was no blind follower of Hobbes; he merely accepted him as one person who had seen the dispensability of the hypothesis of an immaterial soul, but in so doing, he took a much more radical step than Locke ever intended. In his later work, *The Grand Essay*, Coward sought to reply to Broughton's criticisms, asserting that Broughton's Lockean definition of substance, which Broughton, as we have seen, did not really use in his major arguments, was a 'Metaphysical complex of Words' (p. 41). Coward reaffirmed, in all its strength, his doctrine of matter being able to think and of the uselessness of the hypothesis of an immaterial soul.

> Nay when we have framed to our selves an imaginary Existence of that *Substance*, call'd *Immaterial*, yet we find it as unconceivable or more to explain *how* it *Thinks* as Matter itself. Therefore to say *Matter Thinks by the Power of God*, can neither tend to atheism, or Irreligion, and consequently may be a Philosophy no sober Man ought to be ashamed of; . . . (p. 147).

Like the many critics who found Locke's doctrine of non-phenomenalistic substance conducive to scepticism, Coward accused Broughton, by his use of this doctrine, of leading 'head-long into down-right *Scepticisme*'.[3] He did not wish to minimize the difficulties attached to the doctrine of thinking matter, but he sought to show that it was consistent with Christian theology and contained no contradiction in itself.

> I aver it to be *very difficult* to conceive *how* Matter may *think*, but not so difficult as it is to conceive *how* Immaterial Substances can think; neither doth it imply a Contradiction for God to make Matter able to think: I mean, we do not conceive a Contradictory or impossible Idea in our Minds, by conceiving *thinking Matter*.[4]

---

[1] *Second Thoughts*, p. 163.   [2] Ibid., p. 165.
[3] p. 189 of his 'A Brief Answer to Mr. Broughton' (included at the end of *The Grand Essay* as pp. 177–248).   [4] Ibid., p. 194.

The same sort of doctrine as Coward was advocating was also being defended by Henry Layton in a series of tracts. In *Observations upon a Treatise intit'led Psychologia* (1703), Layton attacked Broughton's Lockean doctrine of substance, in the same terms as did Coward. Neither Bentley nor Broughton had shown, Layton argued, that thought cannot be in material things, but had instead pronounced 'magisterially and *ex Cathedra*, that the Idea of Matter and Thought are absolutely incompatible' (p. 91). He explained his positive doctrine in another tract published in the same year, *Arguments and Replies, in a Dispute concerning the Nature of the Humane Soul*.

> The Spirit of Life and Intellect in Man, doth most probably arise from the Breath of Life, and the Blood of our Life. . . . So as these two Principles of Breath and Blood (Material and Unintelligent, tho' they be) seem to effect and produce in the Creature, both Life it self, and all the Faculties there-unto belonging, and that all this *Compositum* is mortal and dies with the Person (p. 7).

He urged that it was the duty of his objector to prove the existence of an immaterial soul, and not his to offer proofs for his doctrine. Like Coward, he sought support for his doctrine from the Scriptures, insisting that he had not sought to demonstrate his conclusion but that he had 'made the opinion of the Soul's Materiality to be more probable, and come nearer the Truth, than that of the Soul's Spirituality, and separate Subsistence hath been, or can be prov'd to be' (p. 14). He denied accepting a mechanical explanation of thought, referring all such activities ultimately to the intervention of God. There was never any intention in Layton's mind of undermining the doctrines of his own Christian faith, as Locke had so frequently been charged with doing. Layton was himself a member of the Church of England, but he explained, in the growing fashion of the day, that he did not accept blindly the dogmas of the Church.

> You mention in two Places my being a Member of the Church of *England*, which I am ready so far to own for my Mother . . . professing to think, That she is the purest Church which I know to be in the World

at this Day; But I do not profess to make her Opinions the Rules of my Belief; or to follow any of her Opinions implicitly . . . The Guides and Powers to which I profess an absolute subjection are but two, *Viz. Scripture* and *Reason*; . . . (pp. 69–70).

Most of Layton's numerous and desultory tracts in defence of his thesis were buttressed by voluminous references to the Scriptures and to ancient authors whom he interpreted as supporting his doctrine. Even while discussing Broughton's attack upon Locke, Layton does not take Locke as the outstanding authority. Once, while writing against Timothy Manlove's *The Immortality of the Soul Asserted* (1697), Layton does directly claim Locke as an authority, but this is not usual in his tracts.[1] As we shall see in the next chapter, not only did he and Coward take up the suggestion of matter being able to think, they also incorporated into their writings several major doctrines of the way of ideas as found in Locke's *Essay*. Locke's epistemology was beginning to be used by the followers of the new radical religious sects; but it was also found in many traditional tracts. Samuel Clarke and John Witty belong to this latter category. Both of these men were concerned to defend the traditional doctrine of the immateriality of the soul against the beliefs of Locke, Coward, and Layton. Both Clarke (*A Second Defense of an Argument . . . in a Letter to Mr. Dodwell,* 1707) and Witty (*The First Principles of Modern Deism Confuted,* 1707) accepted the Lockean doctrine of the unknowability of the essence of substance, as Sherlock had also done much earlier; but both sought to bring this into consistency with the doctrine of the immateriality of the soul. Witty explains that his book was

occasion'd by the late pernicious Attempts of several Persons, who taking advantage of our Concession, of our utter Ignorance of the intrinsic Natures of the Substances or Essences of Spiritual and Material Beings, have thence attempted to invalidate our Evidence for the Existence of any thing Immaterial, and to introduce the Belief of Universal Materialism into the Minds of Men; . . . (pp. 7–8).

In a clear reference to Carroll's attacks, Witty denies his acquiescence in Carroll's charge of Spinozism against Locke.

[1] *Observations upon a Short Treatise, Written by Mr. Timothy Manlove* (1698 ?).

What was the Design of Mr. *Locke*, who denys all Knowledge of Substances, in his famous *Essay concerning Human Understanding*; I won't examine: Whether it was writ with an intention to establish *Spinoza's Material Deity*; or whether all he aim'd at in it was to enquire after the Fundamentals and Extent of Human Knowledge; ... (p. 11).

But he is firm in his denunciation of the implication which Locke drew from the doctrine of the unknowability of the essence of substance. Even though we cannot gain a knowledge of the real essence of spirit or matter, we can, he believed, see that the essential attributes of each, thought and extension, are incompatible (p. 157). To the suggestion that God may be able to annex thought to some system of matter, Witty says that those who argue in this way argue from the fact that 'we know nothing to the contrary' to the conclusion that it is possible (pp. 244–5). But the inconsistency between thought and extension strikes him as too obvious for this suggestion to be tolerable. Hence,

if the *Inconsistency in Nature* 'twixt the known Attributes of any two Substances can be demonstrated; whatever their Essences be, 'tis certain they must be in their intrinsic Natures *Incommunicably* different; and Omnipotence it self can't make those *inconsistent* Attributes coexist in the same Subject (p. 245).

Most of the defenders of the immateriality of the soul against the suggestion of matter being made to think through divine intervention argued, as Witty did, from the inconsistency of thought and extension to the denial of thinking matter. Charles Gildon, author of *A Deist's Manual* (1705) and another close follower of Locke's epistemology, urged the same considerations. The faculty of understanding and extension have nothing in common.

This is the Reason, that none was ever so wild as to suspect, *Thought* to be in any thing, in which we can discover nothing but *Extension*, Divisibility, Solidity, various Figures, and Motion. Who, for Example, that sees a Wooden Bowl in the Green, did ever fancy, that it was indu'd with Thought, or Understanding? We may well therefore deny, that Bodies can think, since we can make no Discovery of any thing in their Nature, that holds any Analogy with Thought (p. 170).

Gildon wrote with Coward's *Second Thoughts* expressly in mind and unquestionably also Locke's digression in the *Essay*. From the admitted fact that no one has ever found evidence of thought being in matter, he concluded that the suggestion of matter being given a power of thought is absurd. Benjamin Hampton, in his *The Existence of Human Soul After Death* (1711), attacked the same two books, alleging openly that

Dr. *Coward* has grounded his Doctrine, that the Soul has no Existence after Death, upon a Saying of Mr. *Locke*, in his *Essay of Human Understanding, viz.* That we do not know but that it is in the Power of God to dispose of Matter so, as to endue it with Understanding. I must confess, when I read that Book, wherein Mr. *Locke* discourses so excellently of the Nature of a Spirit, or Human Soul, telling us, That we know that our Souls are Spiritual Substances, because we think, and that we can have as clear an Idea or Notion of a Spirit, as we can have of Matter, or a Corporeal Substance. I admir'd to find such an odd Conceit as God's giving Understanding to Matter, and that a Man of his great Thought should over-think himself so far as to put himself in doubt, and other Men too . . . whether Men have any Souls at all, or only a little Understanding put in their Heads . . . (pp. 4–5).

Hampton was convinced that the 'conceit' was entirely wrong.

Tho' Mr. *Locke* is so fond of this Child of his Brain, that he would needs set it down for fear of losing it, I suppose for no other Reason, but because it was his own; yet this Child of his is a Monster, for as 'tis certain that God's Power is infinite, and surpasses all Understanding, so 'tis as certain that God is the God of Order and Nature, and it cannot be found in the Universe that he ever gave the Faculty of one Being, to any other Being to whom that Faculty does not naturally belong . . . (pp. 5–6).

God must act in accord with natural law. Even his infinite power cannot transgress the order of nature. For Hampton, Locke was less culpable than Coward, since the latter openly declared that man is just the same as a beast, in that both man and animals think and reason.

Mr. *Locke* in his Essay of human Understanding confest, that tho' we don't know but that it was in the Power of God to have given Understanding to Matter, yet he was most inclinable to believe, that human Soul is a spiritual immortal Substance; and yet while it is clog'd with the Body, does not always think. . . . Now Dr. *Coward* concludes, that since what we call human Soul, does not always think, it is not a spiritual immortal Substance, but only Understanding given to Matter . . . (pp. 24–25).

But like Witty and Samuel Clarke, Hampton accepted *in toto* the Lockean doctrine of the unknowability of substance.

As we have no compleat Idea of immaterial Substance, we have no Idea of Matter, stript of all Qualities and Accidents. All Philosophers own, that the Substance of all material things is the same, diversified by different Accidents and Qualities, as by different Magnitudes, Figures, Motion &c. and yet no Man can tell what pure naked Matter is; . . . We know nothing of any material Beings but their natural Virtues, Powers, Operations, or sensible Qualities; but what that Substance is which we call Matter, and is the Subject of all these different Powers and Qualities, we know not (pp. 33–34).

The controversy between Locke and Stillingfleet over substance had laid down the two alternatives which were followed by most of the subsequent disputants in this discussion of the nature of the human soul. Stillingfleet had agreed in principle to the doctrine of substance advanced in the *Essay*; but, instead of drawing the conclusion concerning the limitations of human knowledge which Locke drew, he preferred to turn to those metaphysical beliefs required by his theology and declare that the existence of immaterial substances was a dictum of reason. Hampton and Witty clearly aligned themselves with this side of the debate, but their acceptance of the Lockean doctrine was even more pronounced than Stillingfleet's. On the other side of the controversy, we find men who accepted both the Lockean doctrine of substance and the suggestion that matter might be able to think, a suggestion that Coward and Layton particularized into a doctrine of the soul as the activating power of the material body. With the idea fixed in the minds of the eighteenth-century writers that any form of materialism entailed atheism, together with their linking of the new Deism to naturalistic doctrines, the way was open for men like Humphrey Ditton, in *A Discourse Concerning the Resurrection of Jesus Christ* (1712), to argue that the doctrine of thinking matter was a deist doctrine, designed to undermine the traditional beliefs in a future state of rewards and punishments. 'Nor are we to imagine, that the Modern *Deists* have cultivated and set about this Notion of *Matter's Thinking*, with any other Design or View, than that of undermining the very Foundations of *Christianity*' (p. 474).[1] The digression which constituted Locke's brief pronouncement upon the long discussion over the relation between immateriality and immortality, a digression whose conclusions arose out of the epistemological doctrine of the limitation of knowledge to the nominal essence, was magnified and carried forward in the debates of the first half of the eighteenth century. Samuel Clarke and Anthony Collins, the friend and follower of Locke, carried on the most extended exchange of tracts on this subject: Clarke maintained against Dodwell that matter is utterly incapable of thought, while Collins sought to show that it was possible for matter to think, and that the immortality of the soul did not depend upon its immateriality.[2] Locke's name appears frequently in this long exchange. Likewise, the radical elaboration of Locke's suggestion by Coward and Layton did not lack its supporters in the eighteenth century. Samuel Strutt, in *A Philosophical Enquiry into the Physical Spring of Human Actions* (1732), argued for this position from four basic premisses: (1) 'that we have no Ideas of Substance, but those which have been receiv'd by our Senses from external Objects'; (2) that 'the only Ideas which we have so receiv'd, are of Matter, or material Substance only'; (3) that 'we have no Reason to conclude, that any part of the human Composition consists of Immaterial Substance; because we have no Ideas of any other Substance than Matter, and because there is nothing (that we know of) in the Nature of Matter, which is incompatible with Thinking'; and (4) that 'it appears most evidently from the Nature of Cogitation, that

---

[1] LeClerc gave a long review of Ditton's book, in which he devoted several pages to Ditton's views on thinking matter. Cf. *Bibliothèque Choisie*, t. xxv, pt. ii, pp. 450–2 (art. vi; 1712).

[2] Cf. esp., Collins's *An Answer to Mr. Clark's Third Defence of his Letter to Mr. Dodwell* (1708), and Clarke's *A Second Defense of an Argument Made use of in a Letter to Mr Dodwel* (1707).

Matter is the Subject of it' (pp. 3-4). Andrew Baxter, in *An Enquiry into the Nature of the Human Soul* (1733), defended the traditional doctrine, taking Locke to task and alleging that Locke's suggestion was based upon 'what Mr. *Locke* elsewhere endeavours to maintain, That our ideas are only *arbitrary combinations*, without connexion to any thing in nature' (p. 86, note r). Baxter went on to give a careful account of the controversy from Bentley and Locke to Collins and Clarke, finding in Peter Browne a sympathetic supporter.[1] The controversy, so far as Locke was involved in it, was brought to a dubious conclusion by John Jackson, who, in his *A Dissertation on Matter and Spirit* (1735), championed Lockean doctrines and put aside the new hypotheses of Berkeley and Watts.

I have taken no notice of a new Hypothesis in Philosophy, which hath been lately advanc'd, *viz.* that there is no such Thing really existing in Nature as *Substance*, either *Material* or *Spiritual*; and that what is so call'd is only an Aggregate of *Properties* without any existent *Subject*: ... (p. vii, note).

Jackson believed that God was the only truly immaterial substance and argued stoutly for the necessary union and even identity of the human soul and body.

This complex and tedious controversy lies to one side in the reception of Locke's epistemological principles, but it has a relevance, as we have seen, to the doctrine of substance and to the belief in the limitations of human knowledge. Perhaps also the general mind–body problem found its reflection in this debate. But even though this controversy and Locke's involvement in it was subsidiary to the major problem of scepticism which concerned his many critics, it took on a great importance in the eyes of Locke's religious contemporaries because it dealt with another doctrine accepted and defended by the believers in natural religion.[2] The doctrine of materialism in its Spinozistic

---

[1] See Browne's *Procedure*, pp. 362–70.

[2] Like many other of Locke's doctrines, this entire controversy was reflected by LeClerc in various reviews in his *Bibliothèque Choisie*. Cf. t. ii, pp. 352 ff., art. xiii; t. viii, pp. 58 ff., art. ii; t. xxi, p. 217, art. vii; t. xxiv, pp. 191 ff.; and t. xxvi, pp. 280 ff., art. iii.

form was, we have seen, forced upon the *Essay* by Carroll, but many another writer credited the doctrine of thinking matter to the deists and to other radical thinkers of the day. In the list of principles underlying deism, a list which was more than once drawn up at the turn of the century, this doctrine takes a prominent place. My concern, however, is more with the epistemological doctrines proper of the *Essay*, their reception, rejection, and absorption by Locke's contemporaries, than it is with the various subsidiary problems engendered by these principles. With the close of the seventeenth century and the beginning of the eighteenth, these epistemological principles —the resting of all knowledge upon ideas, the representative theory of perception, the pretended reduction of knowledge to an empirical basis and the consequent rejection of all innate sources of knowledge, the confusing, semi-phenomenalistic doctrine of substance—found more and more favour among the new deistical sects. No evaluation of Locke's influence upon his countrymen can be complete which does not recognize the role which his epistemology played in the service of these new religious movements. The very fact that many of these principles were absorbed by the orthodox defenders of tradition enabled the new naturalistic movement, in great measure, to catch and spread even while it was being most bitterly attacked.

V

EPISTEMOLOGY AND RELIGION

THE Cartesian development of the logic of ideas together with its English adaptations early in the seventeenth century provided the context from which Locke's epistemology emerged.[1] His epistemology was also rooted in the religious and moral debates of the period. One of the main contentions of the previous chapters has been that Locke's theory of knowledge was developed primarily for application to these debates: that it was accordingly considered by his contemporaries from the point of view of its effects upon religion and morality, and hence commands an evaluation within this context. With very few exceptions, the Lockean doctrines examined in this study elicited response from the seventeenth- and early eighteenth-century writers who were vitally concerned with the problems of man's relation with God, of man's knowledge of God, of the beliefs and dogmas required of the Christian, and fundamentally, of the grounds and doctrines necessary for the moral life. Locke's *Essay* found a place in these contemporary discussions not equalled by any other work in the period which concerned itself with the theoretical questions of human understanding. Its popularity was not solely the result of its literary quality but was in great measure due to the manner in which its doctrines were intimately related to the religious and moral problems of the day. So far as one can validly make inferences to Locke's personality from the few scattered remarks he has left behind, I have suggested that his attitude towards his critics was anything but receptive: he did not show himself ready to learn through debate or prone to believe that his readers could have an insight into these problems which he

[1] For a detailed account of this background, see my 'Locke and the Seventeenth-Century Logic of Ideas', *Journal of the History of Ideas*, October 1955.

himself lacked. With his own interests so firmly rooted in the advances of the period—in the logic of ideas, in the phenomenological-empirical analysis of the problems of knowledge and science, in the naturalization of religion—Locke may actually have been unable to anticipate or to appreciate the disturbance which his careful critique of many of the traditional presuppositions of religion and morality would cause. But we have seen that the first book of his *Essay*, even though its polemic had been amply anticipated by other men in the century (More, Culverwel, Parker, Burthogge), disrupted a long tradition of morality's dependence upon the doctrine of innate sources of knowledge; that even the most basic objectives of that work—the empirical foundation for all knowledge, the representative and symbolic role of ideas— were criticized because of their implicit and far-reaching epistemological scepticism; and that the more positive epistemological doctrines of the *Essay* were discovered to lead inevitably to religious scepticism. Had the story of the seventeenth- and eighteenth-century reception of Locke's epistemology ended at this point, we should have at best a negative, destructive tale, of interest to the historian and to the philosopher concerned with placing the *Essay* in its own context, but not a narrative dealing with any positive applications of the doctrines under examination. One of the more interesting aspects of the analysis of the subject here considered is that not only did the doctrines of knowledge developed by Locke receive careful destructive criticism by his contemporaries, but, at the same time as they were attacked by some, they were knowingly or unknowingly being applied to the immediate problems of religion and morality confronting the men of the period. This positive approach to Locke's theory of knowledge, the ability of his contemporaries to find an application of his doctrines to their practical problems, helps to support the contention that the theory of the *Essay* had its genesis and objective within this area of human conduct. The actual application of Locke's epistemology to religion and morality was begun in the very year

that the *Essay* appeared and continued into the middle of the
eighteenth century. Both the members of the new religious
sects (Deists, Unitarians, Free-Thinkers) and the adherents
to the older tradition found ample use for these doctrines.
But the epistemology of the *Essay* found its most ready
application within the ranks of the Deists and other naturalistic
theologians. Where it is adopted by the traditional theologians
it is usually for the purpose of combating some criticism by the
new sects which had invoked Lockean doctrines, or as a means
of modifying tradition less radically than the Deists demanded.
The absorption within tradition of these principles led to the
general dissemination of the new epistemology of Locke,
making it easier for these doctrines to be accepted finally even
by those most opposed to the growing naturalism in religion.
The epistemology of the *Essay* became so familiar through this
double application, that the theoretical framework of Deism
was given a most favourable impetus and support.

§ 1—*The Charge of Deism Against Locke*

The various sects of Socinianism, Unitarianism, and Deism
were all instances in the seventeenth century of the desire to
rationalize religion by bringing its dictates into conformity
with reason. Leslie Stephen has remarked that it was initially
the strong intermixture of philosophy and religion in the early
part of this century which accounted for the open opposition
between the old and the new forms of religion.[1] When the
analytic tools of philosophy, shaped in the seventeenth century
through the advances made by the sciences, were turned to the
service of religion, the confidence shown in science, that no
important secrets of nature could fail to come under the
control of human reason, was injected into religion.

The calm attitude of the men of science who had been steadily
advancing in the knowledge of the natural world, and by each fresh discovery had given fresh proofs of the power, and wisdom, and goodness
of God, stood forth in painful contrast with the profitless wranglings and bitter animosities of Divines. Men might well begin to ask

[1] *History of English Thought in the Eighteenth Century*, vol. i, pp. 82–85.

themselves whether they could not find rest from theological strife in natural religion? and the real object of the Deists was to demonstrate that they could.[1]

Chillingworth's formulation of the contributory role of reason in religion in his *The Religion of Protestants* (1638) was only the first of the many statements of this theme in the century. All the subsequent attempts at making religion rational, at dispensing with internal sanctions for morality and the knowledge of God, at finding God in nature and moral rules through reason, were met by the orthodox with the various labels of slander which had accrued to terms like 'Socinian', 'Unitarian', or 'Deist'—labels which were meant and understood as synonymous with 'atheist'. In the tracts which sought to defend orthodoxy, the arch-enemy was first Socianism, in its revival in the second half of the century, then Unitarianism, which appeared at about the same time,[2] and finally, in the early years of the eighteenth century, Deism became the dominant foe to be defeated. Deism was in effect the natural issue of the growing concern to establish religion upon natural, as opposed to revealed, grounds. The movement in religion from the middle of the seventeenth to the middle of the eighteenth centuries was steady and in one direction. What Stephen says of the years 1690-6, 'Locke, the Unitarians, Toland, form a genuine series, in which Christianity is being gradually transmuted by larger infusions of rationalism',[3] holds equally well of the period from Toland to Wollaston or Collins.

Although the various non-orthodox sects which appeared in England between 1690 and 1704 (the period from the *Essay* to Locke's death) differed from one another in virtue of certain minor doctrinal points, in studying any one of them we are in effect learning most of the characteristics of all the others. It depends on where one enters the period to decide

---

[1] Abbey and Overton, *The English Church in the Eighteenth Century*, vol. i, p. 181.

[2] The name of Stephen Nye is most often associated with this movement. Cf. his *A Brief History of the Unitarians* (1687).

[3] Stephen, vol. i, p. 111.

which aspect of the general religious movement shall be examined. To study the positive application of Locke's doctrines takes us towards the end of this period and hence leads us into an examination of Deism, the then dominant radical religious sect. While Locke was called a 'Socinian' soon after the publication of the *Essay*, towards the end of the seventeenth and the beginning of the eighteenth century his opponents commonly labelled him a 'Deist'. In both cases, what was being objected to was his emphasis upon a rational religion and the restriction of knowledge to the phenomenal or familiar world. What has come to be called 'Deism' by the historians of religious thought has usually meant those doctrines held by that group of late seventeenth- and early eighteenth-century writers (e.g. Chubb, Blount, Tindal, Toland) who were concerned to deny revealed truth and to set religion upon the foundation of nature. But Overton has correctly pointed out that the Deists did not constitute any organized body of men writing in unison.

They formed no sect, properly so-called, and were bound by no creed. In this sense at least they were genuine 'free-thinkers', in that they freely expressed their thoughts without the slightest regard to what had been said or might be said by their friends or foes. It was the fashion among their contemporaries to speak of the Deists as if they were as distinct a sect as the Quakers, the Socinians, the Presbyterians, or any other religious denomination. But we look in vain for any common doctrine—any common form of worship which belonged to the Deists as Deists.[1]

Overton recognizes that those who usually pass under this name did subscribe to a few common negative tenets, such as the denial of revealed religion, the belief that the Scriptures must be examined critically like any other book, that Jesus Christ is not co-equal with the one God. What the Deists did was to give expression, 'often a very coarse and inadequate expression—to thoughts which the circumstances of the times could scarcely fail to suggest'.[2]

The first reference to a sect of Deists is usually credited to

---

[1] Abbey and Overton, vol. i, p. 178   [2] Ibid., vol. i, p. 190.

the French writer, Pierre Viret, who, in his *Instruction Chrestienne* (1564) says:

I'ay entēdu qu'il y en a de ceste bāde, qui s'appelent Deistes, d'vn mot tout neuveau, lequel ils veulent opposer à Atheiste. Car pour autant qu'atheiste signifie celuy qui est sans Dieu. ils veulent dōner à entendre qu'il ne sont pas du tout sans Dieu, à cause qu'ils croyēt bien qu'il y a quelque Dieu, lequel ils recognoissent mesme pour createur du ciel & de la terre, comme les Turcs: mais de Iesus Christ, ils ne sauent que c'est, & ne tiennent rien ne de luy ne de sa doctrine (vol. ii, p. [8] of Epistre).

The persons whom Viret had in mind in this comment have not been clearly specified, but the characterization which he gives of them could be ascribed to many individuals in England and on the Continent from the earliest years of the seventeenth century. Socinus himself could almost fit this description. Richard Bentley, who gave the first of the Boyle lectures, characterized the Deists as being the same as infidels and atheists in much the same fashion as did Viret.

There are some Infidels among us, that not only disbelieve the *Christian* Religion; but impugn the assertion of a *Providence*, of the *Immortality* of the Soul, of an Universal *Judgment* to come, and of any *Incorporeal* Essence: and yet to avoid the odious name of *Atheists*, would shelter and skreen themselves under a new one of *Deists*, which is not quite so obnoxious.[1]

Bentley's description of Deism includes many of the doctrines for which the *Essay* later became famous. By far the more common mark of Deism was the rejection of revealed religion as a separate source of knowledge, exempt from the ordinary tests of validity, a mark which Leland[2] singled out in his extended analysis of certain leading Deists. Stillingfleet found it necessary to write *A Letter to a Deist* (1677) in which he attacks a particular unnamed person 'who owned the *Being* and *Providence* of God, but expressed a mean Esteem of the *Scriptures*, and the *Christian Religion*' (pref.). The principles which he and the deist held in common involved the existence of God, the concept of God as the creator, that God should

[1] *The Folly of Atheism* (1692), p. 6. This was the first sermon in his series.
[2] *A View of the Principal Deistical Writers* (1754–55), vol. i, p. 3.

be worshipped, that there is a future state of rewards and punishments in another world, and that the New Testament contains many principles 'inducing to Humility and Self-denyal, and to the Honour of God' (pp. 10–11). What was debated was whether the matters of fact reported in the Bible, especially the miracles, were true or no. Similarly, William Stephens published anonymously his *An Account of the Growth of Deism in England* (1696), in which he equated Deism with the denial of all revealed religion (p. 4). He adds to the list of principles accepted by the Deists, or reasons for men turning towards Deism, the dislike of those dogmas which are irrational or above reason, especially that of the Trinity (pp. 19–20). Another anonymous writer confirmed Stephens's general account.[1]

The object of attack in this last-mentioned pamphlet was Humphrey Prideaux, whom the author had credited with championing Locke's reduction of the necessary articles for belief to the one of Christ as the Messiah.[2] The author of this tract had replied by, among other things, calling attention to a person he had known who had returned to revealed religion after reading Locke's *Reasonableness of Christianity*. Leland also considered this work of Locke's an antidote against Deism and natural religion.[3] But Locke's precise relations to Deism are complex. On the one hand there can be little doubt that he never seriously considered himself as an opponent of revealed religion. In the preface to his *Second Vindication* of his *Reasonableness of Christianity*, he wrote:

But, when I had gone through the whole, and saw what a plain, simple, reasonable thing Christianity was, suited to all conditions and capacities; and in the morality of it now, with divine authority, established into a legible law, so far surpassing all that philosophy and human reason had attained to, or could possibly make effectual to all degrees of mankind, I was flattered to think it might be of some use in the world; especially to those, who thought either that there was no need of revelation at all, or that the revelation of our Saviour required the belief of

---

[1] 'Some Reflections on a Book, Entituled, *A Letter to the Deists*', no. 1 of *The Occasional Paper* (1697), p. 10.
[2] See his *A Letter to the Deists* (1697).   [3] Op. cit., vol. i, p. 37.

such articles for salvation, which the settled notions, and their way of reasoning in some, and want of understanding in others, made impossible to them. Upon these two topics the objections seemed to turn, which were with most assurance made by Deists against Christianity; but against Christianity misunderstood. It seemed to me, that there needed no more to show them the weakness of their exceptions, but to lay plainly before them the doctrine of our Saviour and his apostles, as delivered in the Scriptures, and not as taught by the several sects of Christians.[1]

Thus he was not an opponent of revelation, even though he held reason in high esteem and had in common with many men of the period the belief that religion could be made consistent with the demands of reason. But, on the other hand, it is true, as Overton has observed, that Locke had close personal relations with some of the principal deistical writers (e.g. Collins and Tindal) and 'most of the rest show unmistakable signs of having studied his works and followed more or less his line of thought'.[2] It seems to be true that many of the epistemological doctrines of the *Essay* provided material around which the deistical writers could construct their arguments.

Socinianism was much in the minds of Locke's contemporaries; it was a religious movement which did not differ radically from the general deistical temper. Being called a 'Socinian' was in many respects just a prelude to being classed with the Deists. Peter Browne wrote in 1728: 'Our modern Deists, and Freethinkers, and Atheists of all sorts and sizes are likewise the natural Growth and Offspring of Socinianism.'[3] John Milner, in *An Account of Mr. Lock's Religion*, had associated Locke with the Unitarians and the Socinians in virtue of his silence upon the doctrine of the Trinity, and concluded his book by comparing the doctrines of Socinus with those of Locke. John Edwards, who attacked Locke's *Reasonableness of Christianity*, had been one of the more vehement of Locke's slanderers, employing all the damaging epithets of the day.

[1] 'Preface to the Reader', in *Works*, vol. vii, p. 188.
[2] Op. cit., vol. i, pp. 223–4.
[3] *Procedure, Extent, and Limits of Human Understanding*, p. 40.

It is significant that after completing a long attack against what he took to be the Lockean doctrine of clear and distinct ideas as the foundations for all certainty Edwards remarks:

> I had not said so much unless the present Age we live in had required it, for now *Deism* is every where rampant, which is no other then an excessive extolling of Natural Religion, abstract from all Revelation. A *Deist* is one that owns no Scriptures, no Reveal'd or Instituted Religion.[1]

Pairing Toland with Locke, Edwards complained that neither of them stops at 'Exploding an Assertion because it is Common and Vulgar, and because they are willing to broach a new one of their own.'[2] In addition they introduce an entirely new terminology for the purpose of confusing the reader. Locke in particular has made a great advance in this way,

> by his setting up only One Fundamental Article of Christian Religion, by his ridiculing the Resurrection of the same Body, by his Scruples about the Souls Immateriality, by his Notion of Thinking Matter, by his No Natural Conscience, or any such Original Principle in Mens Minds. And both of them have endeavour'd to shake the Fundamentals of Religion by a New Set of Notions about *Reason* and *Clear Ideas*, and the rise of these from *Sensation* and *Reflection* only, and their particular Conceits about *Substances* and *Essences*.[3]

All the troublesome epistemological and ontological doctrines of the *Essay* were thus introduced into Edwards's summary of the particular doctrines of Deism and Socinianism so detrimental to traditional religion. Just how easy was the transfer from Socinian to Deist in the minds of Locke's contemporaries is amply illustrated by John Witty's *The Reasonableness of Assenting to the Mysteries of Christianity* (1707). Lockean principles again figure prominently in his accusations.

> And whereas the Deists would teach us to infer, that because *Ideas are the sole Foundation of our Knowledge and Assent*, therefore *we can't assent to any thing which we have not an immediate Idea of*, and would thence invalidate the reasonableness of our *assent* to *Christian Mysteries* ... (p. 34).

[1] *A Free Discourse concerning Truth and Error* (1701), p. 87.
[2] Ibid., p. 423.   [3] Ibid., pp. 423–4.

Not only did Witty consider the basing of all knowledge upon the way of ideas essential to Deism, but the doctrine of the unknowability of substance is evidenced as an example of the type of vague inferences from ideas allowed by the Deists.

> And thus having Ideas of the inherent Attributes of *Matter*, and *thinking Substances*, and of their necessary dependence on *something* as a support of their Existence, we infer and assent to the Existence of the *Substances* which support them; though what those *Substances* are in their intrinsic Natures we are entirely ignorant. (Ibid.)

Witty had very little sympathy for this kind of guarded inference.

> For the *Socinians* and *Deists* to come over us here with their darling Sophism, that because *Ideas are the sole Foundation of our Knowledge and assent, therefore we can know, or assent to nothing which we have not an immediate Idea of,* is only to shew their assurance; for you see clearly that we have Knowledge of the Existence and different Natures of things, whose intrinsic Natures, or the real *manner of Existence* we have no Ideas of at all; ... (p. 37).

The doctrines which Witty attacked as being both Socinian and deistic were some of the more crucial epistemological doctrines of Locke's *Essay*. One of the opponents Witty had in mind in this attack was Anthony Collins, the friend and follower of Locke. Charles Leslie, writing anonymously in 1707, said that Collins was a champion of the Deists and desired 'no better a Character, than to be thought a true Disciple and Follower of Mr. *Lock* in all his Notions, how erroneous soever they may be thought by some *People*'.[1] Collins was avowedly a defender of free-thinking, his name for what commonly went under the label of Deism, and a champion of many Lockean principles. One of his earliest works, *An Essay Concerning the Use of Reason* (1707), laid down the basic pattern of theory for his thinking. In that work, he defined reason as '*that faculty of the Mind whereby it perceives the Truth, Falsehood, Probability or Improbability of Propositions*', asserting after Locke that all 'Propositions whatever consist of Terms or Words which stand for Ideas

---

[1] *The Second Part of The Wolf Stript of His Shepherds Cloathing*, p. 25.

concerning which some agreement is affirm'd or deny'd ...'
(pp. 3–4). He proceeded to prescribe the general distinctions
between intuitive and demonstrative knowledge which Locke
had made in his *Essay*. 'There are some Ideas join'd in Propositions which the Mind perceives to agree or disagree
immediately or intuitively without the use of Proof or intermediate Ideas to discover that agreement or disagreement ...'
(p. 4). Demonstrative knowledge demands intermediate ideas
in order to find the agreement or lack of agreement which
exists between the propositions and the terms which are
involved in the deduction. Collins also recognized a category
of probable agreement, paralleling Locke's discussions of
probability. His main concern in this work was with establishing the rational grounds upon which knowledge through
testimony could be accepted, since he was concerned with the
validity of the Scriptures and of the facts which they claimed
to report. The general dictum covering assent is once more
taken from the *Essay* of Locke.

> Upon the Mind's perceiving the agreement or disagreement of Ideas
> immediately or by the intervention of Ideas, which have a necessary or
> probable agreement, or by the help of Testimony, there follows an
> Assent of the Mind, which is different according to the different nature
> of the Evidence, whereby the Ideas join'd in a Proposition seem to agree
> or disagree (p. 6).

He distinguishes science, opinion, and faith as degrees of
assent. Besides a trustworthy witness, several other conditions
are required for rational assent to knowledge given by
testimony.

> That the words made use of in the *Relation* stand for known Ideas, or
> Ideas that we are capable of forming; for if they stand for Ideas that we
> know not, or want Faculties to perceive, there are then no objects for the
> Mind to exert it self upon (p. 8).

Moreover, the correlation of words and ideas must occur as
far as possible in accordance with normal usage. Finally, there
cannot be any contradiction between the ideas thus joined
by the person giving the testimony. 'I must not only have
Ideas to the words, but the Ideas must not be repugnant to

one another when put into Propositions nor to what we *know* to be true by the use of our Faculties' (p. 11). Throughout all this discussion, perception is made the criterion of truth.

> If there is a *Criterion*, I desire to know what it is? I know no other but *Perception*: for tho Truth abstractly consider'd consists in the relations of agreement between Ideas; yet being here consider'd relatively to human Understanding, it is not my Truth till I perceive it, nor can I know it to be true but by my own Perception (p. 12).

Witty had complained against Collins's definition of knowledge and then proceeded to attack several other Lockean principles as deistical. Collins had attempted to defend against Clarke Locke's suggestion of matter being able to be given the power of thought, another doctrine considered deistical. In the same year as his previously mentioned book, Witty published another, *The First Principles of Modern Deism Confuted* (1707), in which he sought to show, in opposition to those whom he considered Deists, the immateriality, natural eternity, and immortality of thinking substances, even granting the Deists' assumption that the internal essence of substances is unknown. It is significant, too, that Witty claims in his preface to have had most of this book written before the Clarke–Collins dispute on this question appeared. Thus, he was ascribing these principles to the Deists independently of Collins's application of them. William Carroll had, in the previous year, strongly insisted that both Toland and Tindal were directly inspired by Locke.

> Here are the Titles of some of them [the books by Locke and his followers], *viz. The Reasonableness of Christianity*: and *Christianity not Mysterious*. Those two Titles are different in Sound, but agree in Sense; ... Another Book is lately publish'd, Intituled, *The Rights of the Christian Church*, &c.[1]

The last-named book was written by Mathew Tindal, in 1706, a work which, Carroll charged, 'has been writ by a Gentleman, or a Set of Gentlemen mislead by the Principles establish'd in the *Essay of Human Understanding*.'[2] Tindal

---

[1] *A Dissertation upon the Tenth Chapter of the Fourth Book of Mr. Locke's Essay* 1706), p. 276.   [2] Ibid., p. 277.

had corresponded with Locke concerning an earlier work of his, probably his *Essay Concerning the Power of the Magistrate and The Rights of Mankind in Matters of Religion* (1697), a book concerned with matters of toleration. Tindal sent Locke a copy of this work, expressing his indebtedness to Locke's writings on the same subject.[1] But the only Lockean doctrines present in Tindal's *The Rights of the Christian Church* are the doctrines of a social contract and of a state of nature, neither of which stems from the *Essay*. Collins had pointed out in his *A Discourse of Free-Thinking* (1713) that 'the Reverend Dr. Clarke, and the Reverend Mr. Samuel Bold, and Mr. John Locke are charg'd with Atheism by the Reverend Mr. Carrol' (p. 85), on the ground that they had made the material universe to be the eternal Being or God. It was against such 'Men of Matter and Modification' that George Hickes wrote in his preface to Carroll's *Spinoza Reviv'd* (1709); he described the doctrine of thinking matter as deistical, along with many other principles of the *Essay*. Praising Milner's attack upon Locke, Hickes said:

> The Person who wrote this little Book, was one of the first Magnitude for Learning, much exceeding Mr. *Lock* in Intellectual Acquirements, and not inferior to him in any Intellectual Abilities; and had it been Mr. *Lock's* good Fortune but to have had a good share of his Learning, he had never written those Books, and Letters, for which, to his Ever-lasting Dishonour, the *Deists*, as it were, Canonize his Memory (p. [35] of Prelim. Discourse).

Lee's *Anti-Scepticism* received similar praise from Hickes in the same preface.

> While I am speaking of Books written against Mr. *Lock*, I should be unjust to the Merits of another Priest, the Rev. Mr. *Lee*, should I forbear to mention his Antiscepticism. . . . I am perswaded, had Mr. *Lock* foreseen, that such a Book would have been written against his Essay, he would never have wrote *that*, and if he read it before he dyed, *it* must needs have been Matter of Grief, if not of Humiliation to him, to see his Book, which all the *Atheists*, and *Deists*, and *Scepticks* of the Age cried up for a Performance above whatever had been done by any Philosopher, so perfectly demolished from part to part; . . . (p. [36]).

[1] See Tindal to Locke, 10 January 1696/7, MS. Locke, C. 20, f. 207.

Tindal's *The Rights of the Christian Church* is called deistical, and Hickes makes the charge, repeated by Carroll, that Locke had seen this work in manuscript, a charge for which there seems to be no further evidence. In his preface to his own *Three Short Treatises* (1709), Hickes repeated many of the same accusations: this time tracing the growth of Deism in England to Spinoza. Toland's book and Locke's *Reasonableness of Christianity* are listed among the ten most important deistical books.

Locke was not entirely without his defenders against these various charges of being a Deist or being influential among the Deists. In his review of *Spinoza Reviv'd*, LeClerc scorned to reply to Carroll's ill-mannered attacks upon Locke, pointing to Locke's works as sufficient refutation of these malicious remarks.[1] Especially in relation to Carroll and Hickes, it is wise to keep in mind a point which Jessop has recently made, namely, that there were in general two main sources of dissemination for the deist doctrine in the seventeenth and eighteenth centuries: in the serious books and pamphlets of the day and in the drawing-rooms, coffee-houses, and taverns. In the latter 'it was less decent than it was in books'.[2] Jessop writes to prevent the reader of Berkeley's *Alciphron* from concluding that Berkeley has caricatured the Deists in that work. Undoubtedly some of the more vehement attacks upon the Deists arose from the extravagances of the coffee-house discussions. The mistake which men like Carroll and Hickes made was to write as if the serious writers, such as Locke and Tindal, were advocates of frivolous doctrines like those held by the coffee-house frequenters. LeClerc was certainly just in his condemnation of the method of polemic followed by Hickes and Carroll, insisting that even if Deism was so rampant as these men believed, 'il vaudroit mieux les réfuter, avec plus de calme'.[3] William Whiston also sought to protect Locke from the charges of Deism.

---

[1] *Bibliothèque Choisie*, t. xxi, pt. i, art. ii, pp. 38–39.
[2] Berkeley's *Works*, vol. iii, Editor's introduction to *Alciphron*, p. 6.
[3] Op. cit., p. 39.

Since Mr. *Lock* is here and every where esteem'd an eminent *Free-Thinker*; and that not seldom in the irreligious sense of the Words; nay has been very often esteem'd no better than a *Deist*; I shall here, by way of Vindication of his Memory, and in Hopes that his Authority may make some Impression on all of us, and particularly on the real irreligious *Free Thinkers* themselves, produce unquestionable Evidence of his fixed and last Sentiments about such Matters, from his own Words in two Letters to two of his intimate Friends.[1]

He then quotes from two letters of Locke, the one so briefly as to preclude identification, the other to Collins.[2] But Whiston found little evidence for vindicating Locke from the charges of Deism since the most these quoted passages reveal is that Locke died with a firm conviction in immortality, a doctrine which very few of the Deists ever denied. Edmund Gibson, the Bishop of London, later in the century tried to defend Locke in a similar fashion,[3] but an anonymous writer as late as 1742 published a strong invective, *A Dissertation on Deistical and Arian Corruption*, in which Lockean doctrines once more appear as the foundation for Deism. Part of the blame for the development of Deism, Socinianism, and Arianism, this writer claimed, stems from their inability to distinguish mind from matter, having in mind the Lockean doctrine of substance. The doctrine of ideas as advanced in the *Essay* is taken in a sensualist sense and is then described as a fundamental tenet of the Deists and Arians. John Jackson, an ardent follower of Locke, and Whiston, oddly enough, are charged with being the main leaders of Deism. It was this writer also who defended the doctrine of innate ideas against Jackson and Locke.[4]

§ 2—*The Orthodox Application of Locke's Epistemology*

There can be no doubt that Locke was charged directly with being a Deist by many, and by others with at least being a sympathiser with Deism, and that his doctrines were

---

[1] *Reflexions on an Anonymous Pamphlet, Entituled, A Discourse of Free Thinking* (1713), p. 55.
[2] Locke to Collins, 23 August 1704. Reprinted in *Works*, vol. x, p. 298.
[3] *Second Pastoral Letter* (1730), pp. 5, 6, 35.
[4] Cf. above, p. 71.

considered by most theologians as fundamental to this new movement. The digression concerning the possibility of matter being given a power of thought; the doctrine of substance so carefully circumscribed by the limitations of human knowledge: the entire way of ideas or the method of the ideists insinuated itself into the naturalistic tendencies in religion and found a fertile soil in which to thrive. But the growth of the way of ideas within orthodoxy was no less luxuriant than among the Deists, even though in the case of orthodoxy it worked towards more gradual modifications. With Deism, religion found its anarchists, its advocates for quick and radical changes; the epistemological tools of the *Essay* provided, often unconsciously, means to effect a more gradual revolution in the same direction for many traditional thinkers. In fact, the most careful applications of the Lockean epistemology are to be found among the theologians who were seeking to undermine Deism and Socinianism in the name of tradition. Some of these orthodox writers employed Lockean principles as a means of granting certain doctrines invoked by the Deists, in order, as Witty attempted to show, to derive conclusions antithetical to Deism. Berkeley's modification of Locke's epistemology is the best-known instance of the way of ideas being put to the service of tradition, but many lesser-known writers offer even more interesting examples, since these men often accepted the Lockean position without modification.[1] Locke's doctrines were so much invoked by deistical writers that the defenders of tradition were forced to argue that these doctrines need not be taken as premisses for the deistical conclusions. It was most often the men who were opposing Deism the most vociferously who adopted in detail other Lockean doctrines which, in different contexts, they would have considered deistical. But many men of the period employed Locke's doctrines in the service of tradition quite directly, apparently finding in the way of ideas an estab-

---

[1] Berkeley will not be examined in any detail in this study, but it is useful to recall that, besides the *Alciphron*, which was written explicitly with the Deists as the object of attack, his epistemological treatises were written to combat scepticism and atheism and to establish the incorporeal nature of the human soul.

lished approach convenient to their beliefs. I have already indicated in some detail the extent to which William Sherlock absorbed the doctrine of substance and that of personal identity in the very year that the *Essay* first appeared. The doctrine of substance was used by Sherlock to defend his version of the doctrine of the Trinity. James Lowde, who attacked Locke's rejection of innate sources of knowledge in his *A Discourse Concerning the Nature of Man* (1694), also sought to combat the suggestion that immateriality is not necessary for the immortality of the soul. But like so many who attacked this digression, Lowde took over without question the non-phenomenalistic doctrine of substance of the *Essay*.

But the Essences of things being unknown, the Notion of a Spirit seems as obvious and intelligible, as that of matter: for we may as easily conceive of one thing, to which we attribute cogitation, as its immediate property; as we do of another, to which we ascribe extension and impenetrability (p. 15).

In his defence of the Christian mysteries against Toland, William Payne, *The Mystery of the Christian Faith* (1697), not only accepted the Lockean doctrine of substance, but adopted as well the terminology of ideas and Locke's belief in the limitations of human knowledge.

Now nothing in our own minds, or in visible Nature is perfectly like these [the three parts of the Trinity] or to which we can compare them, or from whence we can draw a Similitude, Representation, or Idea of them, and therefore they are Incomprehensible, and Unconceivable by us, for 'tis by Comparison, and likeness we chiefly know, and conceive things, and 'tis hard to distinguish between Knowledge, Conception, and Imagination; so that what some persons cannot imagine, or cannot have a picture or likeness of in their Fancy, and Imagination, they say they cannot conceive, and therefore some pretend they can have no Conceptions of a Spiritual Substance, and others no Idea of the Trinity, nor even of God, by which they mean they cannot have a Picture or Idea, or likeness of these things in their Imagination (pp. 33–34; cf. pp. 18–23).

Among the theologians who adopted the terminology of ideas, it was common to interpret the term 'idea' as Sergeant and Peter Browne did, as 'image'. Hence, Payne can argue in defence of religion and its mysteries by saying that an image is not necessary for a concept or idea taken in its proper sense. Knowledge and imagination are sharply distinguished. He argues that the doctrine of the Trinity is above reason in the sense that it is incomprehensible in its entirety even after revelation: it is a 'Truth and an object by it self, made known to us purely by Revelation, and such a Complex Idaea or Connexion of Idaeas that we have no other Idaea, Similitude or Representation that exactly answers or comes perfectly up to' this idea or conception of the Trinity (p. 40). As in the writings of Sherlock, the man whom Payne defended against Robert South, Locke's doctrines here again appear in the context of strictly religious issues. Against South's attempts to make the intrinsic nature of matter accessible to human knowledge, Payne pleaded for the unknowability of its nature or its real essence, saying that

we know nothing of that but its outward accidents and a few of its qualities, its colour and figure, and hardness or softness, or the like, but its inward substance, and what is the subject and *Substratum* of these accidents and qualities we know nothing of. How the parts of Matter are united, what makes them so close and inseparable in a solid Stone...is unknown to us; ... (pp. 43–44).

Indeed, Payne did not profess to be able to account for much of the perceptual process which is ancillary to knowledge:

how any of our Senses perceive these Objects, and how we have such Conceptions and Phantasms raised in us by them, which are not in the Objects themselves, (for Bitter and Sweet, Pain and Pleasure, Heat and Cold is not in any of them, nor any thing like them, but only in our selves) and by what secret Powers they excite those Sentiments is as unaccountable as it is obvious (pp. 44–45).

Throughout Payne's long defence of tradition, even though it was a tradition modified in the direction of Sherlock's 'Tri-Trinitarianism', there is no mention of Locke. But the stamp of Locke's epistemology is clearly visible on many pages of his work. The same phenomenon appears in Francis Gastrell's *Some Considerations Concerning the Trinity* (1696), in large part a reply to Toland's *Christianity not Mysterious*.

Toland caused many theologians to reassess their own doctrines and to meet the challenge he had thrown out, a challenge which could not be answered merely by repeating the old verbiage and the customary ambiguous statements concerning the Trinity. Browne developed his doctrine of analogy, as applied to our knowledge of trans-empirical objects, in order to meet Toland's challenge. Gastrell absorbed an unusually large amount of Locke's terminology and doctrines in his attempt to meet Toland's attack and to conciliate the opposing groups. One of the basic distinctions Gastrell invoked for this purpose was that between what can be distinctly conceived and what must be taken on faith. Regarding the latter, he says there are two general conditions requisite: 'That we know the Terms of what we are to assent to' and 'That it imply no contradiction to our former Knowledge' (p. 10), conditions which Collins was to accept later, in his account of the prerequisites for accepting testimony. Gastrell defines truth as 'nothing else but the *agreement or disagreement of its* [a proposition's] *Terms, or the Ideas* expressed by them' (p. 11). Certainty of knowledge and belief is correlated with clarity of the understanding of the terms of the propositions involved. 'From whence it follows, that *Terms* and *simple Idea's* must be *clearly* and *distinctly* understood first, before we can believe any thing *particular* of the *respects* and *relations* they bear to one another, which is the only *proper Object of Faith*' (p. 12). Like Locke, he accepts the doctrine of simple and complex ideas, the former being defined as those 'which are so clear of themselves, that I cannot find clearer to explain them by' (p. 15), or as those 'not distinguishable into different Appearances' (p. 17). Complex ideas are taken in the same strict fashion: 'When I have any Thought or Perception, which is resolvable into several *Idea's*, I call this a *complex* or *compounded Notion*.' (Ibid.) The way of ideas is writ large throughout his treatise.

For this is certain, that every Man is conscious to himself, that he has a power of *perceiving* and *comparing his Perceptions*, and consequently must know, when any thing is presented to his Mind, whether it be perceivable at *one entire view*, and whether the Object have one *uniform appearance* or not: He must be also sensible in a succession of *Idea's*, when the *same* Appearances are *repeated* again, and how often the Representation is *varied* (p. 15).

He goes on in this context to argue that one cannot infer from the variety of ideas to a variety of things without us, or from the sameness of ideas to the sameness of things. The doctrine of nominal essence, the theory of sorting, and the limitations of knowledge to the phenomenalist level are made integral to Gastrell's argument.

> Whether *my Idea's* are agreeable to the *real Natures of things*, or those *Original Patterns* in the Mind of God, I cannot certainly know; but when they are the *same*, and when they differ from one another, I plainly perceive, tho' I cannot always judge of the *Identity* or *Distinction* of Things, according as they are represented to my understanding, under the *same* or *different* Appearances (pp. 17–18).

A 'spirit' is defined as being indivisible, without extension, but he agrees that we can have no idea of the real nature of spirit: 'for all that I conceive, is only several *Idea's* of different particular Actions, which no more express the *Idea* of that Principle from whence they spring, than the *Idea's* of several particular Lines express the *Idea* of that Point they are drawn from'. (Ibid.) The concept of substance which we are able to form is constructed from our experiences, a construction which he feels enables us to approximate to the real essence of the substance in question.

> On the other side, the *real Natures*, and *Essences of Things*, which are allowed to consist in a *simple undivided Unity*, are not conceivable by us at once, but at *different Views*, by *different partial Conceptions*, which the Soul afterwards compounds and calls by *one Name*. Thus when we endeavour to comprehend the Nature and Essence of what we call *Man*, we form, at different times, several confused Notions of *Substance*, *Body*, *Life*, *Sense*, and *Reason*; every one of which is a *complicated Idea*, and to be resolved into a great many others more simple and distinct (p. 16).

The emphasis upon such approximation to real essences through experiental construction is not strong: he is content to rest upon Locke's nominal essence.

With these Lockean doctrines as his fundamental theoretical framework, Gastrell deals with the problem of the Trinity, suggesting that in the doctrine of the Trinity we are merely conceiving of the same idea, i.e. of God, in three different ways. At the same time Gastrell confessed that there is more in this concept than the human mind is able˜to comprehend; thereby he avoided a direct denial of the more traditional interpretations. The twofold analysis of a phenomenalistic and a non-phenomenalistic aspect of substance is thus applied to the Trinitarian controversy as a means of resolving the opposing arguments. As in the work of Payne, so in Gastrell's writing there is no mention of Locke. It is accordingly difficult to determine whether these two men were aware that they were using Locke's epistemology, although it would be equally difficult to believe that they could have incorporated so much of the *Essay* into their writings unconsciously. The three men most immediately involved in this application of Lockean principles—Sherlock, Payne, and Gastrell—presented within tradition a definite modification, but a modification which was still made in opposition to Deism, Socinianism, and Unitarianism. Gastrell could very easily have been one of the new men of ideas about whom Stillingfleet and Sergeant complained, although he is never explicitly mentioned. Carroll and Hickes, however, came to consider him as belonging to Locke's camp, in league with the Deists and Socinians.[1] In a later work, *The Certainty and Necessity of Religion in General* (1697), his Boyle lectures for that year, Gastrell argued at length against the doctrine of matter being able to move itself or to think, adding several other Lockean doctrines to his long list.

Now our *Existence* being granted, the same Consciousness that satisfied us of this, if we carefully attend to what passes within us, will farther inform us, that we are capable of *Thinking, Perceiving,* and *Knowing*; which Capacity. is usually stiled *Understanding*; and that we have a Power of *determining* our selves to *Think* and *not to Think*, or Perceive and not Perceive certain Objects or Ideas . . . (p. 9).

[1] Cf. Hickes's Preliminary Discourse to Carroll's *Spinoza Reviv'd.*

On intuitive knowledge he also clearly follows Locke: 'there are some Ideas or Notions that appear with that Light and. Clearness to our Understandings, that we immediately perceive them in all their Extent, and a necessary Agreement or Disagreement betwixt them, and afterwards the Dependance or Independance of others upon them; . . .' (p. 13; cf. p. 43). The corpuscular theory of perception, elaborated by Boyle and Locke alike, was also accepted by Gastrell. All sensible appearances of body are said to suppose a substance and to come from bulk, number, figure, motion and rest of matter.

> *Solidity*, *Extension*, and *Figure*, I do not only perceive to be *constantly united*, but *necessarily* and *inseparably* to co-exist together in the same *Subject*, which I call *Matter* or *Body*; so that, wherever any one of *these* is found, I certainly conclude from thence, that there are the *other two* also; . . . (p. 60).

Gastrell furnishes one of the more interesting examples of a positive application of Locke's epistemology made by theologians, both in the clarity and in the extent of his adaptation. But there were other men appearing in the first years of the eighteenth century who borrowed from Locke. As we have already seen, Charles Gildon, in *The Deist's Manual* (1705), sought to combat the materialism of Coward; but the twofold source of knowledge, which Locke had made basic in his philosophy, was accepted by Gildon. In the dialogue form in which he presents his ideas, Gildon made one of his characters inquire: 'Whence came you by the knowledge of its [the soul's] *Immortality*? From outward *Sensation*, or inward *Reflection*?' (p. 146). He went on to develop this distinction in some detail.

> There are different ways, by which the Knowledge of Things is convey'd to us, for we know not every thing in the same Manner, or by the same Means. Some we know by the Mediation or Intervention of the Senses: Such are all Corporeal Objects, which make their Approach to the Understanding, by striking on our Senses. Others we know by the Abstraction of the Mind; when we Contemplate and consider the Ideas, that are plac'd in the View of the Mind, without any External Architype which they are like; . . . (p. 155).

'Idea' is sometimes made equivalent to 'image'. The knowledge of self is said to be direct, without the intervention of ideas.

> Thus that *Thinking Substance* within us, which we call the *Soul* or the *Mind*, finds many things Extrinsick to it self, which, as certain Objects, it can consider, survey, and contemplate as it pleases: And besides these, it observes what passes within it self, or is, in other Words, *Conscious of it self* (p. 156).

'Soul' is defined as 'a *Being*, or *Substance, that has Perception, Thought, Will, Reasoning, is Free, and the like*' (p. 157). The definition of knowledge, made famous by Locke, reappears here also; and, like Collins, Gildon concerns himself with the problem of psychological assent: 'When we enquire into the Truth by a Comparison of various Ideas, while they remain so obscure, that we cannot plainly discover their Relation to one another, we sometimes keep them longer under our Consideration' (p. 159). The objective of such deliberation is to gain time in order to discover, if possible, the precise connexion which obtains between these ideas, since assent depends upon the apprehension of the connexion of ideas. 'We must observe, That when our Mind considers Ideas, where Relations to each other have attain'd the highest Perspicuity, we cannot deny our Assent to the Propositions the Mind forms out of them' (p. 161). The representative function of ideas was not developed in much detail by Gildon, although he indicates that he accepted this much of the Lockean epistemology with confidence.

As a champion of traditional religion, John Witty offers a more detailed analysis of the representative nature of ideas. He opens his *The First Principles of Modern Deism Confuted* (1707) with the observation that there are two possible ways in which man can gain knowledge of things: either by knowing the essences of objects and being able *a priori* to deduce their properties, or *a posteriori* by knowing their properties and being able to infer their causes (pp. 1–4). Both ways are concerned with ideas. 'For not the Things themselves, but their *Ideas in us*, are the immediate Objects of Human Understanding in its search after Truth' (p. 4). He briefly develops, in this opening section, the other aspects of the Lockean theory of knowledge: its extension through the combining, separating, comparing, &c., of ideas, distinguishing also intuitive from demonstrative knowledge. Ideas are divided into simple and complex; simple ideas enter the mind through sensation, from which we gain our knowledge of the outside world, and through reflection, from which we gain knowledge of the 'little world within'.

> These *simple Ideas* of whatever Nature, and whether acquir'd from *Sensation*, or *Reflection*, or *both*; whether from one Sense, or more than one; or from *Sensation* and *Reflection* in composition, I reduce under the *first Class* of the Objects of Human Knowledge (p. 17).

Complex ideas comprise the second class of objects of knowledge, while those inferred objects of which we have no immediate ideas (e.g. substance and God) constitute a subclass of complex ideas. He proceeds to develop the entire epistemological structure of Locke's work: the definition of knowledge, the four kinds of agreement and disagreement, &c. Like Gastrell and Browne, Witty sought to make the restriction of analysis to the phenomenalist or nominal level consistent with the necessary inferences of religion concerning non-empirical objects. Accordingly, he had to support the doctrine that causal inferences could be made from known phenomena, taken as effects, to unknown causes.

> From *Effects* of which we have Ideas, we infer *Causes* of which we have often no Ideas, and that *demonstratively*; having no less certain a Foundation for their Existence than this uncontrovertible axiom; That *nothing can't be the Foundation of the Existence or* Operations of any thing: From *Gravitation*, which effects Matter universally as such, we infer a Cause from whence this Effect proceeds, and that as infallibly as we are assur'd by immediate Ideas from *Sensation*, that Matter does actually *gravitate*; . . . (pp. 25–26).

In other words,

> From Extension, Solidity, Figure, Colour, &c. united in one Subject, we infer the *Subject* in which they are united; and that unexceptionably, without any necessity of having an Idea of Matter as it is in it self, or of the inmost Nature of the *Substance* of *Corporeal Being* (p. 27).

But in accepting this doctrine, and in employing the entire

theory of representative perception as well, Witty had to meet, as Locke did, the objection that our knowledge by means of ideas might not be real. By seeking to show that our ideas correctly represent their originals, his intention was to be able to infer from the inconsistency of the ideas of thought and extension to the inconsistency of their existing in reality together; but in trying to illuminate this aspect of the way of ideas, Witty actually modified his previous contention that causal inferences from effects to causes can be made in the absence of any specific information concerning the nature of the cause. The inferences are not made in such a vacuum as he led his readers at first to suppose, but are conducted within a presuppositional context which, if true, lends a large degree of determinateness to the inferred cause. The presupposition involved, if capable of verification, would also lend credence to his belief in the inconsistency between thought and extension. His argument is twofold. (1) Since 'every thing acts necessarily according to its respective Nature', that of which I am conscious in reflection, namely, thinking, self-activity, &c., must correctly represent the act (p. 122). That '*Thought* which makes me conscious, or gives me a reflex *Idea* of my *Thinking*, must make me conscious, or give me a reflex Idea of what I am doing when I *think*; . . .' (p. 123). (2) In the second place, the Cartesian assumption is invoked: 'we can't suppose, that the *primary* Attributes of Things are otherwise in our *Ideas*, than they are in the Things themselves without admitting at the same time, that God has put an invincible deceit upon our Facultys . . .' (Ibid.) Witty did not feel constrained to prove the presupposition of the second argument, but he did seek to support the first. The support which is offered, however, only invokes another series of similarly unsupported presuppositions.

For as nothing can give what it has not, any more than an Effect can be produc'd without a Cause, accordingly nothing can do what is out of its *Power*; but what *Power* any thing has it receives from its respective *Essence* and *Nature*, therefore nothing can act otherwise than according to its respective *Nature*: . . . (p. 125).

Not only does everything refrain from doing what is not in its power, but everything does all that is in its power. To the objection that objects appear to be different under different conditions, and that therefore we have no basis from which to infer the nature of objects in themselves, Witty replies that, though the specific extension may vary, the fact of extension itself never varies. This invariance shows the constancy of the basic qualities of objects (pp. 131–2). To the objection that secondary qualities show that bodies do not always reveal their true natures, Witty argues that bodies reveal themselves through qualities in so far as they can, thus reverting once more to the presupposition of the first argument noted above. He was determined to adhere to the representative theory, while avoiding the scepticism which Locke's earlier critics had disclosed as implicit in that position.

I grant that *Light* and other *secondary* Qualitys have nothing in Bodys in any Measure corresponding to our *Sensations* of 'em; and it must be granted by all, that the *Specific* Powers and Propertys of Bodys are, generally speaking, infinitely too subtle and fine to *represent* themselves *as they are in themselves* to us by the *Mediation* of our gross Organs: But then does it hence follow that, because they can't *represent* themselves to us at all, therefore they don't necessarily represent *themselves*, as far as they can come within the Verge of the finest Senses, according to their Natures, to such Creatures whose organs are fine enough to be affected with their Operations? No such Matter (p. 141).

Witty did not agree with those who held what he called the 'inherent quality' doctrine, which is in reality the position of naïve realism. He may have had men like Sergeant in mind at this point.

And as for those who hold the *inherent-quality* Doctrin, and accordingly maintain that there is heat in the Fire, light in the Sun, &c. adaequately the same as in our Sensations; these Men can't make the Objection I have now answer'd, nor any at all: Inasmuch as they assume not only what I contend for, but much more; not only that the *Primary* but the *Specific* Propertys of Things are in Bodys what they appear in our *Sensations* and *Ideas*; meaning by those Specific Propertys those very Sensations, or something of the like Nature with 'em, which indeed the *secondary* Attributes of Bodys are only the *occasional* Causes of (p. 147).

The same wholesale acceptance of the way of ideas and of the representative theory of perception is found in Joshua Oldfield's *An Essay towards the Improvement of Reason* (1707). This work is a rambling attempt at a comprehensive programme for the advancement of learning, from an analysis of logic and grammar to the examination of the meanings of many terms used in common discourse. The Lockean epistemology is found throughout, sometimes in a slightly garbled language but nevertheless, when it is untangled, clearly borrowed from Locke. Oldfield begins much in the fashion of Witty, by declaring that 'It is very certain, that we know nothing of Things, but as we consciously Perceive, Imagine, or Conceive them', insisting that even in the case of touch and taste, what we immediately attend to is the sensible perception and not the thing itself (pp. 2–3). The word 'tho't' occurs in many places as a substitution for 'idea', e.g. 'Tho't may be consider'd, either absolutely in it self, as what is consciously known, or relatively, as what is understood to refer to somewhat else, whereof it brings the Representations or Report to our Minds: . . .' (p. 3). The representative theory of perception is made one of the basic principles of his system. In fact, Oldfield takes great care to warn his readers against mistaking 'tho'ts' for things.

We commonly overlook the Tho'ts, and our Minds run directly to the Things, whereof we think, so that Tho'ts are generally to our Consideration instead of the Things themselves; and we suppose our selves to consider this or that Thing in it self immediately and directly, when as we cannot possibly take any Cognizance thereof, but under those sensible Perceptions, imaginative Representations, or intellectual Conceptions, which are to us the Natural and Internal Signs of Things, as they are, some way or other objected to our Minds, and sometimes, only, by the Operation of the Phansie, or by the Intellect, conjoining, dividing, and variously disposing, what has been otherwise taken in (p. 4).

Perceptions or thoughts are not always resemblances of things, but they are always notices of something in things. Seeking to overcome some of the opposition to Locke's rejection of innate ideas, Oldfield argues that

Tho' it appears not that we have any innate Ideas, or formed Notions or Principles laid in by Nature, antecedently to the exercise of our Senses and Understandings; yet it must be granted, that we were born with the Natural Faculty, whereby we actually discern the agreement or disagreement of some Notions, so soon as we have the Notions themselves; . . . (p. 5. Cf. p. 7).

He divides his analysis, after the manner of Witty, into a consideration of the ideal or intellectual world, under which he discusses such questions as 'what our Notions or Ideas in themselves are; to what object they refer', and the objective or real world. The ultimate goal of his essay is to lead man to a knowledge of God. Throughout, apprehension, notions, or ideas are made the medium of all thought and of all knowledge.

That other Things cannot be th'ot of by us, but as they are *inwardly presented* in some or other Idea, viz. As perceiv'd imagin'd or conceiv'd: So that the more immediate Object of our Consideration is not properly the very Thing it self without us, but the inward Apprehension we have of it: . . . (p. 8).

The reality of knowledge is advanced (1) by the coherence of various sensations and (2) by invoking the principle that something in the cause was fitted to lead to the idea-effect. Like many other men of the period, Oldfield accepts the Lockean doctrine of substance in its non-phenomenalistic aspect, finding in this doctrine no antithesis to religion nor to the reality of knowledge.

And whereas our Idea of the Substance, in it self consider'd, is very dark and indistinct, being only, that general one of Thing or Somewhat, and this amounting to no more than that it is an Object of Tho't; therefore to help out the Idea, as we can, we consider, that whatever *the Substance* be in it self, it has unquestionably these general Characters, *viz.* (1) That it stands . . . not subjected in another . . . and (2) That it sustains the Form or Make, whereby it is a Being of such a kind, or sort . . . (p. 51).

He recognized the commitments this theory implied for him because of the indirectness of our knowledge.

Reason can tell us somewhat about our sensible Perceptions, as (E. Gr.) that many of them are to be accounted the Effect of some unknown Make and Texture of the sensible Objects, together with some impressed Force, rather than that this should be generally taken for the

Representations or Resemblances of what is subjected in the Thing perceived ... and yet that some of them, especially the Ideas taken in by the Eye, may well be tho't in some sort to represent the Object, particularly as to the External Figure and Shape of the visible Body (p. 160).

He saw the need for developing a theory of signs: 'The matter of every Sign, is always the Subject of a *Relation* to the Thing Signify'd; and all our common Ideas (which are Internal Signs) are plainly so many *Abstractions* from the distinguishing Forms and Characters of Things' (p. 89). He proceeded to develop a fairly detailed theory of meaning, taking into account the expressive character of signs and recognizing many different types of signs, including gestures and music. Oldfield also discusses ideas under the headings of adequate and inadequate, clear and distinct, simple and complex.

Of the two men, Witty and Oldfield, the former was by far the better student of Locke's doctrines. Oldfield's work is poorly written and organized, attempting too much in its comprehension. But both men put the Lockean epistemology to work in the service of religion: Oldfield in a rather nebulous manner and for no specified sectarian purposes, Witty quite openly in his defence of tradition against Deism. Gastrell and Payne had similarly applied the same epistemology in attempts to conciliate the two sides in the dispute over the nature or necessity of the doctrine of the Trinity in religious belief. Peter Browne was perhaps more critical than positive in his approach to Locke's *Essay*, but his *The Procedure, Extent, and Limits of Human Understanding* (1728) constitutes a careful development of one side of the Lockean position, i.e. its sensationalist side. This work was an extension, in its logical details, of his earlier attack against Toland, an attack which presaged his later distinction between ideas and notions, as well as the doctrine that non-empirical knowledge proceeds by analogy. He makes it clear in the opening sections that he and other theologians of his acquaintance had found the doctrine of analogy, as applied to non-empirical knowledge, useful in combating Arians, Socinians, and Deists. (p. 8). He describes his design in this work as follows:

I purpose rightly to state the whole Extent and Limits of human Understanding; to trace out the several steps and degrees of its Procedure from our first and simple Perception of sensible Objects, thro' the several operations of the pure Intellect upon them; till it grows up to its full Proportion of Nature: And to shew, how all our Conceptions of things supernatural are then *grafted* on it by Analogy; and how from thence it extends it self immensely into all the Branches of Divine and Heavenly Knowledge (p. 33).

He holds that all knowledge is limited to what is obtained through our senses and our reason. It is through the senses that the 'Ideas of external sensible Objects are first conveyed into the *Imagination*' (p. 53). He shows the tendency, common in the early eighteenth century, of equating 'idea' with 'image', a tendency of interpreters of Locke which very likely arose out of the opposition which his emphasis upon empirical foundations for knowledge was believed to have to religion. A growing fashion admitted the value and legitimacy of the way of ideas in the restricted realm of sensitive knowledge, reserving for religion the more intellectual provinces of non-sensible knowledge. Browne agreed that the mind first thinks when it begins to sense; but the impressions that are made in this way, whatever be their exact relations with the objects external to the mind, are termed 'ideas'. He illustrates the meaning for the term 'idea' by asking the reader to direct his eyes towards a tree and try to ascertain, after he has closed his eyes, 'whether he retains any Similitude or Resemblance of what he saw; and if he finds any such within him, let him call that an Idea, till a better Word be found' (pp. 58–59). His emphasis on the imaginal character of ideas is lessened when he says that the only relationship required between idea and object is a representative one, that this relation 'answers all the *Ends* of Knowledge in this life' (p. 60). Moreover, he offers the following arguments, which could have been taken from Witty, in favour of the conclusion that the relation of 'belonging to' is one of similarity or resemblance: (1) it is in keeping with the wisdom of God to reveal to us the real natures of objects rather than the imaginary natures (pp. 61–62); (2) objects must operate on our senses 'according to their

own intrinsick Qualities' or their 'respective Nature' (p. 62);
and (3) all objects have the same effects upon the senses of all
men (p. 63). It is integral for Browne's central doctrine of
knowledge of divine things by analogy to limit the term 'idea'
to 'our simple Sensations only, and to the various Alterations
and Combinations of them by the pure Intellect'. (Ibid.) He
takes issue, in other words, with Locke's twofold origin of
ideas. 'Thus the laying down the Ideas of *Sensation* and *Reflection* to be *Alike* the *Original* Sources and Foundation of all
our Knowledge, is one great and fundamental Error which
runs thro' most of the Discourses and Essays of our modern
Writers of Logicks and Metaphysicks' (p. 64). He recognizes
thinking and willing to be the two chief operations of the
mind, arguing that we cannot have any 'ideas' of these operations: 'it is plain that *Thinking* and *Willing* . . . are not Ideas;
but the *Actions* and *Workings* of the Intellect upon *Ideas*'
(p. 65). Not only are the actions of the mind separate from the
conceptions we form of them, but they are not able to be the
subject of 'ideas' proper, since these are interpreted in sensualist terms. Much in the fashion of Malebranche, he argues that
we can have ideas only of objects external to us, preferring
to call our knowledge of the operations of our minds 'conceptions' or, in the fashion of Berkeley, 'notions'. The use of
the term 'idea' as applied to self-knowledge constitutes for
Browne the first step along the erroneous and misleading
road of useless distinctions: those of compound ideas, ideas
of simple modes, of power, of cause, &c.

Referring indirectly (as was his practice) to Locke as 'the
Standard and Oracle of Ideas in our Age' (p. 73), Browne
proceeds to argue (1) that the idea of a thinking matter is
absurd and shameful; (2) that we have more knowledge of
body than we have of spirit; (3) that we have no direct knowledge of spirits at all and especially of God; and (4) that we
do know something of the essential nature of such things as
man and stones. He makes a threefold distinction between
the ideas of sense, the necessary material for all thought,
which enter the mind at first without any intellectual activity;

innate ideas, which he rejects because they are absurd and not necessary; and the so-called ideas of reflection. The only way we come to self-knowledge is by 'an immediate *Consciousness* of the several different ways of its [the mind's] own working upon those Ideas of Sensation lodged in the Imagination' (p. 97). Knowledge of self is thus indirect. 'We have not even the least *Direct Idea* or Perception of the purely spiritual part of us; nor do we discern any more of its *Real Substance* than we do that of an Angel'. (Ibid.) But the necessity of avoiding the second use of the representative theory of perception, that of self-knowledge, in order to be able to maintain his doctrine of an indirect but valid knowledge of divine and non-empirical objects, leads him into a doctrine of the knowledge of the nature of the self strikingly akin to Locke's phenomenalistic doctrine of substance. 'We have no Knowledge of our own Spirit, or of any of its Faculties, but from a conscious Experience of its several Ways of acting upon the Ideas of Sensation' (p. 109). Moreover, when he starts elaborating the details of his doctrine of indirect or non-imaginal knowledge of self and spiritual substances, he finds it necessary to modify the indirectness in a fashion which comes close to destroying his fundamental distinction.

> For our *Conceptions* and Notions may be *Direct* or *Indirect*, as well as our *Ideas*. When they stand in the Mind for their proper and *Original* Objects, and when the Words that express them are taken *Literally* for such Objects, they are *Direct*. . . . But when they are *Substituted* to conceive, and do *Stand for* Divine Immaterial Things, then they become *Indirect* and *Analogical* (pp. 110–11).

Thus, he seems to have altered his position as stated earlier, now limiting the indirectness of spiritual knowledge to divine immaterial things, and placing the knowledge of self on a par with that of physical objects. When the indirectness of our knowledge of things divine is accomplished by means of words and ideas substituted for the objects themselves, our ideas function for Browne in a way not unlike the divine language of Berkeley's philosophy. Indeed, the ways in which Browne and Berkeley strove to meet Toland's challenge are not

so different as historians have been led to believe, despite the
controversy these two men had over the doctrine of analogy.
The way of ideas was modified by both men so as to draw a
firm distinction between ordinary knowledge of common-
sense objects and the special knowledge, demanded by
religion, of God and angels. Berkeley was much more successful in applying this distinction to knowledge of self as well as
to knowledge of God than was Browne; but on the knowledge
of divine objects, the essentials of the two points of view are
more or less the same. Browne went on to try to meet the
challenge of clear and distinct ideas contained in the Toland–
Locke position, defining 'clarity' of ideas as follows: 'an Idea
is at the Height of Perspicuity when it is so evidently and
plainly discerned by the Mind, that it can be distinguished
from all other Ideas at one *View* of the Intellect' (p. 119). He
argues that on this definition even our idea of particular
substances is clear and distinct, since 'the Idea comprehends
all that the Object is naturally disposed to Impress upon the
Sense at once; and all that either the Sense or the *Imagination*
is capable of receiving from one single View' (p. 120). The
acts of the pure spirit or mind are divided into (1) a 'simple
view', or simple apprehension, the 'Survey of those Ideas of
Sensation, in the very Order and Condition they lie in the
Imagination, without *Altering* the Nature or Situation of any
one of them; without passing any *Judgment* or making any
Inferences with Relation to them' (p. 155); (2) judgement, in
which the mind divides, separates, compounds, &c.; and
(3) abstraction. Under the last-named activity, Browne attacks
Locke's doctrine of abstract general ideas along Berkeleian
lines, insisting that 'mankind', for example, 'signifies the Idea
of *One Individual*, which is no otherwise made general, than
by our conceiving all the rest of the same Kind *By* that one;
so that in truth it is the single Idea of any one Individual
which is made to stand for and represent the whole Species'
(p. 187).

Browne was in many ways more of a sensationalist than is
shown by his interpretation of Locke. He recognized the

reality of the various faculties of the mind, but like Locke
subscribed to the *tabula rasa* doctrine.

> At our Birth the Imagination is intirely a *Tabula Rasa* or perfect
> *Blank*, without any Materials either for a *Simple View* or any *Other*
> Operation of the Intellect. We are not furnished with any *Innate* Ideas
> of things material or immaterial; nor are we endued with a Faculty or
> Disposition of forming *Purely Intellectual* Ideas or Conceptions inde-
> pendent of all Sensation: Much less has the human Soul a Power of
> raising up to itself Ideas out of *Nothing*, which is a kind of *Creation*; or
> of attaining any *First Principles* exclusive of all *Illation* or consequential
> Deduction from *Ideas* of *Material* Objects; without which the Mind of
> Man, during its Union with the Body, could never have arrived even to
> a Consciousness of its own *Operations* or *Existence* (pp. 382–3).

Browne never moves very far from this core of sensation, for
knowledge of divine things is acquired or constructed only
by finding analogies within experience. Such constructions
are valid sources of knowledge; but Browne wishes his readers
to recognize the nature of this knowledge, that it involves
close dependence upon experience. In general, he was convinced of the limitations of man's knowledge, limitations
which both Glanville and Locke had voiced before him. All
three men were convinced, however, that though knowledge
is severely restricted it is sufficient for our needs. Browne's
expression of this conviction parallels closely that of Locke.

> Thus short and imperfect is all our boasted Knowledge of Nature;
> we are intirely in the dark as to the inward Structure and Composition of
> the minute Particles of all Bodies; and can with no degree of Certainty
> judge or determine any thing concerning them, but from their outward
> Appearances and sensible Effects; when we attempt any thing beyond
> this, all our Reasonings are full of Confusion and Uncertainty. And yet
> even this purely *Experimental* Knowledge of Nature is however a Degree
> of it aptly suited to our present State and Condition in this Life; it
> answers all the *Reasonable* Ends of our Well-being and Preservation
> (p. 209).

In the same year that Browne's *Procedure* appeared,
Zachary Mayne published *Two Dissertations concerning Sense
and The Imagination* (1728), in which he defends the traditional view of the immateriality of the soul. Here, we note the
same sensationalist tendencies as are found in Browne; but

Mayne was more conscious of the contributions made by reason in the acquisition of knowledge than was Browne. Sense is made entirely subservient to reason, and intelligence is said to make its own notions of objects. Many Lockean doctrines appear in this work, such as the representative character of sense perception and the unknowableness of the real essences of objects.

> As for the Properties or Qualities of Bodies, we understand very few of them, because we do not discover how or by what they are signified; because the Constitution of Bodies, on which they depend, are unknown to us, or not sufficiently discerned by our Senses. But were these thoroughly and exactly perceived by us, they would no doubt appear significative and expressive of the several Properties and Qualities which flow from them, as their natural and immediate Consequences; and they would, as it were, declare and notify them to us (pp. 33–34).

In his essay on the imagination, Mayne equates 'idea' with 'image'. With such an interpretation, he then proceeds to refute the claim that all knowledge comes from ideas (pp. 93 ff.). Perception is distinguished from understanding (p. 103), the latter of which operates, in the manner Sergeant described, with notions. Locke is given credit for propagating the way of ideas, so current in the thinking of men. Mayne undoubtedly wrote with Isaac Watts in mind, for it was Watts who two years previously had given such a strong formulation of the Lockean way of ideas; but he may also have been writing against Berkeley, for Berkeley's *Principles of Human Knowledge* (1710) and his *Three Dialogues* (1713) had also carried forward the logic of ideas, even though these works embodied some fundamental alterations of Locke's theories. As we have already seen, Watts followed Berkeley's elimination of substance, but in the other essentials of the way of ideas he followed Locke more than he did Berkeley. In his *Logick* (1726), he had defined perception, conception, or apprehension as 'the meer simple Contemplation of Things offered to our Minds, without affirming or denying any Thing concerning them' (p. 5). Judgement was taken as that 'Operation of the Mind, whereby we join two or more Ideas

together by one Affirmation or Negation.' (Ibid.) Ideas
became the material of all knowledge and were given their
Lockean, rather than their Berkeleian, definition: 'a *Representation of a Thing in the Mind.* . . . That Notion or Form of
a Horse, a Tree, or a Man which is in the Mind, is call'd the
Idea of a Horse, a *Tree,* or a *Man'* (p. 8). He insisted like
Gastrell and Oldfield that

> It is not the outward Object, or *Thing which is perceived* . . . nor is it
> the very *Perception* or *Sense,* and *Feeling* . . . which is called the *Idea*;
> but it is the *Thing as it exists in the Mind by Way of Conception or Repre-
> sentation,* that is properly called the *Idea,* whether the *Object* be present
> or absent (pp. 8–9).

Watts also distinguishes between outward and inward arche-
types and their corresponding ideas, by calling the ideas of the
latter type pure or mental ideas, and those of the former images.
The general divisions of the *Essay* concerning ideas are repeated, with sensation as the source of our knowledge of
external objects, and reflection the source of our knowledge
of the self and its operations (p. 30). The categories of simple,
complex, compound, collective, real, imaginary, clear, distinct, obscure, &c., reappear, and a careful account of words
and their functions as signs is given. He defines judgement as
the comparing of ideas together (p. 142). In a later work,
Philosophical Essays (1733), he accepts and develops the
distinction between primary and secondary qualities, agreeing
that the representation proper occurs only between primary
ideas and their physical causes (p. 83). Watts, however, was
strongly inclined to accept some version of the doctrine of
innate knowledge,[1] a doctrine for which he was attacked by
another follower of Locke, John Jackson, in his *A Dissertation on Matter and Spirit* (1735).

§ 3—*General Conclusion*

Once more the study of the reception which Locke's epistemological doctrines received from his contemporaries has
carried us into the middle of the eighteenth century. Not only

---

[1] Cf. above, p. 70.

did the various controversies instigated by Locke's doctrines continue into this century: the positive application of these conceptions also became more common. Serious thinkers like the young Berkeley could not avoid analysis and discussion of these prevalent doctrines. Indeed it is not extravagant to claim that Locke's epistemology, with its roots deep in seventeenth-century theology, determined the context and the structure of similar discussions within England throughout the eighteenth and perhaps later centuries. What Aaron says of the whole of Locke's writings is equally true of the epistemological principles of the *Essay*: with these Locke 'secured for posterity the advances which had been made by the most radical and progressive elements of society in the seventeenth century'.[1] The same can be said of his religious views, for here too he was foremost in the ranks of those considered radical and revolutionary. What has not always been appreciated, and never to its fullest extent, is the intimate relation which existed in the minds of Locke's contemporaries between his epistemology and the new movements within religion. It is not very difficult to discern the pervasive influence of Locke's epistemology upon subsequent English and Scottish philosophers, for the very structure and orientation of the writings of men like Berkeley, Reid, or Hume duplicate those of the *Essay*. It is less obvious that the way of ideas was effective in bringing to fruition those radical movements in religion which culminated in the eighteenth century under the single name of 'Deist'. The general tendency in religion throughout Locke's lifetime was towards the natural religion of Collins and Wollaston. In the hands of those who openly professed themselves antithetical to revealed religion and to the many complex mysteries required by traditional religious beliefs, Locke's clear-cut jettisoning of much of the traditional verbiage and the strong direction towards empirical, phenomenalist analysis exemplified in the *Essay* became tools to be exploited. But the religious scene in this period of criticism and growth is complicated by three

[1] *John Locke*, pp. 307–8.

distinct movements. Opposed to the radical detractors of revealed religion, to the rationalizers of mysteries, was a large band of strict fundamentalists who suspected the least modification of their beliefs and dogmas. These men were busy attaching slanderous labels to their opponents, and were concerned with maintaining the doctrine of the Trinity as inexplicable but necessary for Christianity (Stillingfleet, Edwards). They were the defenders of Athanasianism, the doctrine that ' "there is but one living and true God", but that "in the Unity of this Godhead there are three Persons, of one substance, power, and eternity".'[1] They were also the men who objected most strongly to the introduction of new terminology or new modes of analysis. But aligned with tradition were also other men of a less tenacious and more open temperament who, either consciously or unconsciously, effected modifications in religion of a less radical and more gradual nature than those called for by the Deists. These were the men who gave Locke's epistemology its most extensive application. Some of these writers applied only small portions of the Lockean doctrines, while rejecting other aspects of the *Essay*, as Sherlock accepted the Lockean doctrine of substance but rejected the whole of Book One. Others, such as Witty, Gastrell, or Oldfield, took over almost all of the essentials of the Lockean theory of knowledge. It was in the hands of these men, even more than in those of the Deists who appealed to Locke's epistemology, that the new tendencies within religion were most aided and abetted by the theoretical structure of the *Essay*. The application by the Deists was flashy and superficial; that of the traditionalists much more penetrating, perceptive, and positive.

What the application of the various epistemological doctrines of Locke's *Essay* accomplished under the guidance of the less rigid traditionalists was an alteration in the presuppositions felt to be necessary for religion. The change taking place in religion during this period was from the presupposition of an innate source of morality to an external, critical construc-

[1] Abbey and Overton, op. cit., vol. i, p. 481.

tion of moral rules and precepts; from the belief that, in order to understand the Trinity and human personal identity, an intimate knowledge of substance was required, to the realization that the required beliefs could be retained while relinquishing the confused and difficult notions which they formerly seemed to entail. A major shift in the intellectual temper of the country was under way. The new science, the new emphasis upon observation in medicine, the rationalism within religion, the empiricism within philosophy, all served to propel this reorientation of thought. The seventeenth century introduces the forces which lead to a movement away from metaphysics towards empiricism; from scholastic reliance upon definitions and predetermined schemes of thought, to an impartial phenomenological analysis of knowledge; from a simple, direct form of realism to a complex, representative position embodied in the generally accepted way of ideas; from making theory of knowledge harmonize with the requirements of religious beliefs and theological dogma, to the reverse: to making theology keep in step with the demands of the phenomenological analysis of knowledge. The emphasis on clarity and distinctness raised to prominence by Toland's and Locke's writings served to lead men to revise their conceptions, to discard many obscure notions. Some of the intricacies of the new epistemology formulated by Locke could not be absorbed even by the more pliable traditionalists, such as his suggestion that matter might be able to acquire a power of thought. The necessity of immateriality for immortality was a belief not easily shaken, although there were men ready to champion this suggestion and to develop it to lengths not conceived of nor tolerated by Locke (e.g. Coward, Layton). Likewise, the denial of innate sources of knowledge proved difficult for more than one otherwise resilient follower of tradition to accept. There were undoubtedly many among these receptive men of tradition who perceived the dangers of these radical rejections and innovations, who trusted more to a tradition which did not conform to the current standards than they did to the clarifications of the deist and naturalist theologians. But by the middle of the eighteenth century the general result of the religious controversies was a definite modification of tradition in the direction of naturalism and a simplification such as Locke had demanded in his *Reasonableness of Christianity*. The indirectness of knowledge necessitated by the way of ideas was no longer viewed as a hindrance to religion, and the limitations of knowledge circumscribed by Locke were accepted as consistent with religious belief in non-empirical objects. On the one hand, the spheres of religion and science, of theology and ordinary experience, were drawn farther apart through these restrictions; for men like Browne saw the need of defending religion by conceding to the Lockean analysis of ideas its sphere of legitimacy, while reserving for religion the area of analogical representation. But, on the other hand, religion had been brought closer to the confines of experience and observation. It lost some of its former loftiness and mystery, but it had become more a part of the ordinary world. Experience and observation were generally accepted as the point of departure for any theological speculation.

Within the area of secular thought, the logic of ideas had won the day by the mid-years of the eighteenth century. The terminology and concepts of the *Essay* were widely diffused throughout theological as well as secular writings. Logical treatises of the eighteenth century, such as those of Oldfield and Watts, incorporated large parts of the *Essay* almost verbatim. The corpuscular analysis of perception championed by Boyle and Cudworth, together with the distinction of primary and secondary qualities, had acquired respectability by the eighteenth century. The importance of close attention to the meaning of words, and to the way in which words carry meanings and serve as signs for non-linguistic events, had also gained some prestige by the time Oldfield and Watts began writing, despite the indifference to this aspect of the *Essay* evidenced as late as 1702 by Henry Lee. But not all of the epistemological difficulties posed by the seventeenth-century exponents of the way of ideas had been resolved by the mid-eighteenth century. Even within religious discussions, the problems of the reality of knowledge and the adequacy of the representative character of ideas were seriously questioned and considered. The important problem—faced by Hobbes, Digby, and Burthogge, and most of the other men writing upon problems of knowledge—of accounting for the immaterial principles and ingredients in knowledge had by no means been solved. This particular aspect of the epistemological problem was lost in the maze of the dispute over the immateriality of the human soul. These more subtle and theoretical aspects of the way of ideas were left for the more specialized thinkers of the eighteenth century to deal with: the theologians concerned to find practical application for Locke's epistemology had to accept, as Locke had likewise done, the common-sense convictions about the reality of knowledge and the adequacy of our representations, invoking well-known axioms in their support.

Thus, the epistemology which Locke inherited from his predecessors, and to which he turned initially because of certain unspecified difficulties encountered in religious discussions, played a major role in the controversies which troubled his contemporaries, stimulating first violent reaction and condemnation and then gradual acceptance and application by radicals and conservatives alike. The duality of this tradition which taught simultaneously the phenomenalistic restriction of human knowledge and the necessity of positing real essences in nature, led to some confusions; but, like those unsolved issues of real knowledge and representation, this aspect of the new way of ideas was pushed to one side. Locke did not himself belong to the Deists, although he found many of their beliefs quite sympathetic; but he was clearly a member of that group of theologians and laymen who worked within tradition towards the modifications in theory and dogma which became actual later in the eighteenth century. He belonged to this group not only in virtue of his specifically religious convictions and statements, but more importantly because the epistemology which he formulated in his *Essay*

concerning Human Understanding moved in the same direction as the theological tendencies of the less rigid traditionalists. Locke may not have consciously co-ordinated these
two sides of his thought; but what he failed to unite, his
contemporaries were quick to join together. Product of his
society and its controversies, Locke's doctrines received their
critical scrutiny and their practical application from the theologians of his country. What he failed to clarify through the
purifying air of debate with his contemporaries continued, for
the most part, unclarified into the eighteenth century. The
problems of epistemology raised by Locke were not solved by
his contemporaries, but the general theory of knowledge, as
well as the terminology in which he expressed that theory,
constituted the foundations of the important shiftings in the
intellectual—religious, moral, and logical—temper of the
succeeding century.

BIBLIOGRAPHY

CONTEMPORARY SOURCES

A. Manuscript Material

Lovelace Collection of Locke manuscript material in the Bodleian Library, Oxford.

> The collection comprises a large number of letters to and from Locke, together with important philosophical and religious papers, and most of his journals. The collection has been arranged and catalogued by Prof. W. von Leyden, of Durham University. It is to his painstaking care that all subsequent researchers on Locke owe a great debt of gratitude. For his own description of this collection, see his articles 'John Locke's Unpublished Papers' (in *Sophia*, anno XVII, n. 1; gennaio-marzo 1949; pp. 73–80), 'Notes concerning Papers of John Locke in the Lovelace Collection' (in *The Philosophical Quarterly*, January 1952, pp. 63–69), and pp. 1–7 in *John Locke: Essays on the Law of Nature*, edited by W. von Leyden. References to this collection in this study are indicated as 'MS. Locke'.

Letter of Jacques Bernard to Pierre Desmaizeaux, dated 6 May 1705. British Museum Add. Sloane MS. 4281, fol. 144.

Letter of A. Houdart de la Motte to Desmaizeaux, dated 16 July 1720. British Museum Add. Sloane MS. 4286, fol. 242.

> The above two letters are part of a collection of Pierre Desmaizeaux's correspondence, British Museum Add. Sloane MS. 4281–9. These two letters are concerned with a paper which Desmaizeaux had apparently written in criticism of Locke. Through the persuasion of La Motte and Bernard, he desisted from publishing it.

Letters from the Abbé Du Bos to Nicholas Thoynard (or Toinard) d'Orléans. Bibliothèque Nationale MS. Fr. n.a. 560.

> Many of these letters have reference to Locke. They are reprinted in their entirety by Paul Denis, in his *Lettres Autographes de la Collection de Troussures Classées & Annotées*, published at Beauvais in 1912.

B. Books

ANONYMOUS. A Dissertation on Deistical and Arian Corruption: Or, Plain Proof, that the Principles and Practices of Arians and Deists are founded upon spiritual Blindness, and resolve into Atheism; and have contributed greatly to the Infidelity and Profaneness of the present Age. Where Mr. JACK—N's Dissertation on Matter and Spirit, Mr. Lockes's Essay, &c. are particularly examined, &c. London, G. Strahan, 1708. 8°. 68 pp.

—— Fides et Ratio collatae, ac suo utraque loco reddittae, adversus Principia J. Lockii . . . Cum accessione triplici 1. De fide implicita. . . . 2. De SS. Scripturarum certitudine ac sensu. 3. De perfectione et felicitate in hac vita. Edidit et praefatus est P[ierre] Poiret. Amstelaedami, 1708. 8°.

—— Faith & Reason Compared . . . In Answer to certain Theses (drawn from Mr. Lock's Principles) Concerning Fancy & Reason. With a New Preface concerning *Reason, Philosophy, Morality & Religion*. London, 1713.

> A translation of *Fides et Ratio collatae*; the British Museum copy has a note: Ex dono authoris—D.C.H., possibly a Mrs. Hungerford.

ANONYMOUS. The Mischief of Persecution Exemplified; By a True Narrative of the Life and Deplorable End of Mr. John Child . . . Also A Discourse of the Nature and Office of Conscience [on pp. 1–8] . . . Attested by us, Tho. Plant, Benj. Dennis. May 7, 1688. . . . London, Tho. Fabian, 1688. 4°. 46 pp.

—— A Philosophick Essay concerning Ideas, According to Dr. *Sherlock's* Principles. Wherein His Notion of them is Stated, and his Reasonings thereupon Examin'd. In a Letter to a Friend. London, B. Bragg, 1705. 4°. 24 pp.

> This tract is a most interesting attempt at a summary and synthesis of the dispute of the nature and role of ideas in knowledge at the turn of the century. It is clearly and concisely written and reveals an intimate knowledge of the doctrines of Malebranche, Norris, Sherlock, and Locke. In composition the author has employed a deductive manner of exposition working from axioms and definitions to conclusions. The tract serves as a natural bridge between seventeenth- and eighteenth-century developments of the way of ideas, that is, between Locke and Berkeley. It would be valuable to learn who the author was. I have been able to uncover nothing definitive in this respect, but two possible candidates may be cited. In the auction catalogue made for the sale of Anthony Collins's library by Thomas Ballard for 18 January 1730/1, this tract is credited to 'Tho. Burnet'. This may have been Thomas Burnet, D.D., sometime prebendary of Salisbury and Boyle lecturer for 1726. In his *An Essay upon Government* (1716) and in his *The Argument Set forth in a late Book, Entitled Christianity as old as the Creation* (1730–2), he employs and praises the deductive manner of writing from definitions, axioms, corollaries, &c. However, this Burnet does not seem to have written anything prior to 1716, and I have found no other authority for ascribing the above tract to him. Another possibility is that it was written by Robert South, but my only basis for this suggestion is that in a letter to Locke, dated 18 July 1704 (MS. Locke C.18, ff. 175–6) South tells Locke that he has drawn up some remarks upon Sherlock's 'Digression'. However, he confesses that he thinks his remarks unworthy of publication (a sentiment of humility also found in this tract), and urges Locke to reply to Sherlock.

ARNAULD, ANTOINE. La Logique ou L'Art de Penser: Contenant, Outre les Regles communes, Plusieurs Observations nouvelles, propres à former le jugement. 3. éd., reveuë & augmentée. Paris, C. Savreux, 1668. 12mo. 473 [6] pp.

B., F. A Free but Modest Censure On the late Controversial Writings and Debates of The Lord Bishop of Worcester and Mr. Locke; Mr. Edwards and Mr. Locke; The Honble Charles Boyle, Esq; and Dr. Bently. Together with Brief Remarks on Monsieur Le Clerc's Ars Critica. By F. B., M.A. of Cambridg. London, A. Baldwin, 1698. 4°. 31 pp.

> According to the *D.N.B.* (article on John Edwards) the section on the debate between Edwards and Locke was written by Edwards; there is, however, no authority given for this statement and I have found no intimation of the authorship for the other sections.

BATES, WILLIAM, D.D. Considerations of the Existence of God, and of the Immortality of the Soul, With the Recompences of the future state: For the Cure of Infidelity, the Hecktick Evil of the Times. London, J. D. for Brabazon Aylmer, 1676. 8°. 8 p.l., 292 pp., 6 l.

[BAXTER, ANDREW] An Enquiry into the Nature of the Human Soul; Wherein the Immateriality of the Soul Is evinced from the Principles of Reason and Philosophy. London, James Bettenham [*ca.* 1733]. 4°. 6 p.l., 376 pp.

BAYLE, PIERRE. Œuvres Diverses de Mᵣ. Pierre Bayle . . . Contenant tout
ce que cet Auteur a publié sur des matieres de Theologie, de Philosophie, de Critique, d'Histoire, & de Litterature; excepté son Dictionnaire Historique et Critique. La Haye, Chez P. Husson [et al.], 1727–31.
folio. 4 vols.

—— Dictionnaire Historique et Critique. Seconde Edition, Revuë, corrigée & augmentée par l'Auteur. Rotterdam, Reinier Leers, 1702. folio.
3 vols.

—— Reponse aux Questions d'un Provincial. Rotterdam, Reinier Leers,
1704–7. 12ᵐᵒ. 5 vols.

BECCONSALL, THOMAS, B.D., Fellow of Brasenose College, Oxford. The
Grounds and Foundation of Natural Religion, Discover'd, In the
Principal Branches of it, in Opposition to the Prevailing Notions of the
Modern *Scepticks* and *Latitudinarians*. With An Introduction con-
cerning the Necessity of Revealed Religion. London, W. O. for A.
Roper, 1698. 8°. xi, vi, [44] 256 pp.

BENTLEY, RICHARD. The Folly and Unreasonableness of Atheism Demonstrated from The Advantage and Pleasure of a Religious Life, The
Faculties of Human Souls, The Structure of Animate Bodies, & The
Origin and Frame of the World: In Eight Sermons Preached at
the Lecture Founded by The Hon—. Robert Boyle, Esquire; In the
First Year MDCXCII. London, J. H. for H. Mortlock, 1693. 4°.
8 nos. in 1 vol.

> All eight sermons were first issued separately with separate title-pages; the second
> sermon going into several editions. I note here only the first two, and most impor-
> tant sermons of this series.

—— The Folly of Atheism, And (what is now called) Deism; Even with
Respect to the Present Life . . . Preached, Being the First of the
Lecture . . . March the VII 1691/92. London, for T. Parkhurst, 1692.
4°. 40 pp.

—— Matter and Motion cannot Think: Or, A Confutation of Atheism
from the Faculties of the Soul. A Sermon Preached April 4, 1692.
Being the Second of the Lecture . . . London, for T. Parkhurst, 1692.
4°. 39 pp.

—— The Second Edition. London, for Tho. Parkhurst, 1692. 4°. 40 pp.

> A new typesetting of the first edition.

—— The Third Edition. London, J. H. for Henry Mortlock, 1694. 4°.
33 pp.

> Some minor textual changes occur in this edition.

[BEVERLEY, THOMAS]. Christianity The Great Mystery. In Answer to a
late Treatise, Christianity not Mysterious [by John Toland]: That is
Not Above, Not Contrary to Reason. In Opposition to which is
Asserted Christianity is above Created Reason, in its pure Estate. And
contrary to Humane Reason, as Fallen and corrupted: and, therefore
in proper senses, Mystery. Together with a *Postscript* Letter to the
Author, on his Second Edition Enlarg'd. By T. B. London, for W.
Marshal, 1696. 4°. 2 p.l., 13–44, 41–56 pp.

BLOUNT, CHARLES. The Oracles of Reason: Consisting of [16 articles] . . . In several Letters to Mr. *Hobbs* and other Persons . . . By *Char. Blount*, Esq; Mr. *Gildon* and others. London, Printed 1693. 12ᵐᵒ. 12 p.l., 226 pp.

> The sixth article is 'Of Immortality of the Soul' and the fifteenth is entitled 'That the Soul is Matter'.

[BOLD, SAMUEL]. A Discourse Concerning the Resurrection of the Same Body: With Two Letters Concerning the Necessary Immateriality of Created Thinking Substance. London, S. Holt for A. and J. Churchill, 1705. 8°. 6 p.l., 206 pp.

> Dated at end 10 Sept. 1703.

—— Some Considerations On the Principal Objections and Arguments Which have been Publish'd against Mr. Lock's Essay of Humane Understanding. London, for A. & J. Churchill, 1699. 8°. 1 p.l., 60 pp.

> Reprinted in his: A Collection of Tracts, Published in Vindication of Mr. Lock's Reasonableness of Christianity . . . And of his Essay Concerning Humane Understanding. London, A. & J. Churchill, 1706. 8°. 5 nos. in 1 vol.

[BOYLE, ROBERT]. The Christian Virtuoso: Shewing, That by being addicted to *Experimental Philosophy*, a Man is rather Assisted, than Indisposed, to be a *Good* Christian. The First Part. By T. H. R. B. Fellow of the Royal Society. In the Savoy, Edw. Jones, 1690. 8°. 9 p.l., 120 pp.

—— Experiments, Notes, &c. about the Mechanical Origine or Production of Divers particular Qualities. London, E. Flesher, 1675. 8°. 3 p.l., 21 pp.

> 'Advertisements Relating to the following Treatises', followed by 12 separately paged treatises.

—— The Origine of Formes and Qualities, (According to the *Corpuscular Philosophy*,) Illustrated by *Considerations* and Experiments, (Written formerly by way of *Notes* upon an *Essay* about Nitre). Oxford, H. Hall, 1666. small 8°. [54], 433 pp.

BROUGHTON, JOHN, M.A., Chaplain to Duke of Marlborough. Psychologia: Or, An Account of the Nature of the Rational Soul. In Two Parts. The First, An Essay concerning the Nature of the Human Soul. London, W. B. for T. Bennet, 1703. 8°. 7 p.l., [23], 418 pp., 7 l.

> The second part, paged continuously with the first, has a separate title: A Vindication of the Nature of the Human Soul, &c.

BROWNE, PETER, Senior Fellow of Trinity College, Dublin. A Letter in Answer to a Book Entituled, *Christianity not Mysterious* [by Toland] As also To all Those who Set up for Reason and Evidence In opposition to Revelation and Mysteries. London, for Robert Clavell, 1697. 8°. 1 p.l., 180 pp.

[——] The Procedure, Extent, and Limits of Human Understanding. London, for W. Innys, 1728. 8°. 4 p.l., 477 pp.

[BULLOKAR, JOHN] lexicographer. An English Expositor: Teaching the Interpretation of the hardest words used in our Language. With Sundry

Explications, Descriptions, and Discourses. By I. B., Doctor of Physicke. London, John Legatt, 1616. small 8°. Signatures: A–P⁴.

BURNET, GILBERT, Bishop of Salisbury. An Exposition of the Thirty-nine Articles of the *Church of England*. Written by Gilbert, Bishop of Sarum. London, by R. Roberts for Ri. Chiswell, 1699. folio. 4 p.l., xxiv, 396 pp.

[BURNET, THOMAS] Master of the Charterhouse. Remarks upon an Essay concerning Humane Understanding: In a Letter Address'd to the Author. London, M. Wootton, 1697. 4°. 15 pp.

—— Second Remarks upon an Essay concerning Humane Understanding, In a Letter address'd to the Author. Being a Vindication of the First Remarks, Against the Answer of Mr. Lock, At the End of His Reply to the Lord Bishop of Worcester. London, M. Wootton, 1697. 4°. 30 pp.

Locke's copy is in the Yale University Library.

—— Third Remarks upon an Essay concerning Humane Understanding: In a Letter Address'd to the Author. London, M. Wootton, 1699. 4°. 27 pp.

Locke's copy is in the Yale University Library. It has many of his manuscript notes in the margins.

BURTHOGGE, RICHARD, M.D. The Philosophical Writings of Richard Burthogge. Edited with introduction and notes by Margaret W. Landes. Chicago, Open Court Pub. Co., 1921. xxiv, 245 pp.

Contains his *Organum Vetus & Novum*, reprinted in full; his *An Essay upon Reason* (a shortened version) and *Of the Soul of the World*, in full.

—— Causa Dei, Or An Apology for God. Wherein The Perpetuity of Infernal Torments is Evinced, and Divine both Goodness and Justice (that notwithstanding) Defended . . . London, Lewis Punchard, 1675. 8°. 10 pl., 422 pp.

—— An Essay upon Reason, and the Nature of Spirits. London, J. Dunton, 1694. 8°. 3 p.l., 280 pp.

Dedicated 'To the Learned Mr. John Lock'.

[——] Of the Soul of the World; and of Particular Souls. In a Letter to Mr. Lock, occasioned by Mr. Keil's Reflections upon an Essay lately published concerning Reason. By the Author of that Essay. London, Daniel Brown, 1699. 8°. 46 pp.

—— Organum Vetus & Novum. Or, A Discourse of Reason and Truth. Wherein the Natural Logick common to Mankinde is briefly and plainly described. In a Letter to the most Honoured Andrew Trevill, Esq. London, for Sam. Crouch, 1678. 8°. 73 pp.

[BURTON, ROBERT]. The Anatomy of Melancholy. What it is, With all the kindes, causes, symptoms, prognostickes, & severall cures of it. By Democritus Iunior. Oxford, Iohn Lichfield, 1621. 4°. 2 p.l., 783 [784]–[791] pp.

CARPENTER, RICHARD, D.D., & Pastor of Sherwell in Devon. The Conscionable Christian: Or, The Indevour of Saint Paul, to have and discharge a good conscience alwayes towards God, and men: laid open and applyed in three Sermons. London, F. K. for John Bartlett, 1623. 4°. 3 p.l., [4] 119 pp.

CARROLL (or CAROLL or CARROL), WILLIAM. A Dissertation upon the Tenth Chapter of the Fourth Book of Mr. Locke's Essay . . . Wherein the Author's Endeavours to Establish Spinoza's Atheistical Hypothesis, more especially in that Tenth Chapter, are Discover'd and Confuted. London, J. Matthews, 1706. 8°. 4 p.l., xv, 292 pp.

—— A Letter to the Reverend Dr. Benjamin Prat. Wherein The Dangerous Errors in a late Book, Intituled, An Essay concerning the Use of Reason in Propositions [by Anthony Collins] are Detect'd, Confuted, and gradually Deduc'd from the very Basis of all *Atheism*, upon which alone they are Bottom'd. By William Caroll. London, for Richard Sare, 1707. 4°. 24 pp.

—— Remarks upon Mr. Clarke's Sermons, Preached at St. Paul's against *Hobbs*, *Spinoza*, and other *Atheists*. . . . London, Jonathan Robinson, 1705. 4°. 1 p.l., 42 pp.

[——] Spinoza Reviv'd. To which is added A Preliminary Discourse . . . by the Reverend Dr. George Hicks. London, J. Morphew, 1709. 8°. 1 p.l., [57] pp., 6 l., 179 pp.

The unnumbered 57 pages constitute Hickes's Preface.

—— Spinoza Reviv'd. Part the Second. Or, A Letter to Monsieur *Le Clerc*, Occasion'd By his *Bibliothèque Choisie, Tom.* 21. By William Carrol. London, John Morphew, 1711. 8°. 1 p.l., 76, [2] pp.

CHAMBERS, EPHRAIM. Cyclopaedia: Or, An Universal Dictionary of Arts and Sciences. . . . The Whole intended as a Course of Antient and Modern Learning. London, J. & J. Knapton, 1728. folio. 2 vols.

CHARLETON, WALTER. The Darkness of Atheism Dispelled by the Light of Nature. A Physico-Theologicall Treatise. London, J. F. for Wm. Lee, 1652. 4°. 25 p.l., 335 pp.

[——] Epicvrvs's Morals, Collected Partly out of his owne Greek Text, in Diogines Laertius, And Partly out of the Rhapsodies of Marcus Antoninus, Plvtarch, Cicero, & Seneca. And faithfully Englished. London, Henry Herringman, 1656. 4°. 2 p.l. [37] p., 1 l., 184 pp.

[——] The Immortality of the Human Soul, Demonstrated by the Light of *Nature*. In Two Dialogues. London, Wm. Wilson, 1657. 4°. 7 p.l., 188 pp.

[——] Natural History of the Passions. In the Savoy, T. N. for James Magnes, 1674. 8°. 24 p.l., 188 pp.

Largely an adaptation of Jean-François Senault's *De l'Usage des Passions* (Paris, 1641).

—— Physiologia Epicuro-Gassendo-Charletoniana: or, A Fabrick of Science Natural, upon the hypothesis of Atoms . . . The first part. London, Thomas Heath, 1654. folio. 475 pp.

CHILLINGWORTH, WILLIAM, M.A. Oxon. The Religion of Protestants A Safe Way to Salvation. Or An Answer to a Booke Entitled Mercy and Trvth, Or, Charity maintain'd by Catholiques, Which pretends to prove the Contrary. Oxford, Printed by Leonard Lichfield, 1638. large 4°. 16 p.l., 413, [1] pp.

CLARKE, SAMUEL, M.A., Rector of St. James, Westminster. A Demonstration of the Being and Attributes of God: More Particularly in Answer to Mr. *Hobbs*, *Spinoza*, And their Followers: Wherein the Notion of *Liberty* is Stated, and the Possibility and Certainty of it Proved, in Opposition to *Necessity* and *Fate*. 2d ed., corrected. Being the Substance of Eight Sermons Preach'd in the Year 1704, the Boyle Lectures. London, Will Botham, 1706. 8°. 8 p.l., 206 pp.

—— A Second Defense of an Argument Made use of in a Letter to Mr. *Dodwel*, To Prove the Immateriality and *Natural Immortality* of the Soul. In a Letter to the Author of *A Reply to Mr.* Clarke's *Defense*, &c. [i.e. Anthony Collins]. London, W. B. for James Knapton, 1707. 8°. 1 p.l., 54 pp.

[COCKBURN, MRS. CATHARINE TROTTER] A Defence of the Essay of Human Understanding, Written by Mr. *Lock*. Wherein its Principles with reference to *Morality*, *Reveal'd Religion*, and the *Immortality of the Soul*, are consider'd and Justify'd: In Answer to Some Remarks on that Essay [by T. Burnet]. London, Will Turner, 1702. 8°. 4 p.l., 70 pp.

[COLLINS, ANTHONY] A Discourse of Free-Thinking, Occasion'd by The Rise and Growth of a Sect call'd Free-Thinkers. London [J., J., & P. Knapton] 1713. 8°. vi, 178 pp.

[——] An Essay Concerning the Use of Reason in Propositions, The Evidence whereof depends upon Human Testimony. London, Printed in the Year 1707. 8°. 56 pp.

[——] A Letter to the Learned Mr. Henry Dodwell; Containing Some Remarks on a (pretended) Demonstration of the Immateriality and Natural Immortality of the Soul, In Mr. Clark's Answer to his late *Epistolary Discourse*, &c. London, for A. Baldwin, 1707. 8°. 16 pp.

[——] A Reply to Mr. Clark's Defence Of his Letter to Mr. *Dodwell*. With a Postscript relating to Mr. *Milles's* Answer to Mr. *Dodwell's* Epistolary Discourse. London, Printed in the Year 1707. 8°. 48 pp.

[——] Reflections on Mr. Clark's Second Defence of his Letter to Mr. *Dodwell*. London, by J. Darby, 1707. 8°. 61 pp.

[——] An Answer to Mr. Clark's Third Defence Of his Letter to Mr. *Dodwell*. London, for A. Baldwin, 1708. 8°. 94 pp.

[——] A Philosophical Inquiry Concerning Human Liberty. London, for R. Robinson, 1717. 8°. vi, 115 pp.

[COWARD, WILLIAM] M.D. The Grand Essay: Or, A Vindication of Reason, and Religion, against Impostures of Philosophy. Proving according to those Ideas and Conceptions of Things Human Understanding is capable of forming to it self. 1. That the Existence of any *Immaterial Substance* is a Philosophic Imposture, and impossible to be conceived. 2. That all Matter has Originally created in it, a principle of Internal, or Self-Motion. 3. That Matter & Motion *must* be the Foundation of *Thought* in Men and Brutes. To which is Added, A Brief Answer to Mr. Broughton's Psycholo. &c. By *W. C.* M. D. C. M. L. C. London, for P. G., 1704. 8°. vi, 197, 177–248 pp.

[COWARD, WILLIAM] The Just Scrutiny: Or, a Serious Enquiry into the *Modern Notions* of the Soul. I, Consider'd as *Breath of Life*, or a Power (not *immaterial Substance*) united to Body, according to the H. Scriptures. II, As *a Principle Naturally Mortal, but Immortaliz'd by Its Union with the Baptismal Spirit*, according to *Platonisme* lately Christianiz'd. With a Comparative Disquisition Between the *Scriptural* and *Philosophic State* of the Dead; and some Remarks on the Consequences of such Opinions. By *W. C.* M. D. London, John Chantry [*ca.* 1703]. 8°. 1 p.l., 221 pp.

[———] Second Thoughts Concerning Human Soul, Demonstrating the Notion of *Human Soul*, As believ'd to be a Spiritual Immortal Substance, *united to Human Body*, To be a Plain Heathenish Invention, And not Consonant to the Principles of *Philosophy, Reason,* or *Religion;* But the Ground only of many *Absurd,* and *Superstitious Opinions,* Abominable to the Reformed *Churches,* And Derogatory in General to True Christianity. London, for R. Basset, 1702. 8°. 12 p.l., 457 [3] pp.

[———] Farther Thoughts concerning Human Soul, In Defence of Second Thoughts; Wherein The weak Efforts of the Reverend Mr. *Turner,* and other less significant Writers are occasionally Answer'd. By the Author of Second Thoughts. London, for Richard Bassett, 1703. 8°. 12 p.l., 155 [3] pp.

CROUSAZ, J. P. DE, Professeur en Philosophie & en Mathématique dans l'Académie de Lausanne. La Logique, ou Systeme de Reflexions, Qui peuvent contribuer à la netteté & à l'étendue de nos Connoissances. Seconde Edition, revue, corrigée & augmentée considerablement. Amsterdam, L'Honoré & Chatelain, 1720. 12ᵐᵒ. 3 vols.

CUDWORTH, RALPH, D.D., Master of Christ's College Cambridge. A Treatise concerning Eternal and Immutable Morality. London, J. & J. Knapton, 1731. 8°. xii pp., 4 l., 303 pp.

——— The True Intellectual System of the Universe: The First Part; Wherein, All the Reason and Philosophy of Atheism is Confuted; and Its Impossibility Demonstrated. London, R. Royston, 1678. large 4°. 10 p.l., 899 pp., 46 l.

CULVERWEL, NATHANAEL, M.A. An Elegant and Learned Discourse of the Light of Nature, With severall other Treatises. London, T. R. and E. M., 1654 . 4°. 7 p.l., 183, 207 pp.

Dedication and 'To the Reader' dated 10 Aug. 1652.

——— The same. London, by Tho. Roycroft for Mary Rothwell, 1661. 4°. 8 p.l., 175, 212 pp.

Substantially the same as the 1654 edition, except for the addition of italicization and capitalization throughout.

DIGBY, SIR KENELM. Two Treatises, in the one of which, The Nature of Bodies; in the other; The Nature of Mans Soule; is looked into: in way of discovery, of The Immortality of Reasonable Soules. Paris, Gilles Blaizot, 1644. folio. 22 p.l., 466 pp.

DITTON, HUMPHREY, Master of the New Mathematical School in Christ's-Hospital. A Discourse Concerning the Resurrection of Jesus Christ. In Three Parts . . . Together with An Appendix concerning the Impossible Production of *Thought*, from *Matter and Motion:* The *Nature* of *Humane Souls*, and of *Brutes*: The *Anima Mundi*, and the Hypothesis of the *To Παν*; as also, concerning *Divine Providence*, the *Origin of Evil*, and the *Universe* in General. London, by J. Darby, 1712. 8°. xvi, 568 pp.

EARBERY, MATTHIAS. An Answer to a Book intitled, Tractatus Theologico Politicus [of Spinoza]. London, for Charles Brome, 1697. 8°. 8 p.l., 189 pp.

EDWARDS, JOHN, B.D. A Brief Vindication of the *Fundamental Articles* of the Christian Faith, As also Of the *Clergy, Universities* and *Publick Schools*, from Mr. *Lock's* Reflections upon them in his Book of *Education*, &c. With some Animadversions on two other late Pamphlets, viz. Of Mr. Bold and a Nameless *Socinian* Writer [Stephen Nye and his *Agreement of the Unitarians*]. London, for J. Robinson, 1697. 8°. 4 p.l., 125 pp.

—— A Free Discourse concerning Truth and Error, Especially in Matters of Religion . . . Also A Preface containing some Brief Remarks on the late *Reflections on Humane Learning*. London, for Jonathan Robinson, 1701. 8°. xlviii, 483 pp.

> In the Preface Edwards tells us that this work had its origins in a sermon he preached before King Charles II at Newmarket on the text John xviii. 38, in answer to Pilate's question 'What is truth?' (First published in 1698 in his *Sermons on Several Occasions and Subjects.*) The only similarity in content is a vague reference in the sermon to 'eternal laws of reason' and 'natural notions' which may indicate some belief in innate ideas, developed in the above work.

—— The Socinian Creed: Or, A Brief Account Of the Professed *Tenets and Doctrines* of the Foreign and English *Socinians*. Wherein is shew'd The Tendency of them To *Irreligion* and *Atheism*. With Proper *Antidotes* against them. London, J. Robinson, 1697. 8°. 12 p.l., 264 pp.

—— Socinianism Unmask'd. A Discourse Shewing the Unreasonableness Of a Late Writer's Opinion Concerning the Necessity of only *One Article* of *Christian Faith;* And of his other Assertions in his late Book, Entituled, The Reasonableness of Christianity . . . and in his *Vindication* of it. With a Brief Reply to another (professed) Socinian Writer. London, for J. Robinson, 1696. 8°. 8 p.l., 142 pp.

—— Some Thoughts Concerning the Several Causes *and* Occasions of Atheism, Especially in the Present Age. With some Brief Reflections on *Socinianism*: And on a Late Book Entituled The Reasonableness of Christianity. . . . London, for J. Robinson, 1695. 8°. 4 p.l., 126 pp.

FERGUSON, ROBERT. The Interest of Reason in Religion; With the Import & Use of Scripture-Metaphors; And The Nature of the Union Betwixt Christ & Believers. . . . London, Dorman Newman, 1675. 8°. 11 p.l., 657 pp.

[FOWLER, EDWARD] Bishop of Gloucester. The Principles and Practices, Of certain Moderate Divines of the Church of England, (greatly misunderstood) Truly Represented and Defended; Wherein (by the way) Some Controversies, of no mean Importance, are succinctly discussed:

In A Free Discourse between two Intimate Friends. In III Parts. London, Lodowick Lloyd, 1670. 8°. xxvi, 348 pp.

GAILHARD, JEAN, Gent. The Epistle and Preface To the Book against the Blasphemous Socinian Heresie Vindicated; And the Charge therein against Socinianism, made Good. In Answer to Two Letters. London, J. Hartley, 1698. 8°. 90 pp.

—— The Blasphemous Socinian Heresie Disproved and Confuted . . . With Animadversions upon a late Book called, Christianity not Mysterious [by Toland]. London, R. Wellington, 1697. 8°. 21 p.l., 344 pp.

GASTRELL, FRANCIS, Student of Christ Church, Oxon. The *Certainty* and *Necessity* of Religion in General: Or, The First Grounds & Principles of Humane Duty Establish'd; In Eight Sermons Preached . . . at the Lecture for the Year 1697, founded by the Honorable *Robert Boyle*, Esquire. London, for Tho. Bennet, 1697. 8°. 2 p.l., xi, 257 pp.

[——] Some Considerations Concerning the Trinity: And The Ways of Managing that Controversie. London, Printed, and Sold by E. Whitlock, 1696. 4°. 6 p.l., 52 pp.

[——] A Defence Of some Considerations Concerning the Trinity, &c. In Answer to the Reflections made upon them, in a late Pamphlet, Entituled, *An Essay concerning the use of Reason, &c.* [by Anthony Collins] In a Letter to the Author. London, for Henry Clements, 1707. 8°. 1 p.l., 35 pp.

GIBSON, EDMUND, Bishop of London. The Bishop of *London's* Second Pastoral Letter to the People of his *Diocese*; Particularly, to those of the two great Cities of *London* and *Westminster*. Occasion'd by some late Writings, in which it is asserted, 'That Reason is a sufficient Guide in Matters of Religion, without the Help of Revelation'. London, for Sam. Buckley, 1730. sm. 4°. 1 p.l., 80 pp.

GILDON, CHARLES. The Deist's Manual: Or, A Rational Enquiry into the Christian Religion. With some Considerations on Mr. Hobbs, Spinosa, the Oracles of Reason [by Charles Blount], Second Thoughts [by Wm. Coward], etc. To which is prefix'd a Letter, from the Author of The Method with the Deists [Charles Leslie]. London, A. Roper, 1705. 8°. 15 p.l., xvi, 36, 301 pp.

GLANVILL, JOSEPH, F.R.S. Essays on several Important Subjects in Philosophy and Religion. London, by J. D. for John Baker & H. Mortlock, 1676. 4°. 7 nos. in 1 vol.

Contents: I. Against Confidence in Philosophy (pp. 1–33)—II. Of Scepticism and Certainty (pp. 35–66)—III. Modern Improvements of Useful Knowledge (56 pp.) —IV. The Usefulness of Real Philosophy to Religion (43 pp.)—V. The Agreement of Reason and Religion (28 pp.)—VI. Against Modern Sadducism in the Matter of Witches and Apparitions (61 pp.)—VII. Anti-fanatical Religion and Free Philosophy. In A Continuation of the New Atlantis (58 pp.).

—— Plus Ultra: Or, The Progress and Advancement of Knowledge Since the Days of Aristotle. In an Account of some of the most Remarkable Late Improvements of Practical, Useful Learning: To Encourage Philosophical Endeavours. Occasioned By a Conference with one of the *Notional* Way. London, James Collins, 1668. 8°. 6 p.l., [24], 149 pp.

GLANVILL, JOSEPH. Scepsis Scientifica: Or, Confest *Ignorance*, the way to
Science; In an Essay of The Vanity of Dogmatizing, and Confident
Opinion. With a Reply to the Exceptions of the Learned Thomas Albius
[i.e., Thomas White]. London, E. Cotes, for Henry Eversden, 1665. 4°.
17 p.l., 184 pp.

> 'Imprimatur Octob. 18. 1664'. 'The "Vanity of Dogmatizing" recast and some
> passages omitted'.—*D.N.B.*, vol. vii, p. 1288.

—— SCIR$_I^E$ tuum nihil est: Or, The Authors Defence of The Vanity
of Dogmatizing; Against the Exceptions of The Learned Tho. Albius
In his Late Sciri. London, E. C. for Henry Eversden, 1665. 4°.
8 p.l., 92 pp.

—— The Vanity of Dogmatizing: Or Confidence in Opinions Manifested
in a Discourse of the Shortness and Uncertainty of our Knowledge
And its Causes; With some Reflexions on Peripateticism; and An
Apology for Philosophy. London, by E. C. for Henry Eversden, 1661.
8°. 16 p.l., 250 pp.

HALE, SIR MATTHEW, Chief Justice. The Primitive Origination of Mankind, Considered and Examined According to The Light of Nature.
London, Wm. Godbid, 1677. folio. 5 p.l., 380 pp.

HAMPTON, BENJAMIN, of the Middle Temple. The Existence of Human
Soul After Death: Proved from *Scripture, Reason and Philosophy*.
Wherein Mr. *Lock's* Notion that Understanding may be given to Matter,
Mr. *Hobb's* Assertion that there is no such thing as an Immaterial
Substance . . . and all such other Books and Opinions, are briefly and
plainly confuted . . . London, for S. Popping, 1711. 8°. 1 p.l., ii, 44 pp.

HARRIS, JOHN, M.A., F.R.S. Lexicon Technicum: Or, An Universal
English Dictionary of Arts and Sciences Explaining not only The *Terms*
of *Art*, But the Arts Themselves. London, Dan. Brown, 1704. folio.

—— Vol. ii. London, Dan. Brown, 1710.

> A new edition and revision of the 1704 volume.

HARTCLIFFE, JOHN, B.D., Fellow of King's College, Cambridge. A Treatise
of Moral and Intellectual Virtues; Wherein their Nature is fully explained, and their Usefulness proved, as being The best Rules of
Life. . . . London, C. Harper, 1691. 8°. 23 p.l., 414 pp.

> 'Imprimatur. Nov. 20. 1690.'

[HAWORTH, SAMUEL] M.D. Ἀνθρωπωλογία, Or, A Philosophic Discourse
Concerning Man. Being the Anatomy Both of his *Soul* and *Body*.
Wherein The *Nature, Origin, Union, Immateriality, Immortality,
Extension,* and *Faculties* of the one, And The *Parts, Humours, Tempera-
ments, Complexions, Functions, Sexes,* and *Ages*, respecting the other, are
concisely delineated. By *S. H.* Student in *Physic*. London, for Stephen
Foster, 1680. 8°. 18 p.l., 211 pp.

HEARNE, THOMAS. Remarks and Collections of Thomas Hearne. Oxford,
Clarendon Press for Oxford Historical Society, 1885–1921. 11 vols.

HERBERT, EDWARD, 1st Baron Herbert of Cherbury. De Veritate. Provt
Distingvitur A Revelatione, A Verisimili, A Possibili, Et A Falso.
Hoc Opvs condidit Ed. Herbert, Miles Ord. Bal. et Leg. S^{mi}. Regis

M. Brittaniae in Gallia. Et Vniverso Hvmano Generi Dicavit. 1624. 4°. 1 p.l., 227 pp.

HICKES, GEORGE. Three Short Treatises . . . Formerly Printed, And now again Published . . . In Defense of the Priesthood, and *True Rights of the* Church, against the Slanderous and Reproachful Treatment of the Clergy, in a late Book of Pernicious and Blasphemous Doctrines, falsely Intituled, *The Rights of the* Christian Church [by Matthew Tindal]. London, for W. Taylor, 1709. 8°. 43 p.l., 17 pp. *and* 3 separately paged numbers.

—— Two Treatises, One of the Christian Priesthood, The Other of the Dignity of The Episcopal Order. First Written, and Afterwards Published to obviate the Erroneous Opinions . . . in a late Book Entituled, The Rights of the Christian Church. With a large Prefatory Discourse In Answer to the said Book. 3d ed. enlarged. London, W. B. for Richard Sare, 1711. 8°. 2 vols.

HILL, OLIVER. A Rod for the Back of Fools: In Answer to Mr. John Toland's Book, Which he calleth, *Christianity not Mysterious.* . . . London, at Ed. Evets, 1702. 8°. 34 pp.

JACKSON, JOHN, M.A., Rector of Rossington (Yorkshire) A Dissertation on Matter *and* Spirit: With Some Remarks on a Book, Entitled, *An Enquiry into the Nature of the humane Soul* [of Andrew Baxter]. London, for J. Noon, 1735. 4°. viii, 56 pp.

KING, WILLIAM, Archbishop of Dublin. De Origine mali. Authore Guilielmo King, S. T. D. Episcopo Derensi. Londini, Benj. Tooke, 1702. 8°. 2 p.l., 214, [26] pp.

—— An Essay on the Origin of Evil. Translated from the *Latin*, with large *Notes;* tending to explain and vindicate some of the Author's Principles Against the Objections of Bayle, Leibnitz, the Author of a *Philosophical Enquiry concerning Human Liberty* [i.e. Anthony Collins]; and others. To which is prefix'd A Dissertation concerning the Fundamental Principle and immediate Criterion of Virtue . . . With some account of The Origin of the Passions and Affections. London, W. Thurlbourn, 1731. large 4°. lvi, 330 p., 1 l.

[LAYTON, HENRY] Arguments and Replies, In a Dispute concerning the Nature of the Humane Soul. Viz. Whether the same be *Immaterial, Separately Subsisting*, and *Intelligent:* Or be *Material, Unintelligent* and *Extinguishable* at the *Death* of the Person. London [n.p.] 1703. 4°. 112 pp.

[——] Observations upon a Sermon Intituled, *A Confutation of Atheism from the Faculties of the Soul* aliàs, *Matter and Motion cannot think*: Preached April 4. 1692 [by Richard Bentley]. By way of Refutation. [n.p., n.d.] 4°. 19 pp.

> The date which appears as part of the title of Layton's numerous anonymous 'Observations' is the date of the publication of the work he is attacking. With one exception all his 'Observations' are undated with reference to their own publication, and were all issued without a title-page.

[——] Observations upon a Treatise intit'led Psychologia: Or, An Account of the Nature of the Rational soul [by John Broughton] [n.p., 1703] 4°. 132 pp.

[LAYTON, HENRY] Observations upon a Short Treatise, Written by Mr. *Timothy Manlove*: Intituled, *The Immortality of the Soul Asserted*; and Printed in *Octavo* at London. 1697. [n.p., n.d.] 4°. 128 pp.

[———] Observations upon a Treatise Intituled, A Discourse concerning the Happiness of Good Men in the next World . . . By Dr. Sherlock. Printed at London, 1704. [n.p., n. d.] 4°. 115 pp.

LE CLERC, JEAN. Logica: Sive, Ars ratiocinandi. Autore, Joanne Clerico. Londini, Awnsham & Johan. Churchill, 1692. 12ᵐᵒ. 6 p.l., 182 pp.

  Dedicated to Robert Boyle.

——— Ontologia: Sive De Ente in genere. Londini, Awnsham & Johan. Churchill, 1692. 12ᵐᵒ. 4 p.l., 70 pp.

  Dedicated to Locke.

LEE, HENRY, D.D. Anti-Scepticism: Or, Notes upon each Chapter of Mr. Lock's Essay concerning Humane Understanding. With an Explication of all the Particulars of which he Treats, and in the same Order. In Four Books. London, for R. Clavel & C. Harper, 1702. folio. 3 p.l., 5 l. [of Preface], 7 l., 342 pp.

LEIBNIZ, GOTTFRIED WILHELM. Die philosophischen Schriften von Gottfried Wilhelm Leibniz. Hrsg. von C. J. Gerhardt. Berlin, Weidmann, 1875–90. 7 vols.

[LESLIE, CHARLES] The Second Part of The Wolf Stript of His Shepherds Cloathing: In *Answer* to a Late Celebrated *Book* Intituled The Rights of the Christian Church Asserted [by Matthew Tindal]. Wherein The Designs of the *Atheists, Deists, Whigs, Commonwealths-Men*, &c. and all sorts of Sectarists against the Church, are plainly laid Open and Expos'd. Humbly offer'd to the Consideration of Her Majesty And the *High-Court* of Parliament. By one call'd An High-Church-Man. With my Service to Dr. *Tindall* and Mr. *Collins*, &c. Sold by the Booksellers of London and Westminster, 1707. 4°. 2 p.l., 75 pp.

[———] A Short and Easie Method with the Deists. Wherein, The Certainty of the Christian Faith is Demonstrated . . . In a Letter to a Friend. The Second Edition. To which is Added, a Second Part To the Jews. . . . London, for C. Brome, 1699. 8°. xxiv, 424 pp., 8 l.

LOCKE, JOHN. The Works of John Locke. A new edition, corrected. London, T. Tegg, 1823. 10 vols.

——— Extrait d'un Livre Anglois qui n'est pas encore publié, intitulé *Essai Philosophique* concernant *L'Entendement*, où l'on montre quelle est l'étendüe de nos connoissances certaines, & la maniere dont nous y parvenons. Communiqué par Monsieur Locke. (*In* Bibliothèque Universelle et Historique de l'Année 1688, t. viii, pp. 49–142.)

[———] An Essay Concerning Humane Understanding. In Four Books. London, Printed for Thomas Basset, and sold by Edw. Mory, 1690. large 4°. 6 p.l., 362 pp., 11 l.

  The first edition, first issue.

——— Essai philosophique concernant l'Entendement Humain, ou l'on montre quelle est l'etendue de nos connoissances certaines, et la maniere dont nous y parvenons. Traduit de l'Anglois de Mr. Locke, Par Pierre Coste, Sur la Quatrieme Edition, revûë, corrigée & augmentée par l'Auteur. Amsterdam, Henri Schelte, 1700. 4°. 29 p.l., 936 pp., 11 l.

LOCKE, JOHN. An early draft of Locke's Essay, together with excerpts from his journals. Edited by R. I. Aaron and Jocelyn Gibb. Oxford, Clarendon Press, 1936. xxviii, 132 pp.

—— An Essay concerning Human Understanding, By John Locke. Collated and Annotated, with Prolegomena, Biographical, Critical, and Historical. By Alexander Campbell Fraser. Oxford, Clarendon Press, 1894. 2 vols.

—— Essays on the Law of Nature; the Latin text with a translation, introduction, and notes, together with transcripts of Locke's shorthand in his Journal for 1676. Edited by W. von Leyden. Oxford, Clarendon Press, 1954. xi, 292 pp.

[——] The Reasonableness of Christianity, As delivered in the Scriptures. London, for Awnsham and John Churchill, 1695. 8°. 2 p.l., 304 pp.

LOWDE, JAMES. A Discourse Concerning the Nature of Man, Both in his Natural and Political Capacity Both as he is a Rational Creature, and Member of a Civil Society. With an Examination of some of Mr. Hobbs's Opinions relating hereunto. London, T. Warren, 1694. 8°. 13 p.l., 243 pp.

—— Moral Essays; Wherein some of Mr. Lock's and Monsi^r Malbranch's Opinions are briefly examin'd. Together with an answer to some chapters in the Oracles of Reason [by Charles Blount], concerning Deism. London, J. White, 1699. 12mo.

[MALEBRANCHE, NICOLAS] De la Recherche de la Verité. Ou l'on traitte de la Nature de l'esprit de l'homme, & de l'usage qu'il en doit faire pour éviter l'erreur dans les Sciences. Paris, André Pralard, 1674–8. 8°. 3 vols.

MANLOVE, TIMOTHY. The Immortality of the Soul Asserted, and Practically Improved.... London, by R. Roberts for Nevill Simmons, 1697. 8°. 160 pp.

[MAYNE, ZACHARY] Two Dissertations concerning Sense and The Imagination. With an Essay on Consciousness. London, for J. Tonson, 1728. 8°. 1 p.l., vi, 231 pp.

[MILNER, JOHN] B.D. An Account of Mr. Lock's Religion, Out of his Own Writings, and in his Own Words. Together with some Observations upon it, and a Twofold Appendix. I. A Specimen of Mr. Lock's Way of Answering Authors.... II. A brief Enquiry whether Socinianism be justly Charged upon Mr. Lock. London, J. Nutt, 1700. 8°. 2 p.l., 188 pp.

MOLYNEUX, WILLIAM, M.P., F.R.S. Dioptrica Nova. A Treatise of Dioptricks, In Two Parts. London, Benj. Tooke, 1692. 4°. 7 p.l., 301 pp. and 43 folded plates.

MORE, HENRY. An Antidote against Atheisme, Or, An Appeal to the Natural Faculties of the Minde of Man, whether there be not a God. London, Roger Daniel, 1653. 8°. 16 p.l., 164 pp., 3 l.

MORE, HENRY. The Immortality of the Soul, So farre forth as it is demonstrable from the Knowledge of Nature and the Light of Reason. London, J. Flesher, 1659. 8°. 18 p.l., 549 pp., 9 l.

MORNAY, PHILIPPE, seigneur du Plessis-Marly. The Soule's Own Evidence, for its Own Immortality . . . First compiled in French . . . afterward turned into English . . . And now re-published By John Bachiler, M.A. London, M.S. for Henry Overton, 1646. 4°.

NABBES, THOMAS. Microcosmus. A Morall Maske, presented with generall liking at the private house in Salisbury Court, and heere set down according to the intention of the Authour Thomas Nabbes. London, Richard Oulton, 1637. 4°. 3 p.l.; signatures: B–G4.

NICHOLLS, WILLIAM, M.A., D.D. A Conference with a Theist. Containing An Answer to all the most Usual Objections of the Infidels Against the Christian Religion. In Four Parts. London, T. W. for Francis Saunders [et al.], 1698, 1697-9. 8°. 4 vols.

NORRIS, JOHN, Rector of Bemerton, near Sarum. Cursory Reflections upon a Book call'd, An Essay concerning Human Understanding. 44 pp., 1 l.
Included at the end of his *Christian Blessedness* . . . London, S. Manship, 1690.

—— An Essay Towards the Theory of the Ideal or Intelligible World. Designed for Two Parts. The First considering it Absolutely in it self, and the Second in Relation to Human Understanding. London, S. Manship, 1701-4. 8°. 2 vols.

[NYE, STEPHEN] The Agreement of the Unitarians, with the Catholick Church. Being also A full Answer, to the Infamations of Mr. *Edwards*; and the needless Exceptions, of my Lords The Bishops of *Chichester*, *Worcester* and *Sarum* . . . Part I . . . Printed in the Year MDCXCII. 4°. 64 pp.

[——] A Brief History of the Unitarians, Called also Socinians. In four Letters, Written to A Friend [i.e. to Thomas Firmin]. Printed in the Year 1687. 8°. 184 pp.

[——] A Discourse of Natural and Reveal'd Religion in Several Essays: Or, The Light of Nature, A Guide to Divine Truth. London, J. Newton, 1691. 8°. 2 p.l., 363 pp.

OLDFIELD, JOSHUA. An Essay towards the Improvement of Reason; in the Pursuit of Learning and Conduct of Life. London, for T. Parkhurst, 1707. 8°. 25 p.l., viii, 424 pp., 6 l.

PARKER, SAMUEL, D.D., Bishop of Oxford. A Demonstration of the Divine Authority of the Law of Nature, And of the Christian Religion. In Two Parts. London, M. Flesher, 1681. 4°. 3 p.l., xlii pp., 4 l., 427 pp.

—— A Free and Impartial Censure Of The Platonick Philosophie, Being a Letter Written to his much Honoured Friend Mr. N. B[athurst]. Oxford, W. Hall, 1666. 4°. 3 p.l., 112 pp.

—— Tentamina Physico-Theologica De Deo: Sive Theologia Scholastica . . . Duobus Libris comprehensa: Quorum Altero De Dei Existentiâ adversus Atheos & Epicureos ex ipsis Ipsorum Principiis disputatur. Altero De Ejusdem Essentiâ & Attributis . . . Londini, A. M. venales apud Jo. Sherley, 1665. 4°. 12 p.l., 418 pp.

PAYNE, WILLIAM, D.D. The Mystery of the Christian Faith and of the *Blessed Trinity* Vindicated, and the *Divinity of Christ* Proved. In Three Sermons . . . In the Press before his Death, and by himself ordered to be published. London, for Richard Cumberland, 1697. 8°. 1 p.l., 103 pp.

PEARSON, JOHN, Bishop of Chester. An Exposition of the Creed. London, Roger Daniel, 1659. 4°. 8 p.l., 785 pp.

PERRONET, VINCENT, A.M. A Vindication of Mr. *Locke*, from the Charge of giving encouragement to Scepticism and Infidelity, and from several other Mistakes and Objections of the Learned Author of the Procedure, Extent, and Limits of Human Understanding [i.e. Peter Browne]. In Six Dialogues. Wherein is likewise Enquired, Whether Mr. *Locke*'s True Opinion of the Soul's Immateriality was not mistaken by the late Learned Mons. Leibnitz. London, for J., J., and P. Knapton, 1736. 8°. 6 p.l., 124 pp.

—— A Second Vindication of Mr. *Locke*, Wherein his Sentiments relating to Personal Identity Are clear'd from some Mistakes of the Rev. Dr. *Butler*, in his Dissertation on that Subject. And the various Objections rais'd against Mr. *Locke*, by the late learned Author [i.e. Andrew Baxter] of *An* Enquiry *into the* Nature *of the* Human Soul, are consider'd. To which are added Reflections on some passages of Dr. Watt's Philosophical Essays . . . London, for Fletcher Gyles, 1738. 8°. 8 p.l., 132 pp.

PRIDEAUX, HUMPHREY, D.D. A Letter to the Deists: Shewing, *That the Gospel of Jesus Christ is no* Imposture; *but the Sacred Truth of God.* London, by J. H. for W. Rogers, 1697. 8°. 1 p.l., 152 pp.

RAY, JOHN, F.R.S. Miscellaneous Discourses Concerning the Dissolution and Changes of the World. Wherein The Primitive Chaos and Creation, the General Deluge . . . [&c., &c.] are largely Discussed and Examined. London, Samuel Smith, 1692. small 8°. 13 p.l., 259 pp.

S., M. A Philosophical Discourse of the Nature of Rational and Irrational Souls. By M. S. London, Richard Baldwin, 1695. 4°. 3 p.l., 34 pp.

SCLATER, WILLIAM, B.D. A Key to the Key of Scriptvre: *Or* An Exposition with Notes, vpon the Epistle to the Romanes. . . . London, Printed by T. S. for George Norton, 1611. 4°. 3 p.l., 388 p.; 1 l.

[SERGEANT, JOHN] The Method to Science. By J. S. London, Printed by W. Redmayne, 1696. 8°. 4 p.l., [62] 429 pp.

[——] Solid Philosophy Asserted, Against the Fancies of the Ideists: Or, The Method to Science Farther Illustrated. With Reflexions on Mr. Locke's *Essay* concerning *Human Understanding.* By J. S. London, Printed for Roger Clevil, 1697. 8°. 1 p.l., [14 p. of 'Epistle'], [xxxvi p. of Preface], 460 pp., 12 l.

Locke's copy of this book, with his numerous manuscript notes, is in the library of St. John's College, Cambridge.

[——] Transnatural Philosophy, or Metaphysicks: Demonstrating the Essences and Operations of all Beings whatever, which gives the *Principles* to all other Sciences. And Shewing the Perfect Conformity of *Christian Faith* to *Right Reason*, and the Unreasonableness of *Atheists*, *Deists*, Anti-trinitarians, and other Sectaries. With an Appendix,

Giving a *Rational Explication* of the Mystery of the most B. Trinity. By J. S. London, Printed by the Author, 1700. 8°. 484 pp., 1 l.

SHERLOCK, WILLIAM, D.D., Dean of St. Paul's, Westminster. A Digression concerning Connate Ideas, or Inbred Knowledge. pp. 124–164 *in his* A Discourse Concerning the Happiness of Good Men, Part I. London, W. Rogers, 1704. 8°.

—— A Vindication of Dr. *Sherlock's* Sermon concerning The Danger of Corrupting the Faith by Philosophy. In Answer to some Socinian Remarks. London, for W. Rogers, 1697. 4°. 2 p.l., 40 pp.

—— A Vindication of the Doctrine of the Holy and Ever Blessed Trinity, and the Incarnation of The Son of God. Occasioned By the Brief Notes on the creed of St. Athanasius [anonymous] and the Brief History of the Unitarians, Or Socinians [by Stephen Nye], and containing an Answer to both. London, for W. Rogers, 1690. 4°. 4 p.l., 272 pp.

'Imprimatur, Jun. 9. 1690.'

—— A Defence of Dr. Sherlock's Notion of A Trinity in Unity, In Answer to the Animadversions upon his Vindication of the Doctrine of the Holy and Ever Blessed Trinity. With a Post-Script Relating to the Calm Discourse of a Trinity in the Godhead. In A Letter to a Friend. London, W. Rogers, 1694. 4°. 1 p.l., 112 pp.

[SOUTH, ROBERT] Animadversions upon Dr. *Sherlock's* Book, Entituled A Vindication of the Holy and Ever-Blessed Trinity, &c. By a Divine of the Church of England. The Second Edition with some Additions. London, for Randal Taylor, 1693. 4°. 1 p.l., xix, [3] 382 pp.

[——] Tritheism charged upon Dr *Sherlock's* New Notion of the Trinity. And the Charge made good, in an Answer to the Defense of the said Notion against The *Animadversions* upon Dr. *Sherlock's* Book, Entituled, A Vindication of the Doctrine of the : . . Trinity. By a Divine of the Church of England. London, for John Whitlock, 1695. 4°. 12 p.l., 316 pp.

—— Twelve Sermons Preached upon Several Occasions. Six of them never before Printed. London, J. H. for Thomas Bennet, 1692. 8°. 4 p.l., 639 pp.

SPRAT, THOMAS, D.D., F.R.S., Bishop of Rochester. The History of The Royal Society of London, For the Improving of Natural Knowledge. London, T. R. for J. Martyn, 1667. 4°. 8 p.l., 438 pp.

[STEPHENS, WILLIAM] B.D., Rector of Sutton, Surrey. An Account of the Growth of Deism in England. London, for the Author, 1696. 4°. 32 pp.

STILLINGFLEET, EDWARD, Bishop of Worcester. The Works of That Most Eminent and Learned Prelate, Dr. Edw. Stillingfleet, Late Lord Bishop of Worcester. Together with His Life and Character. In Six Volumes. London, J. Heptinstall for Henry & George Mortlock, 1710–13. folio. 6 vols.

Stillingfleet's biography contained in the first volume was also issued separately under the title: The Life and Character of That Eminent and Learned Prelate, The Late Dr. Edw. Stillingfleet. . . . (London, J. Heptinstall, 1710. 8°. 149 pp.) According to Thomas Hearne's note in his copy (now in the Bodleian Library) its author was Timothy Goodwin, or Godwin. This edition of his Works, however, was made by Richard Bentley, Stillingfleet's chaplain.

[STILLINGFLEET, EDWARD] A Letter to a Deist, In Answer to several *Objections* against the *Truth* and *Authority* of the Scriptures. London, by W. G., 1677. 8°. 3 p.l., 135 pp.

—— Origines Sacrae, Or A Rational Account of the Grounds of Christian Faith, as to the Truth and Divine Authority of the Scriptures, And the matters therein contained. London, R. W. for Henry Mortlock, 1662. 4°. 18 p.l., 619 pp.

—— A Discourse in Vindication of the Doctrine of the Trinity: With An Answer to the Late *Socinian* Objections Against it from *Scripture, Antiquity* and *Reason.* And A Preface concerning the different *Explications* of the *Trinity,* and the Tendency of the present Socinian Controversie. The Second Edition. London, J. H. for Henry Mortlock, 1697. 8°. 1 p.l., lxii, [3] 292 pp.

—— The Bishop of Worcester's Answer to Mr. Locke's Letter concerning Some Passages Relating to his Essay of Humane Understanding, Mention'd in the Late Discourse in Vindication of the Trinity. With a Postscript in answer to some Reflections made upon that Treatise in a late *Socinian* Pamphlet. London, J. H. for Henry Mortlock, 1697. 8°. 154 pp.

—— The Bishop of *Worcester's* Answer to Mr. *Locke's* Second Letter; Wherein his Notion of Ideas Is prov'd to be Inconsistent with it self, And with the Articles of the Christian Faith. London, J. H. for Henry Mortlock, 1698. 8°. 178 pp.

[STRUTT, SAMUEL] A Philosophical Enquiry into the Physical Spring of Human Actions, and the Immediate Cause of Thinking. London, for J. Peele, 1732. 8°. 1 p.l., 53 pp.

[TINDAL or TINDALL, MATTHEW] The Reflexions on the XXVIII Propositions touching the Doctrine of the Trinity, In a Letter to the Clergy, &c. [n.p.] Printed in the Year MDCXCV. 4°. 36 pp.

[TOLAND, JOHN] *Christianity not Mysterious:* Or, A Treatise Shewing That there is nothing in the Gospel Contrary to Reason, Nor Above it: And that no Christian Doctrine can be properly call'd a Mystery. London, Printed in the Year 1696. 8°. xxxii, 176 pp.

—— Letters to Serena: Containing I. The Origin and Force of Prejudices. II. The History of the Soul's Immortality among the Heathens. III. The Origin of Idolatry, and the Reasons of Heathenism. As also, IV. A Letter . . . showing Spinosa's System of Philosophy to be without any Principle or Foundation. V. *Motion Essential to Matter*; in Answer to some remarks by a Noble Friend on the *Confutation* of Spinosa. London, Bernard Lintot, 1704. 8°. 1 p.l., [48] 239 pp.

[——] Pantheisticon. Sive, Formula Celebrandae Sodalitatis Socraticae, In Tres Particulas Divisa; Quae Pantheistarum, sive Sodalium, Continent I, Mores et Axiomata: II, Numen et Philosophiam: III, Libertatem, et non fallentem Legem, Neque fallendam . . . Cosmopoli, MDCCXX. 8°. 3 p.l., 89 pp.

VIRET, PIERRE. Instruction Chrestienne en la Doctrine de la Loy et de l'Evangile: & en la vraye philosophie & theologie tant naturelle que supernaturelle des Chrestiens: & en la contemplation du temple &

des images & oeuures de la providence de Dieu en tout l'univers. . . .
Geneve, Iean Rivery, 1564. folio. 2 vols.

> Vol. 2 has title: Exposition de la Doctrine de la Foy Chrestienne, touchant la vraye cognoissance & le vray service de Dieu. . . .

[WARD, SETH] Bishop of Salisbury. A Philosophicall Essay Towards an Eviction

of The { Being and Attributes of God. / Immortality of the souls of men. / Truth and Authority of Scripture.

Together with an Index of the Heads of every particular Part. Oxford, by L. Lichfield, 1652. small 8°. 8 p.l., 152 pp.

WATTS, ISAAC. Logick: Or, The Right Use of Reason in the Enquiry after Truth, With A Variety of Rules to guard against *Error*, in the Affairs of Religion and Human Life, as well as in the Sciences. The Second Edition, Corrected. London, John Clark, 1726. 8°. 3 p.l., 365, [5] pp.

[——] Philosophical Essays on Various Subjects, viz. Space, Substance, Body, Spirit, The Operations of the Soul in Union with the Body, Innate Ideas, Perpetual Consciousness, Place and Motion of Spirits, the departing Soul, the Resurrection of the Body, the Production and Operations of Plants and Animals; With some Remarks on Mr. Locke's Essay on the Human Understanding. To which is subjointed A Brief Scheme of Ontology, Or The Science of Being in general with its Affections. By I. W. London, Richard Ford, 1733. 8°. xii pp., 2 l., 403 pp.

WHICHCOTE (also WHICHCOT and WHITCHCOTE), BENJAMIN. Select Sermons of Dr. Whichcot. In Two Parts. London, Awnsham & John Churchill, 1698. 8°. 10 p.l., 452 pp.

WHISTON, WILLIAM, M.A. Reflexions on an Anonymous Pamphlet, Entituled, a Discourse of Free Thinking [by Anthony Collins]. London, for the Author, 1713. 8°. 55 pp.

WILKINS, JOHN, Bishop of Chester. Of the Principles and Duties of Natural Religion: Two Books. London, A. Maxwell, 1675. 8°. 9 p.l., 410 pp.

WITTY, JOHN, M.A., of St. John's College, Cambridge. The First Principles of Modern Deism Confuted. In A Demonstration of the *Immateriality*, Natural *Eternity*, *Immortality* of *Thinking* Substances in general; and in particular of Human Souls. Even upon the Supposition that we are intirely ignorant of the *Intrinsic Nature* of the *Essences of Things*. London, for John Wyat, 1707. 8°. 2 p.l., xxix, [6] 301 pp.

[——] The Reasonableness Of Assenting to the *Mysteries* of *Christianity* Asserted and Vindicated. With some Remarks Upon a Book Entitul'd *An Essay concerning the Use of Reason* . . . [by Anthony Collins] In a Letter to a Friend. London, for John Wyat, 1707. 8°. 81, [1] pp.

[WOLLASTON, WILLIAM, M.A.] The Religion of Nature Delineated. [n.p.] Printed in the Year MDCCXXII. 4°. 158 pp., 1 l.

WOTTON, WILLIAM, B.D., Chaplain to the Earl of Nottingham. Reflections upon *Ancient* and *Modern* Learning. London, by J. Leake, for Peter Buck, 1694. 8°. [32] 359 pp.

C. Periodicals

Acta Eruditorum anno 1682–1731 publicata. Lipsiae, J. Grossium [*et al.*], 1682–1731. 4°. 50 vols. monthly.

The Athenian Gazette: or Casuistical Mercury, Resolving all the most Nice and Curious Questions proposed by the Ingenious. vols. 1–14, no. 29; 17 March 1691–8 August 1694. London, J. Dunton, 1691–4. 4°.

Running title: The Athenian Mercury.

ATHENIAN SOCIETY, London. The Young-Students-Library. Containing Extracts and Abridgments of the Most Valuable Books Printed in England, and in the Forreign Journals, From the Year Sixty-Five, to This Time. To which is Added, A New Essay upon all sorts of Learning; Wherein the Use of the Sciences Is Distinctly Treated on . . . Printed in the Year 1691. London, John Dunton, 1692. folio. 3 p.l., xviii, 479 pp.

Bibliothèque Universelle et Historique de 1686–1693. t. 1–26. Amsterdam, Wolfgang, Waeberge, [*et al.*] 1686–94.

Edited by Jean Le Clerc, J. Cornand de la Crose, and Jacques Bernard. Continued as Bibliothèque Choisie.

Bibliothèque Choisie, pour servir de suite à la Bibliothèque universelle. Par Jean Le Clerc. t. 1–28. Amsterdam, H. Schelte, 1703–13.

Continued as Bibliothèque ancienne & moderne.

Censura Temporum. The good or ill tendencies of Books, Sermons, Pamphlets, &c. impartially considered [by Samuel Parker], in a dialogue between Eubulus and Sophronius. vols. 1–2; vol. 3, nos. 1–3. [Jan.] 1708–[March] 1710. London, for H. Clements, 1708–10. 4°.

The Compleat Library: Or, News for the Ingenious. Containing several original pieces, with an historical account of the choicest books newly printed in England and in the forreign journals. As also, the State of Learning in the World. By a London divine [Richard Wolley] vols. [1]–2; vol. 3, nos. 1–4; May 1692–April 1694. London, for J. Dunton, 1692–4. 4°.

'A continuation of the Young Student's Library and a perfecting of that Undertaking.'

Gentleman's Journal; or, The Monthly Miscellany. Edited by P. A. Motteux. vols. 1–3. Jan. 1692–Nov. 1694. London, 1692–4. small 4°.

Histoire des Ouvrages des Savans, par Henri Basnage de Beauval. t. 1–24. sept. 1687–juin 1709. Rotterdam, Reinier Leers, 1687–1709. 8°.

A sequel to Nouvelles de la République des Lettres.

London Gazette. Nos. 1–23, as Oxford Gazette, 1665–6. folio. Oxford, 1665–6. nos. 24–4107, as London Gazette. 5 Feb. 1666–22 March 1705. London 1666–1705. folio.

Mémoires pour l'Histoire Des Sciences & Des beaux Arts. Janvier/ Février 1701–75. t.[1]–265. Trévoux, L'Imprimerie de S. A. S., 1701–75. 12ᵐᵒ.

Also known as 'Mémoires de Trévoux'. Absorbed by Journal des Savants.

Mémoires pour servir à l'Histoire des Hommes Illustres dans la république des lettres. Avec un catalogue raisonné de leurs Ouvrages. [Edited by P. Nicéron] Paris, Briasson, 1729–45. small 8°. 43 vols.

Memoirs for the Ingenious. . : . In Miscellaneous Letters. By J. Cornand de la Crose. vol. 1, nos. 1–12. Jan.–Dec. 1693. London, H. Rhodes, 1693. small 4°.

> Continued as Memoirs for the Ingenious, or, The Universal Mercury, Vol. 1, no. 1. Jan. 1694.

Mercurius Eruditorum, or News for the learned World. 1691 (5–12 August).

Miscellaneous Letters, Giving an Account of the Works of the Learned, Both at Home and Abroad . . . 17 Oct. 1694–19 Dec. 1694; Jan.–March 1696. Vol. 1, nos. 1–10; vol. 2, nos. 1–3. London, 1694–6. Weekly.

Nouvelles de la République des Lettres. mars 1684–mai/juin 1718. Amsterdam, H. Desbordes [et al.], 1684–1718. 8°. 40 vols.

> Founded by Pierre Bayle, and edited by him to Feb. 1687; continued by D. de Larroque, J. Barrin, and others to April 1689; from Jan. 1699 on, edited by Jacques Bernard.

The Occasional Paper . . . nos. I–X. London, 1697–8. 4°.

> The following three numbers are of special interest:
>   I. contains 'Some reflexions on a Book Entituled, *A Letter to the* Deists'.
>   III. Reflexions upon Mr. Toland's Book, Called *Christianity not Mysterious:* with some Considerations about the use of Reason in Matters of Religion.
>   VII. 'Shewing the Usefulness of Human Learning in *Matters of Religion*; Contrary to the Suggestions of some *Sceptical* Men, in their late Pamphlets.'

SECONDARY SOURCES

AARON, R. I. John Locke. London, Oxford Univ. Press, 1937. ix, 328 pp.
—— 2nd ed. Oxford, Clarendon Press, 1955. x, 323 pp.

ABBEY, CHARLES J., and JOHN H. OVERTON. The English Church in the Eighteenth Century. London, Longmans, Green and Co., 1878. 2 vols.

ASCOLI, GEORGES. La Grande-Bretagne devant l'opinion française au XVIIᵉ siècle. Thèse pour le doctorat . . . Paris, J. Gamber, 1930. 2 vols.

ASPELIN, GUNNAR. Locke and Sydenham. (*In Theoria*, vol. xv, 1949. Lund [1949] pp. 29–37.)

BARNES, ANNIE. Jean LeClerc (1657–1736) et la République des Lettres. Paris, E. Droz, 1938. 280 pp., 2 l.

BASTIDE, CHARLES. Anglais et Français au XVIIᵉ siècle. Paris, F. Alcan, 1912. xii, 362 pp.
—— John Locke, ses théories politiques et leur influence en Angleterre. Les Libertés politiques—L'église et l'état—la Tolérance. Thèse pour le doctorat . . . Paris, E. Leroux, 1906. 3 p.l., 397 pp.

BRANDT, FRITHIOF. Thomas Hobbes' mechanical conception of nature. Copenhagen, Levin & Munksgaard, 1927. 399 pp.

> Translated from the Danish edition of 1921 by Vaughan Maxwell and Annie I. Fausbøll.

230 BIBLIOGRAPHY

BREDVOLD, LOUIS I. The Intellectual Milieu of John Dryden, Studies in Some Aspects of Seventeenth-Century Thought. Ann Arbor, University of Michigan Press, 1934. viii, 189 pp.

CASSIRER, ERNST. Das Erkenntnisproblem in der Philosophie und Wissenschaft der neueren Zeit. 3 Aufl. Berlin, Bruno Cassirer, 1922–3. 3 vols.

CHRISTOPHERSEN, H. O. A Bibliographical Introduction to the Study of John Locke. Oslo, J. Dybwad, 1930. 134 pp. (Skrifter utgitt av det Norske Videnskaps-Akademi i Oslo. II. Hist.-Filos. Klasse. 1930. no. 8.)

COURTINES, LÉO PIERRE. Bayle's Relations with England and the English. New York, Columbia University Press, 1938. x pp., 1 l., 253 pp.

CRAGG, G. R. From Puritanism to the Age of Reason. A Study of Changes in Religious Thought within the Church of England, 1660 to 1700. Cambridge, University Press, 1950. vi, 247 pp.

DENIS, PAUL. Lettres Autographes de la Collection de Troussures Classées & Annotées. Beauvais, Imprimerie du Dépt. de l'Oise, 1912. xv, 665 pp. (Publications de la Société Académique de l'Oise, t. 3.)

Abbé DuBos's correspondence occurs on pp. 1–225.

DUMAS, GUSTAVE. Histoire du Journal de Trévoux depuis 1701 jusqu'en 1762. Thèse pour le doctorat de l'Université . . . Paris, Boivin & cie, 1936. 210 pp.

FOX-BOURNE, H. R. The Life of John Locke. London, Henry S. King, 1876. 2 vols.

GIBSON, JAMES. Locke's Theory of Knowledge and its Historical Relations. Cambridge, University Press, 1931. xiv, 338 pp.

GRAHAM, WALTER JAMES. The Beginnings of English Literary Periodicals. A Study of Periodical Literature 1665–1715. New York, Oxford University Press, 1926. iv pp., 2 l., 92 pp.

GRÜNBAUM, JACOB. Die Philosophie Richard Burthogges (1637–1698). Inaugural-Dissertation. . . . Bern, J. Kleiner, 1939. v, 93 pp.

HALLAM, HENRY, F.R.A.S. Introduction to the Literature of Europe, in the Fifteenth, Sixteenth, and Seventeenth Centuries. 4th ed. London, John Murray, 1854. 3 vols.

HEFELBOWER, SAMUEL GRING. The relation of John Locke to English deism. Chicago, Ill., The University of Chicago Press [1918]. vii, 188 pp.

HÖFFDING, HARALD. Geschichte der neueren Philosophie. Eine Darstellung der Geschichte der Philosophie von dem Ende der Renaissance bis zu unseren Tagen. Leipzig, O. R. Reisland, 1895–6. 2 vols.

JESSOP, T. E. Editor's Introduction to Alciphron. In vol. 3 of the Works of George Berkeley... Edited by A. A. Luce and T. E. Jessop. London, T. Nelson [1950].

JOHNSTON, GEORGE ALEXANDER. The Development of Berkeley's Philosophy. London, Macmillan, 1923. vii, 400 pp.

KING, PETER, 7th baron King. The Life of John Locke, with extracts from his Correspondence, Journals, and Commonplace Books. London, H. Colburn, 1829. 8°. xi, 407 pp.

—— A New Edition. With Considerable Additions. London, Henry Colburn and Richard Bentley, 1830. 8°. 2 vols.

LAMPRECHT, STERLING POWER. The Rôle of Descartes in Seventeenth-Century England. *In* Studies in the History of Ideas. Edited by the Department of Philosophy of Columbia University. New York, Columbia University Press, 1935. Vol. iii, pp. 179–240.

LASSWITZ, KURD. Geschichte der Atomistik vom Mittelalter bis Newton. Hamburg, Leopold Voss, 1890. 2 vols.

Contents: Bd. 1: Die Erneuerung der Korpuskulartheorie. Bd. 2: Höhepunkt und Verfall der Korpuskulartheorie des siebzehnten Jahrhunderts.

LECHLER, GOTTHARD VICTOR. Geschichte des englischen Deismus. Stuttgart, J. G. Cotta, 1841. xvi, 488 pp.

LELAND, JOHN, D.D. A View of the Principal Deistical Writers That Have Appeared in England in the last and present Century. . . . London, for B. Dod, 1754–5. 8°. 2 vols.

—— A Supplement to the First and Second Volumes of the *View* of the *Deistical Writers* . . . With A Large Index to the Three Volumes. London, for B. Dod, 1756. 8°. xvi, 368 pp., 20 l.

LOMBARD, A. L'Abbé Du Bos, un initiateur de la pensée moderne (1670–1742). Thèse pour le doctorat . . . Paris, Hachette, 1913. 2 p.l., viii, 614 pp.

LYON, GEORGES. L'Idéalisme en Angleterre au XVIIIᵉ Siècle. Paris, F. Alcan, 1888. 2 p.l., 481 pp., 1 l.

MACKINNON, FLORA I. The philosophy of John Norris of Bemerton. Baltimore, Md., The Review Pub. Co. [1910]. 2 p.l., iii, 104 pp. (Psychological Review publications. The Philosophical Monographs . . . vol. 1, no. 2.)

MCLACHLAN, H. The religious opinions of Milton, Locke, and Newton. [Manchester] Manchester University Press, 1941. vii, 221 pp.

MCLACHLAN, H. JOHN. Socinianism in Seventeenth-Century England. [London] Oxford University Press, 1951. viii, 352 pp.

MAYO, THOMAS F. Epicurus in England (1650–1725). Dallas, Texas, The Southwest Press [1934]. xviii, 237 pp.

MUIRHEAD, JOHN H. The Platonic Tradition in Anglo-Saxon Philosophy. Studies in the History of Idealism in England and America. London, G. Allen & Unwin [1931]. 446 pp. (The Library of Philosophy series.)

OLLION, H. La Philosophie générale de John Locke. Thèse pour le doctorat . . . Paris, F. Alcan, 1908. 482, [1] pp.

PICARD, GABRIEL. Le Thomisme de Suarez. *In* Archives de Philosophie, t. xviii, Cahier I. Paris, 1949. pp. 108–28.

PORTER, NOAH. Marginalia *Locke*-a-na. *In* The New Englander and Yale Review, vol. xi (new series), July 1887; New Haven, 1887. pp. 33–49.

RÉMUSAT, CHARLES DE. Histoire de la Philosophie en Angleterre depuis Bacon jusqu'à Locke. Paris, Didier & cⁱᵉ, 1875. 2 vols.

RIVAUD, ALBERT. Histoire de la Philosophie. Paris, Presses Universitaires de France, 1948–50. 3 vols.

STEPHEN, LESLIE. History of English Thought in the Eighteenth Century. 3d ed. London, Smith, Elder & Co., 1902. 2 vols.

WERNER, KARL. Franz Suarez und die Scholastik der letzten Jahrhunderte. Regensburg, G. J. Manz, 1861. 2 vols.

WINDELBAND, WILHELM. Lehrbuch der Geschichte der Philosophie. Hrsg. von Heinz Heimsoeth. 14., ergänzte Aufl. Tübingen, J. C. B. Mohr, 1950. xlvii, 656 pp.

YOLTON, JOHN W. Locke's Unpublished Marginal Replies to John Sergeant. *In* Journal of the History of Ideas, vol. xii, Oct. 1951. New York, 1951. pp. 528–59.

—— Locke and the Seventeenth-Century Logic of Ideas. *In* Journal of the History of Ideas, vol. xvi, Oct. 1955. pp. 431–52.

INDEX

(References in bold-face figures are to the more important discussions)